Dialogue on the Internet

Dialogue on the Internet

Language, Civic Identity, and Computer-Mediated Communication

RICHARD HOLT

Civic Discourse for the Third Millennium
Michael H. Prosser, Series Editor

Westport, Connecticut
London

Library of Congress Cataloging-in-Publication Data

Holt, Richard, 1949–
    Dialogue on the Internet : langauge, civic identity, and
    computer-mediated communication / Richard Holt.
        p. cm. — (Civic discourse for the third millennium)
    Includes bibliographical references and index.
    ISBN 1-56750-679-8 (alk. paper)
      1. Internet—Social aspects.   2. Internet—Political aspects.
    3. Telematics—Social aspects.   4. Civil society.   5. Communication in
    politics.   6. Communication in social action.   7. Dialogism (Literary
    analysis)   8. Discourse analysis.   I. Title.   II. Series.
    HM851.H66   2004
    302.23'1—dc22   2004046060

British Library Cataloguing in Publication Data is available.

Library of Congress Catalog Card Number: 2004046060
ISBN: 1-56750-679-8

First published in 2004

Praeger Publishers, 88 Post Road West, Westport, CT 06881
An imprint of Greenwood Publishing Group, Inc.
www.praeger.com

Printed in the United States of America

The paper used in this book complies with the
Permanent Paper Standard issued by the National
Information Standards Organization (Z39.48-1984).

10   9   8   7   6   5   4   3   2   1

*To my mother, Jeanne Holt, of beloved memory,
and my father, George E. Holt.
The hard work and sacrifice of these two
extraordinary people have made
everything possible.*

Contents

Acknowledgments

Above all, my deepest gratitude is to my wife, Dr. Hui-Ching Chang. Quite literally, this book is as much due to her persistent efforts at organizing and editing as it is to my writing. Moreover, she has helped at times of extreme stress and demands related to her own work, always selflessly and without complaint. I can never thank her enough—but I have dedicated the rest of my life to trying.

I would also like to thank Dr. Michael Prosser, who in 1999 recognized from my paper at the Rochester Conference on Human Rights and Responsibilities the potential that dialogism holds for opening up our views of human communication and furthering the causes of peace and understanding and who encouraged me to contribute this volume to this fine series. My gratitude as well to my outstanding colleagues at Northern Illinois University, who rescued me from an intellectual and moral wasteland, and who have unstintingly provided me with strong support—financially, emotionally, and spiritually—for the writing of this book; I am especially grateful to our nonpareil leader, Dr. Lois Self, and my longtime friend, Dr. Joseph Scudder. Lastly, in the spirit of the public discourse for which the book argues, I should also mention that the great majority of material herein was composed in three places where people gather to read, talk, and drink lots of coffee: my local Barnes and Noble bookstore (102 Commons Drive, Geneva, IL); Borders bookstore (3935 East Main, St. Charles, IL); and the best coffee shop ever, the Caribou (201 North Randall Road, Batavia, IL). I extend my humblest gratitude to the long-suffering staffs in these fine places of business.

Chapter 1

The World in the Post and the Page

The entire world is literally in every e-mail post you read and write on the Internet, and in every page you visit or compose on the Web. This is because, once uttered, neither the post nor the page is any longer owned by its composer. Rather, it is cast into a stream of ongoing discourse, thus becoming a property jointly owned (and fought over) by its composer and any person who may read it. The meaning of a post or a page (or any other spoken or written message) is not set, but is achieved collaboratively in the struggle over what it represents among those in the whole world—those who write, read, and represent it. Because meaning is inescapably social, all society (the world) must be included in the category of those who fashion the meaning of any Internet utterance. No matter how seemingly ordinary, any Internet interaction represents a nexus at which the vast universe of Internet users and their innumerable utterances coalesce—this is the "world" in the post and the page.

The preceding paragraph summarizes a view of communication and thought known as "dialogism" and a mode of communicating known as "dialogue." Those espousing dialogistic perspectives are comfortable with, and indeed celebrate, multiplicity. In many ways the dialogical perspective resonates well with the familiar idiosyncratic features—immediacy, interconnectivity, global range—of Internet communication, features that make it noticeably different from many previous forms of communication. For these reasons, as well as other reasons to be explored at length in this discussion, Internet communication is ideally suited to exploration by dialogic means, and depth exploration of the meanings of such utterances poses a significant challenge to those interested in Internet communication.

Among the multitude of possible forms of Internet expression that deserve attention, I have chosen to focus on one of the most important: civic discourse. The Internet and the Web have continued to increase in significance as tools of civic discourse, being used by both traditional politicians and by nontraditional activists. For those wishing to disseminate messages related to civic life, Internet communication offers great advantages in terms of range, extent, variety, and speed. As more Internet users have been brought into civic discourse, there has naturally occurred a dramatic increase in the number of voices clamoring for attention. Since civic discourse involves the airing of many, frequently conflicting, perspectives, the dialogic perspective proves especially suitable for analyzing it.

The goal of this book is to offer an expanded conception of dialogue to analyze selected Internet civic discourse. This extended conception of dialogue is achieved, not only by using dialogical methods to bring out alternative interpretations of Internet utterance, but also by contrasting these readings with insights from nondialogical perspectives. These latter views are called "monological," and their distinction from dialogical standpoints is explained in greater detail later in this chapter. Such "dual readings," as I call them, rely on the rich and diverse heritage of dialogism, leading to a deeper understanding of the role played by computer-mediated communication (CMC) in civic discourse, especially its two most prevalent forms, e-mail discussion messages (EDMs) on the Internet and Web pages/sites on the World Wide Web. I will further argue that, despite limitations that prevent their full use in today's society, we have reason to hope that a better understanding of EDMs and Web pages/sites can lead to their more effective use in civic discourse, resulting in a more open and productive culture for the propagation of ideological and political thought.

To prepare for these explorations, however, I will first deal with some conceptions (and misconceptions) about the Internet, this "new medium" that, over time, becomes increasingly more prominent in our lives. In many ways, the Internet is still a mystery, yet elements central to the discussion can be grasped, provided one begins at the beginning, with a systematic definition of some key terms.

THE INTERNET

Despite the increasing involvement of the Internet in daily life, and the correspondingly greater familiarity of users with Internet concepts and terminology, much about this new form of communication remains puzzling. Since in this book I focus on the use of the Internet in civic discourse, in its two most widely used forms (e-mail discussion messages and Web pages/sites), it will be helpful to explain some terms essential to understanding this particular focus. In this section, I define these concepts, trusting that a shared understanding of these few terms will help unfold the dialogic (and monologic) aspects of the specific examples analyzed in later chapters. I then use these common understandings to explore the richness and complexity of the Internet, and how these lead to problems faced by those who try to analyze Internet discourse in all its bewildering complexity.

Key Terms Defined

Defining computer and other terms is particularly important since, in popular usage, these terms either take on a multiplicity of meanings (often far removed from their formal definitions) or they are used, inappropriately, as synonyms for one another. A common understanding of the technical meaning of these terms may help preclude misunderstandings later on.

The Internet

The first term to clarify is the *Internet*, defined as the worldwide collection of networks and gateways that use TCP/IP (Transfer Control Protocol/Internet Protocol) to communicate with one another.[1] The Internet has been called "a network of networks" (Jansen, 2002, p. 218); although there are many internets (small "i"), what is called "the Internet" is a cooperative system by which messages are forwarded through linked computer systems across the world. The core of the Internet is a set of high-speed lines for communicating between primary nodes, or host computers, which in turn encompass thousands of smaller networks. The Internet was designed so that no single computer or network controls it. This means one or more nodes can malfunction without interrupting the Internet as a whole or causing it to shut down. This idea was based on a perceived need for the government to have access to a working communication system should other systems be shut down in a nuclear war. Margolis (1999) has called this unusual approach "anarchy by design" (p. 283).

The World Wide Web

Although often mistakenly used as a synonym for the Internet, the *World Wide Web* (more commonly, simply "the Web") is defined as the set of interlinked hypertext documents on servers around the world. These servers use HTTP (HyperText Transfer Protocol) to translate documents written in HTML (HyperText Markup Language).[2] The World Wide Web is part of the Internet, but is not synonymous with it. Similarly, not all Internet servers are on the World Wide Web. Two features of the Web important to this discussion are that, first, each page (that is, screenful) is identified by a unique address called a "URL" (Uniform Resource Locator),[3] and second, links to these URLs can be placed in any HTML document or, for that matter, e-mail message. This ability to link pages to one another gives the Web an extraordinary flexibility by making it possible for one location to involve others.

There can also be confusion over the terms *Web page* and *Web site* (sometimes, "website"). A Web page is a document in HTML code, with associated files for supporting materials such as pictures, sound, and so on. The Web page document, along with supporting materials, is in a directory on a particular computer and is assigned a unique URL. The term *page* can be confusing; when viewed by a browser, a page may extend down several lengths of the screen. Even if the page is several screens in length, the screen displayed according to the formatting in the HTML document is still considered simply as a single page.

A Web site is technically a collection of pages arranged hierarchically. The HTML documents (that is, pages) comprising a Web site, along with supporting materials, are usually grouped around common themes with links to interconnect the various parts of the site. Sites can be very simple with just one or a few pages, or extraordinarily complex with thousands of pages interacting with extensive databases.

E-Mail

The term *e-mail* (short for electronic mail), having become so much a part of modern life, is more widely and accurately understood. E-mail is the exchange of text messages and computer files through a communications network, generally between computers or terminals. As use of e-mail has increased, computer users have joined together in groups (forums) to communicate via e-mail on topics of mutual interest. Although all depend on e-mail as the primary form of communication, these forums can be of various kinds; two of the most common are *mailing lists* and *newsgroups*. Mailing lists are set up so that a contribution to a "discussion" occurs when an individual member posts a message to the list. This message is then simultaneously posted to the e-mail addresses of everyone else on the list. If the list is *moderated*, the message must be approved by a list member whose role is to screen messages for appropriate content, so there is a delay before the message is distributed. If the list is *unmoderated*, posts are forwarded to list addresses automatically.

The newsgroup is a slightly different kind of forum. In newsgroups (unless one accesses them through a search engine) one needs a newsreader program, a special kind of software, to read posted messages.[4] Like mailing lists, messages posted by individual members are forwarded to all members, but unlike mailing lists, they become part of a public data source available to anyone through Web pages.[5] In other words, one does not need to be a member of the group to read messages. The largest, oldest, and most extensive collection of newsgroups is Usenet.

The Bewildering E-World

The new world of Internet discourse has presented scholars with a problem of analysis different from any other in the history of communication studies. Two factors in this problem are the Internet's size and its diversity. Internet discourse takes place in a medium that "allows, for the first time, the communication of many to many, in chosen time, on a global scale" (Castells, 2001, p. 2). The Internet is far too big and too varied to understand by means of many of the communication models we commonly use. Moreover, Internet size and diversity are connected. Diversity results from a multitude of combinations arising from the participation of the vast number of Internet users. Finally, the sheer volume of information exchanged through Internet communication is staggering. One recent book quotes a researcher who estimates that at any given moment "the equivalent of a small library, 15,000 to 30,000 books, is in transit over the Internet" (Weinberger, 2002, p. 19).

A good example illustrating this problem is e-mail discussion groups whose messages (EDMs) are analyzed in Chapter 3. The number of discussion groups is probably uncountable. On Usenet alone,[6] files are "grouped into approximately 75,000 newsgroups" (Henderson, 2003, p. 256) in an impressive array of special interest categories

(McLaughlin, Osborne, & Smith, 1995; Spencer & Lawrence, 1998). There are also many instances of an older form of group posting resource, the BBS (bulletin board system).[7] Still other groups on nonpublic systems use LISTSERV software,[8] and increasingly, groups are formed on commercial sites, such as Yahoo!Groups (www.yahoogroups.com) that offers groups access to very sophisticated programs for group discussion, in return for placing paid advertisements in messages and elsewhere.

The task of analyzing Internet discourse is further complicated by the diversity of forms of expression in which one encounters it. Internet discourse occurs in a host of languages, voices, tones, and inflections, and in Internet discourse one finds both the most and least elevated human expression—regardless of how "elevated" is defined—as well as accounts of the "best" and "worst" in human experience.

For example, the breathtaking diversity in e-mail discussion groups (Weinberger, 2002, p. 108) leads to a bewildering variety of messages that defy neat classification and could drive a composition teacher to distraction. In e-mail discussion groups we sometimes find ourselves on the frontier of human verbal expression. Many times the only rules seem to be those that listmembers themselves agree on and even these are repeatedly contestable. Weinberger (2002) says that

> the Web is a mess. . . . It consists of voices proclaiming whatever they think is worth saying, trying on stances, experimenting with extremes, being wrong in public, making fun of what they hold sacred in their day jobs, linking themselves into permanent coalitions and drive-by arguments, savoring the rush you feel when you realize you don't have to be the way you've been. (p. 23)[9]

Not only does participation in e-mail groups frequently teeter on disorder, the variation in forms of expression seems frantic. As a result, for many, not only is careful, "by-the-book" written composition not encouraged, it can be cruelly lampooned by other posters. Moreover, each group will, over time, develop its own unique expressions, shorthand, and abbreviations meaningful to cognoscenti but opaque to outsiders. Adoption of such terms works to make utterances in e-mail discussions even more idiosyncratic.

Another factor contributing to the confusion is that the Internet was designed to resist control structures that help define other venues of communication (Segaller, 1999). In other words, not only did Internet developers adhere to principles such as freedom from constraint, they have worked very hard to arrange matters so the Internet would stay that way. Throughout its development, key aspects of the Internet—such as open code (Castells, 2001, p. 38), hacking and other breaches of security (Mitnick & Simon, 2002; Schneier, 2000), and positions taken against censorship (Lessig, 1999, p. 232)—have been oriented toward an almost obsessive resistance to authority. This quality places even more uncertainty on attempts to understand Internet discourse. Far from being a venue that limits forms of expression, the Internet seems determined to go in the opposite direction, multiplying them without the constraints that work to limit variety in other forms of discourse.

The above observations are as true of Web pages/sites as they are of EDMs. Regulation of any form of Internet discourse is anathema to many of those responsible for creating and maintaining the Internet. To these individuals, the Internet symbolizes a spirit of freedom, the last form of expression that has not been largely co-opted and controlled by commercial institutions. Although we cannot know for certain, Web pages/sites may be even more diverse than EDMs, because of their much greater capacity to add visual and other features.

With an understanding of these key elements of the "bewildering e-world," one can perhaps begin to see why Internet communication provides a suitable environment for the propagation of civic discursive messages. The Internet offers possibilities for sharing, connecting, and participating, involving a far greater number of individuals, from a significantly more diverse range of cultures and backgrounds, than any previous form of communication. In the following, I explore the qualities of civil society, and their connection to Internet communication, in greater detail.

Internet Discourse as Civic Participation

The notion of civic participation is of course a cornerstone of democratic process, as is the use of civic discourse as a means to participate. By civic discourse I mean utterances, either written or spoken, that function to maintain society, particularly civil society. Modern life has seen civic processes increasingly mediated by the Internet, which has become one of a number of channels (two other predominant ones are television and radio) used to construct civic life.

Traditionally, civil society has been seen as that portion of social life related to the management of human interaction in a democracy. Not wishing to get entangled in the contentious disputes over what the term *democracy* means, I endorse what Posner (2003) refers to as "Concept 1 democracy," or the loftier, more idealistic, and (he argues) more academically inclined notion of democracy (p. 130). Posner contrasts Concept 1 with Concept 2 democracy, an idea based on Schumpeter (1947). Concept 2 democracy, also called "elite democracy," is, in the words of Posner, "realistic, cynical, and bottom-up" and, ultimately, "pragmatic" (p. 130).

The tenets of Concept 1 democracy are enunciated by Dahl (1989). Each participant in a democracy should be able to experience effective participation, have voting equality at the decisive stage, have enlightened understanding, and have control of the agenda. That these represent unrealistic ideals is noted by Dahl himself: "I take for granted that a perfect democratic process and a perfect democratic government might never exist in actuality. They represent ideas of human possibilities against which actualities may be compared" (p. 109). Nevertheless, I assume that our understanding of Internet utterance, as a tool of civic discourse, is still in its very preliminary stages, and therefore, that the most useful idea of it is the one that will do the most good in expanding the problem space in how we think about it. The more useful candidate for this purpose is Concept 1 democracy. If we become bogged down in the messy, dark realities of Concept 2 democracy, we stand little chance of developing the optimism to carry us forward to a new vision of the Internet in civic discourse.

Although this will be shown in much more detail in subsequent discussion, I should point out here that, in either the Concept 1 or Concept 2 view, democracy involves communication. The far more extensive opportunities for communication presented by the Internet make it an optimal means for communicating civic discursive utterances. This is particularly so in the United States (which has led the way in developing the Internet), where one of the most precious freedoms is freedom of expression. Freedom of expression hinges on the belief that better civic solutions emerge from open discussion. Indeed, it would not be too much to say that freedom of expression is the mainspring driving democracy, no matter how or where it is manifested. An important feature of early, optimistic predictions about how the Internet and the World Wide Web would change the face of civic life had to do with the Internet's (purportedly) "wide open" architecture that was thought more likely to encourage participation.[10]

The Internet, broadly conceived, provides the venue for e-mail, while its more limited subelement, the World Wide Web, defines the setting for Web pages/sites. Furthermore, e-mail discussion (as contrasted with person-to-person e-mail) is mediated by computer software, as in newsreaders (for newsgroups) or LISTSERV software (for the management of mailing lists), while the display of Web pages/sites relies on HTTP protocols as well as markup languages such as HTML, XML (Extensible Markup Language),[11] and so on, that define how pages will appear in the Web browser. Through all of these developments, discourse about civic matters, ranging from civil activism to contemplation of one's role in society to presidential politics, has changed. While the change might not yet have been as thoroughgoing as originally predicted (no new medium lives up to the buoyant predictions made when it is first introduced), and while there is still much room for growth, the landscape for civic discourse is now different, as I will show from the analysis of data in Chapter 3 ("E-Mail Discussion Messages") and Chapter 4 ("Web Sites as Means for Propagating Civic, Political, and Ideological Concepts").

Next, I delve further into specific points concerning the relation between the Internet and public/civic discourse. I look at both the potential for the Internet to play a key role in the propagation of civic utterances and some of the current limitations that may be keeping this potential from being fully realized.

EDMs and Web Pages/Sites: Channels for Civic Discourse

With an understanding of the role played by the Internet in civic participation, I now turn to establishing a rationale for focusing on two of the most prevalent forms of Internet communication (EDMs and Web pages/sites), as well as comments on the relationship between these two forms and civic discourse. Of the many types of Internet discourse available, EDMs and Web pages/sites present not only the greatest volume of material for analysis but are also the most readily accessible. Beyond this, EDMs and Web pages/sites are ideal for studying Internet communication as civic discourse, for a number of reasons. For one thing, like some forms of civic discourse (for example, public speeches or letters to the editor), but unlike others (for example, production of television messages), people with only basic familiarity with computers can create and alter Internet messages. This is most evident in e-mail, which many use regularly, but it is also becoming progressively truer of Web pages/sites, which are increasingly easier to construct and change. Moreover, apart from the still limited availability of computers and connection to the Internet in many countries, the architecture of both the Internet and the Web is designed to encourage open participation. Also, the reach of e-mail and the World Wide Web, spanning the entire world, means that most utterances have the potential to engender responses from any other computer user, anywhere.

Apart from EDMs and very basic Web pages/sites, other forms of what might be called "enhanced Internet/Web communication" (that is, communication that, due to its sophistication, is only found on a comparative minority of pages/sites) also play a significant role in civic and public discourse. For example, both retrievable sound and video recordings have had an impact on how news is delivered or perceived by users of the Internet. As I will show in Chapter 4, U.S. presidential candidates now regularly use video and audio files on their Web sites as a comparatively low-cost way of propagating messages to large numbers of receivers simultaneously. Prior to such technology, the only way a candidate could get a video or audio message to the voter was to buy air time for it, subject to "equal-time" provisions. Now, not only can video/audio feeds be instituted on the Web site for a fraction of the cost of broadcast airing, the link to the presentation is often coordinated, for example, with an e-mail message that can be sent to thousands of addressees at once.

However, despite the great potential of such technological innovations to change the face of civic discourse, I want to focus on what is currently most readily available to the greatest number of computer users. Enhancements such as video presentations are not in wide enough use, nor available to enough propagators or perceivers, to be helpful to a majority of computer users. On the other hand, nearly every user who can access the Internet can join, or even start, an e-mail discussion group. Likewise, nearly every person connected can design and put pages/sites on the Web (particularly through "free" host sites such as Tripod[12]) with only a bare minimum of training. While there is no question that technological enhancements once thought exotic are becoming more common and can be expected to continue to increase as computers become more sophisticated, these and other "high-level" augmentations are still currently the property of the comparatively privileged few. EDMs and Web pages/sites are forms of public discourse widely available to many more people, even those who do not personally own computers, but who can access the Internet through public venues such as libraries or cybercafes. With this picture of the rapidly shifting cyber-scape in mind, I now turn to the specific aspects of EDMs and Web pages/sites that make them useful for civic discourse.

EDMs, Web Pages/Sites, and the Democratic Process

Despite its flaws (for a particularly trenchant summary of these, as applied to the political arena, see Graber, 2003, pp. 152–153), the Internet and "classic" (ideal) democracy intersect in several areas. In the following, I consider three facets of Internet communication that resonate with democratic principles: (1) as a means to contribute to forums for persuasion, (2) as a means for a greater number of users to participate, and (3) as a means to create a climate for debate.

Internet Communication as a Means to Contribute to Forums for Persuasion

There is no question that Internet communication has changed the face of persuasion in public/civic discourse. Internet communication is more immediate in that distances of time and space between communicators have dramatically lessened, permitting persuasive messages a much wider and quicker dissemination than ever before. However, some of the persuasive techniques that teachers tell their students to rely on in "real-life" situations are not necessarily as effective when used in Internet communication. Rarely, for example, do EDM discussions conform to the dictates of formal reasoning or "proper" debate.

Perhaps because of these qualities, EDM forums, and to a somewhat lesser extent Web pages/sites, have a strong sense of immediate, visceral participation lacking in other more traditional forums for persuasion. On the Internet, you can say what you want in some forum or other, for the most part nearly free of censorship. Moreover, what you say can potentially reach a much wider audience. Thus, for those frustrated at not being able to express themselves in conventional channels of public discourse (not everyone has the money to buy air time on television or radio or space in newspapers, or the assertive personality needed to be heard in face-to-face forums), the Internet is an ideal channel. The drawback is that, given the vast expanse of the Internet, one's utterance is likely to be lost in the vast amorphous sea of information. However, at least on lists or newsgroups, one can often be assured that at least some interested parties encounter one's persuasive message directly, and may even respond, not just to oneself but to all the other list/group members as well.

A number of unique features of Internet communication function to encourage its use in forums for persuasion. For example, people are protected by anonymity, in that very little is known of the real person who composes the post or the page. Hence, users are more free to say what is really on their minds, though this of course can be a mixed blessing, since many use this protection as an excuse to descend to the basest levels of communication (for example, through "flaming"[13] in discussions or placing offensive utterances on Web pages).

Another feature that encourages participation in forums for persuasion is that, at least for the moment, Internet communication is, comparatively speaking, unregulated. This is probably less a matter of governmental disinterest than an inability for any regulator even to grasp what the Internet/Web really is, including its size, what it accomplishes, how far it extends, and so on. Those who would try to regulate civic discourse on the Internet must first deal with the question of precisely what is being regulated and who is involved. Because Internet communication can be anonymous, this regulatory task is especially daunting.

Those responsible for maintaining the Internet seem anxious to protect their reputation as defenders of the "last frontier" of free expression. In disputes over whether to be lenient concerning expression (as when people are allowed to use sexually abusive or threatening language in discussion groups) or restrict it (as when people propose banning such utterances), the Internet community tends toward leniency. Supporters of freedom of Internet expression often cite the "slippery slope" argument: over time, governments tend to endorse more, not less, regulation and the process of regulating Internet speech, once begun, might tend to exclude more and more communication until users of the Internet may someday face the same situation broadcasters confront today. Broadcasters on the public airwaves are controlled by the threat that they will not have their licenses renewed should they broadcast forms of communication that violate federal law or community practice. Ironically, these advocates emphasize that, although federal broadcast regulation began with a desire to protect access, over time it has also come to represent restriction. Similarly, many in the Internet community tend to suspect any regulation, no matter how seemingly benign. One could add to this concern another: if Internet speech is regulated, the willingness of people to participate in forums for persuasion might lessen and the potential of the Internet to serve as a way for people to engage in civic discourse would also suffer.

Internet Communication as a Means for a Greater Number of Users to Participate

Another ideal of democracy has to do with including the greatest possible number of participants in the democratic process. Participation of individuals in Internet-based communication has grown along with growing access to these venues, as well as the increased availability of computer hardware and software. For several reasons, communicating through these venues expands participation in civic discourse.

One quality of Internet communication leading to increased opportunities for participation in civic discourse is that many discussion groups and sites do not have very stringent requirements for participation (though there are, of course, notable exceptions). In line with the greater degree of anonymity, it is difficult, not to say impossible, for anyone wishing to monitor qualifications for membership to confirm that participants are who they say they are. As a result, for many discussion groups, the only requirement for membership is simply that one sign up. Many people, for whom membership in groups in "real life" might be problematic, find it a liberating experience to express themselves about issues of concern in the "presence" of similarly inclined others.

Another feature of Internet discourse that makes it ideal for increased civic participation is that there are widely varying levels of what can be classified as "participation," ranging from "lurking" (that is, just reading messages, and not posting messages) to occasional posting/responding to full participation in a discussion as a key, frequently contributing participant. Participation in civic discourse takes on more threatening qualities when it is done face to face, or even via mass media (as in the extraordinarily popular venue of radio call-in talk shows). These problematic elements include facing aggressive or hostile opposition from either opponents or moderators, such as the risk of being "shouted down" for expressing a controversial viewpoint. While Internet communication can hold some of these same terrors (Seabrook, 1997), in that people who respond to one's posts or react to one's pages/sites can be extraordinarily cruel and insulting, at least one does not have to face the opponent. Usually the worst that can happen in e-mail is that one is presented with a response that seems to necessitate a reply. Not only can one choose to reply or not, one can take a longer time to compose that reply than if one had to come up with a response on the spot.

Also, the Internet medium is ideal for discussing competing or alternative ideologies. If we view ideology in its simplest form, simply as a system of meaning, then we must assume, with Bakhtin, that communication inevitably involves a clash of meaning systems, simply because what one person knows cannot be even approximately the same as what another knows (see Holquist, 1990, p. 21). This means the communication venue that stands the best chance of gaining the most participation is the one in which competing viewpoints (based on variant ideologies) are easiest to transmit and receive. On these requirements, the Internet is clearly an attractive form of communication, being open to many, largely unregulated, and widespread enough to guarantee a broad dissemination of utterances.

Not only does the Internet utterance, by its nature (for example, apparently infinite connectivity), seem inherently more "democratic" than other kinds of utterance, it is this quality that makes it easier for people separated by aspects of their lives (for example, where they live, cultural background, and so on) to exchange messages with each other. Although contacts such as these can often require sophisticated coordination, as in public relations events in which entertainers or authors "meet" the public, answering questions from them "in real time," it can also be done through far less sophisticated Internet resources. In Chapter 4, for example, I discuss a feature that U.S. presidential candidate Al Gore had on his Web site called the "Interactive Town Hall," a Web page to which visitors could post questions for the candidate to answer.[14] A forum such as this provides an ideal opportunity for a candidate and people across the country, or even the world, to interact, and be seen interacting, over the Internet.

Internet Communication as a Means to Create a Climate for Debate

The ability of the Internet to unite those of disparate backgrounds has great potential for fostering debate and discussion of issues in the civic arena. In many cases, differences of opinion about, for example, political issues arise from lack of familiarity with the perspectives of other people. In other words, political disputes often arise as much out of unfamiliarity with others as they do from "true" differences of opinion. Regardless of the points at which they begin, people who stand in opposition can nearly always, in a democratic, civic society, benefit from learning more about an issue through becoming more familiar with those who hold opinions different from their own. Internet communication creates a climate in which multiplicities of connections provide a great number and variety of opportunities for ideas to be shared.

Furthermore, the Internet can foster debate and discussion through an interesting feature nearly unique to the medium: message archiving. The written format of, for example, EDM lists (which regularly archive their past messages) permit the interested observer to read, at his or her leisure, past debates on a given issue. Particularly through the use of search engines that combine the massive archives of Usenet groups (this service was formerly called "DejaNews [deja.com]"[15] but is now one of several searchable databases under the management of Google [www.google.com]), it is possible to find a voluminous amount of public discussion on just about any subject. Thus, anyone wishing to sample opinion in this part of the public sphere can do so through the simplest of search requests. Indeed, this is exactly the procedure I followed to find the two message sequences (threads) analyzed in Chapter 3, after examining hundreds of message sequences from vastly different newsgroups.

Another way both EDMs and Web pages/sites can realize debate and discussion is through their ability to link to other pages/sites or messages throughout the Internet, thus allowing composers of utterance to have at their fingertips the most extensive reference library in the history of communication—and all it takes to give the visitor access is the simple procedure of highlighting a bit of text in either the EDM or on the Web page and specifying it as a link to another cyberspace location. This means that in addition to joining together different points of view between more or less immediate interactants (for example, in the simplest case, the poster of an EDM message and another poster who replies directly to it), Internet utterance has the ability to involve others as "participants" in the dialogue. The climate for debate is thus greatly enhanced, in that both the numbers of people involved (and their personal repositories of knowledge), as well as the amount of information capable of being cited as evidence, are substantially increased.

The effects of this interconnectivity can be quite dramatic. I will show, for example, that in the thread composed by the group discussing the case of Wen Ho Lee (Chapter 3) that a poster, early in the thread, copies into a message an entire article taken from the Web site of *Newsweek* magazine. This article, together with reactions to it, are reposted, either in whole or in part, numerous times in the rest of the messages, as posters after the first message utilize their e-mail software's capacity to requote the article. In what other venue could one have messages that summarize a piece of writing, together with all the posted reactions to it, sequentially displayed in a single format, and moreover, for there to be the capability of such an artifact available at the touch of a button (in this case, the key that activates the "reply to" function in the e-mail program)? The Internet is, as Lessig (2002) puts it, a "commons," that is, an area accessible to many individuals. Such a commons is essential in any conception of democracy, and despite Lessig's reservations about the diminishing amount of freedom in the Internet's layers of access, there is no question that the medium is unique among communication channels in its ability to bring together individuals of vastly divergent backgrounds to communicate with each other.

Limitations in Realizing the Potential of Internet Communication as Civic Discourse

While both EDMs and Web pages/sites have significant potential for use in the arena of civic discourse, they also present some pitfalls. The flexibility and wide open character of EDMs and site utterances lead to problems that run somewhat counter to the ideal of free and open exchange of information in the ideal civic culture. However, these problems are usually seen as inevitable, given the nature of the medium, and indeed as a small price to pay for such a unique form of expression.

First, we must face the fact that comparatively little, if any, information on the Internet can be verified. In more traditional forms of communication, such as newspaper publication or broadcasting, those who fashion utterances can be held to account for what they say. Although things are changing very slowly with respect to the Internet, at present very little discourse on it is similarly monitored. Were one to attempt such regulation, one would face the perpetual problems of Internet size and scope. Even if, for example, it were possible to regulate one site by forbidding certain utterances or banning certain utterers, it is easy for the offending communicator to shift to another site or group, and moreover nearly immediately apprise numerous others of the new location. Thus, the truth or falsity of what is posted on the Internet is left entirely to the poster.

Furthermore, on the Internet, possibilities for manipulating information seem endless. Perhaps the aura of precision attached to computers makes it seem as if what is on the Internet must be "correct" or "real" in some special sense. However, manipulation by people who design Web sites or participate in discussion groups can give the patina of legitimacy to information that is highly questionable. A dramatic example is parody sites, such as those propagated by the Yes Men, a collection of Net guerillas who describe themselves as "a genderless, loose-knit association of some three hundred imposters worldwide" (Ramasastry, 2002). The Yes Men have been involved in construction of some notorious parodies, including one of the World Trade Organization's (WTO) site (www.gatt.org) that prompted a WTO demand that the site be shut down (the Yes Men had sent out e-mails that announced, among other things, that the WTO intended to dissolve itself and create a new organization focused on human rights rather than business interests [Ramasastry, 2002]). The Yes Men have taken the process of making "fake" sites one step further by offering special software that allows users to copy sites and to change the language to more satirical phrasing. These and many other examples of users "playing with" site utterances demonstrate that any Internet utterance must be regarded with caution.

Of course, false or doctored information is a problem in any venue of communication (witness the recent scandals concerning story fabrication at the *New York Times* [Frank, 2003]), and the Internet certainly is not the only form of communication where lies come to seem like the truth. However, aside from our inability to verify the truth or falsity of the information found on pages and sites, the ability of designers/communicators in cyberspace to link to other parts of the Internet makes the provision of bad information even more dangerous. For example, a "legitimate" document might contain information through links to other Web sites that has not, quite innocently enough, been checked by the composer, while a spurious document could easily have an air of legitimacy due to using what appear to be highly respectable Internet sources.

The possibility of false information being taken for true runs counter to the ideal of civic discourse. Civic discourse is supposed to provide a forum in which the "best"—that is, the truest and most appropriate—ideas will gain increasing acceptance through being exposed to open debate. Indeed, given the propensity of the Internet to generate questionable utterances, it is possible to conceive of an interesting and potentially informative clash of various representations in Internet venues, none of which are true.[16]

While the composer and user of Internet communication may feel that information conveyed via the Internet is a case of "let the buyer beware," it is difficult to check every reference, keeping up to date on whether the information on a site is reliable. Even more problematic, though, the "tree" structure of Internet linkages presents even more tenebrous pitfalls. For example, an individual might have checked his or her own site for accuracy; nevertheless, it would be too much to demand that he or she thoroughly check the linkages on the site to which his or her site links, or the links from those links, and so on—and this is not even to mention all the pages that contain links to the site in question. At some point, one simply trusts to two dubious principles: first, the rather Gricean notion that most people are fundamentally honest and do their best to provide good information to others (Grice, 1975); and second, that most users of the Internet are aware of the questionable nature of anything they encounter on the Internet and therefore develop a distrust of it.

Another problem that can render the Internet problematic as a channel for civic discourse is the sheer volume of information available. Though one cannot easily establish this empirically, it is probably not too much to say that the amount of information available on any given issue is incomprehensible. Beyond primary sources, one can extend linkages into secondary, tertiary, and even further levels, with comparative ease. The simplest search through a widely used search engine such as Google (whether for Usenet messages or Web pages/sites) customarily yields thousands of links. In other words, just reading the information from the Internet is difficult enough, but the branching complexities of the search present another problem to anyone who wants to use this material in civic discourse. It becomes enormously difficult to sort through the information one obtains. Anyone who has used the Internet to do research has encountered this problem: one difficulty with "grazing" for Internet information is that one is taken (usually by the parameters of a search engine) into areas connected only marginally to one's area of interest. Unless one sets up extremely restrictive search criteria—a strategy that can severely limit the scope of results—the Internet provides a frightening number of "blind alleys" to snare the unwary. In an oddly paradoxical way, the user who must cope with information overload may return in frustration to previous knowledge with which she or he is more familiar, thus obviating the Internet's purported advantage in bestowing information, an outcome that is, of course, also antithetical to the ideals of civic discourse.

In the realm of civic discourse, such seemingly limitless possibilities can prove to be a problem, because one gets overloaded with data, and yet it is so easy to link to this data in EDMs and Web pages/sites that one can come to think that linking to another source performs the same function as citing evidence to support an argument in conventional rhetoric. Combined with the problems of not being able to verify the accuracy of information, the user who relies on cyberutterances as sources for civic discourse stands in serious danger of coming to depend on information that is superfluous, trivial, inaccurate, or outright wrong. The availability of information on the Internet merely increases the odds that "bad" information will find its way into public debates (and this is in addition to information of lesser quality that finds its way onto the Internet from other sources such as speeches, published articles, and so on).

These conditions, however, lead to another problem bearing on use of the Internet in civic discourse. The problems just described relate to conditions as they exist in the United States, whose population constitutes by far the most extensive body of Internet users (Juliussen & Petska-Juliussen, 1998). Beyond the United States, one can often be confronted with a considerably more pessimistic picture of the future of the Internet. Use of the Internet for American-style civic discourse in some other countries is limited by such factors as the availability of computers, development of infrastructure for electronic transmission of signals, and policies of authoritarian governments to control the content of Internet discourse. Nevertheless, I will take the position that it is in the United States, the cradle of what is arguably one of the most enduring and successful human experiments in self-governance, that we find the seeds for a beginning of a new phase in our understanding of the potential for civic discourse. It is this understanding, developed more thoroughly, that will lead to realizing the potential of Internet discourse and provides other cultures a template—of which the Internet will be an integral part—for democratic self-expression.

We now have some better understanding of the role of the Internet in civic discourse, its benefits and problems, as manifested in its two most widely used communication forms, EDMs and Web pages/sites. These understandings prepare us to pursue the question of why Internet utterance is in some ways less well understood than other forms of communication, and also why EDMs and Web pages/sites currently are used in civic discourse at somewhat less than their full potential. I would argue that one answer lies in current lack of in-depth understanding of the nature of Internet messages, especially when compared to the much greater understanding we have about other forms of communication. The ideas we use to discuss other forms of communication take on different meanings when we apply them to the Internet. The reach of the Internet is much vaster; its potential for audience feedback much more immediate; and the ability for people to participate in the production of messages on it much more extensive, than with perhaps any other form of communication. As has proved the case in the past, with other "new" media, the tools applied to the analysis of more established, better known, forms of media are usually deficient, though we rely on them because they are the best we have and we do gain some insight from them.

Access to the Internet will continue to increase, as will cultural adjustment to its central role in civic and other aspects of daily life. Without a more sophisticated understanding of Internet utterance, we risk seeing Internet communication, as civic discourse and otherwise, not in terms of how it actually functions, but in terms of conventional models of communication that do not fit its unique features. We can thus better prepare for accelerated technological change if we understand how the Internet works in incorporating messages into the construction of the fabric of civic life.

THE NEED FOR A NEW METHOD: PROPOSED INTEGRATION

The preceding discussion has brought out both the promise and the pitfalls of Internet communication as a way of actualizing the ideals of civic society, setting the stage for the method I will propose both as a solution to the problems of understanding Internet utterance, and, ultimately, as the basis for improving it as a means of civic discourse. This method involves considering Internet utterance in both its monologic and dialogic aspects. In the following, I elaborate these two important terms, often thought of as opposites, and then turn to a discussion of why integration of the two perspectives offers the opportunity for a much more comprehensive understanding of Internet utterance.

Monologism and Dialogism

In this section, I offer a provisional distinction between *monologism* and *dialogism*, and will continue to define these concepts as I explore dialogism's roots (Chapter 2) and analyze EDMs and Web pages/sites (Chapters 3 and 4, respectively).

My approach to Internet discourse is built around two ideas: monologism (as an adjective, *monological*, as a mode of communication, *monologue*), which in discourse and thought suggests order and predictability; and dialogism (as an adjective, *dialogical*, as a mode of communication, *dialogue*), which suggests uniqueness and unpredictability. These two terms describe fundamentally different ways of looking at cognition and communication, and in one form or another, have always been part of human intellectual perspectives. However, like most useful ideas, the so-called distinction between monologism and dialogism is best seen as a contrast between two convenient metaphors, rather than as a hard and fast division resulting in nonoverlapping categories. In fact, it could be argued that monologism and dialogism really define each other, in that monologism represents widely endorsed, institutionally sanctioned, predominant views (though not often explicitly acknowledged as such), whereas dialogism can be understood as the alternative to monologism. To put it another way, we comprehend monologism by considering dialogism, and vice versa.[17]

Dialogism is most commonly associated with Mikhail Bakhtin (1895–1975), perhaps the most influential Russian literary and cultural critic of the modern era. Nevertheless, as Bakhtin scholar Michael Holquist (1990) points out, Bakhtin never used the word *dialogism*, and Holquist is even hesitant to use that term to describe Bakhtin's work, though he does so as "a synthetic means . . . for categorizing the different ways he meditated on dialogue" (p. 15). Bakhtin described novels as being either primarily monologic (that is, primarily characterized by a single, controlling authorial voice that dominates the text, even when other voices are included) or primarily dialogic (primarily characterized by numerous voices interacting with one another and no one voice controlling).

By extension, then, language or communication that is predominantly monological (it can never be purely monological, but only tend in that direction) is constructed according to a dominant system of thought (for example, a Supreme Court decision is written according to strict formal reasoning and style, and with reference to established legal precedent). Monological views resonate with the information-processing model of cognition; the code model of language; and the transmission model of communication (see, for example, Shannon & Weaver, 1949). Like Bakhtin's monological novel type, in monologic discourse of all kinds, alternative conceptions of the ideas involved are kept firmly under the control of the author, according to the dictates primarily of the written mode of expression (for example, formal logic, rules for composition, denotative definitions, and so on). Monologism also frequently involves reducing the world to constituent parts that can be thought about rationally and verified empirically. Language and knowledge are viewed as being independent of the individual who knows them and speaks/writes about them. In monologism, one can trust in what one knows and can rely on language to convey that knowledge to others, even though, as individuals, humans seldom live up to the standards of perfection of the monologic model. Most of what we learn through formal education is based on primarily monological discourse.

Language or communication that is predominantly dialogical (it can never be purely dialogical, but only tend in that direction) is constructed so as to allow the interactive presence of multiple perspectives on phenomena (for example, a free-for-all, anything-goes exchange in an unmoderated Internet chat room[18]). Dialogism resonates with subjective modes of cognition; transactional models of language (see, for example, Watzlawick, Beavin, & Jackson, 1967); and dynamic, nonlinear models of communication. Like Bakhtin's dialogical novel type, in dialogic discourse of all kinds, alternative conceptions of the ideas involved are given free rein, functioning in ways that call to mind the spoken mode of expression (for example, multivocality, informality, lack of precision, collaborative construction of meaning, and so on).

Dialogism resists the idea of constructing discourse according to an overriding, dominant system of thought. Rather, the focus of dialogism is on *relations* and *context*, which vary according to the specific circumstances in which discourse occurs. Thus, the "same" words can mean different things when used in different specific circumstances. Moreover, concepts underlying language are unavoidably interdependent, and "real life" can neither be described in monological terms nor can its constituent components be separated from one another. Language and knowledge are viewed as dependent on who the knower or the speaker/writer is, and on his or her relationship to all others and to specific circumstances in which thought and language are used. What we know is open to interpretation and although we must rely on language to express knowledge, we cannot assume this knowledge is stable or independent of context. Regardless of monological standards of perfection, dialogism assumes that each individual has a unique view of the world and that this view has validity as a reference point to think about the world. Typically, dialogism does not receive broad support in formal education; indeed, the ways by which we learn to question the primarily monological foundations of thought in formal education could be characterized as dialogic.

As noted, no discourse should be seen as either monologic or dialogic. Any utterance, written or spoken, however, usually will indicate which way the author intends it to be taken. If the author seems to want to have the utterance taken in only one, or a few, ways (a nasty letter from a collection agency, for example, seldom appears to invite dissent), then we would say that her or his utterance tends toward monologism (single word/thought). On the other hand, if the author seems to invite a multiplicity of viewpoints (for example, leading a brainstorming session about ways to improve efficiency on the shop floor at one's workplace), or in some other way surrender control of the discourse, then her or his utterance tends toward dialogism (many words/thoughts).

Language used in specific sociohistorical situations (which is to say all language) always involves elements tending both to monologism and dialogism. The monological features of language include grammatical rules, denotative definitions of words, rules of composition, and so on; these features render language at least partially understandable, regardless of who is uttering it and who is listening to or reading it. At the same time, dialogism as well as common sense tells us that each utterance is also completely unique unto itself and will never be repeated, nor will different people understand it the same way from one occurrence to the next. These considerations mean that no utterance can be considered understandable to any other person, except in the crudest and most basic ways. Since utterance has both monological and dialogical qualities, all utterances are predictable, yet unpredictable; stable, yet constantly changing; classifiable into common categories, yet unique.

The situation just described, the unavoidable joining of regular–irregular aspects of language, has a well-known name given to it by Bakhtin: *heteroglossia*, or "other voicedness." Heteroglossia advances the idea that one who introduces an utterance into the stream of discourse must choose, out of an infinite number of ways to express thought (suggestive of the irregular, relentlessly divergent, aspects of language), only one way, created and understood primarily according to conventional categories of language such as grammar, sentence structure, understanding of conversation conventions, and so on (suggestive of the regular aspects of language) (Bakhtin, 1981). Bakhtin wished to highlight the idea that every utterance represents a choice of form of expression by the utterer, even though the utterer's unique configuration of perceptions guarantees that no one else will understand, even approximately, what the utterance means (because those who encounter the utterance also have unique perspectives of their own).

While the fact that living language comprises both monological and dialogical tendencies makes ordinary communication frustrating, it also provides the communication analyst with a useful tool, particularly when applied to an emergent form of communication such as Internet discourse. The union, in living language, of monological/dialogical features means that any given piece of discourse can be examined for aspects of either quality, depending on the needs of the analyst. Realization of this duality presents many more possibilities for probing the meaning of utterance, a feature that proves particularly valuable in the case of Internet discourse, whose breathtaking range of expression, multivocality, and thoroughgoing diversity make it resistant to primarily monological models derived from the study of more conventional forms of communication.

This is not to say that, by improving our ability to analyze Internet utterances, we will make it possible to fully use them as tools of civic discourse. Beyond understanding Internet utterances, a host of technical, physical, and psychological problems prevent people from having the capability, or the willingness, to participate in civic life through computer-mediated communication (Graber, 2003; Putnam, 2000). Nevertheless, despite these obstacles, understanding the dialogic (and monologic) nature of Internet utterance is a good place to begin, perhaps because the monological and the dialogical represent an analog to the two, often contradictory, features of civic discourse: the need to systematize discourse to provide a structure of control (as through legislation and regulation), and the need, as a matter of principle, to embrace even the most widely divergent views (as through protection of the right to free expression, even if it violates prevailing social norms).

An Integrated Approach

In Chapters 3 and 4, I employ a "dual reading" method whereby it is possible to consider Internet discourse, first, in monological terms (called the "standard reading") and then, in dialogical terms (called the "utterance reading"). The dual reading approach allows the analyst to bypass certain obstacles standing in the way of analyzing Internet discourse, particularly the two forms on which I concentrate: EDMs and Web pages/sites.

Chief among these obstacles is the fact that almost all conventional communication theory is based on monological perspectives. This has led to a preponderance of structural/functional explanations of EDMs and Web pages/sites as artifacts of communication. Although there have been some attempts to avoid primarily monological analysis of Internet communication, these attempts for the most part have gone too far the other way, in that they privilege an almost entirely subjective approach that insufficiently acknowledges the advantages of the monological perspective. Perhaps because of the relatively short time Internet communication has been studied, the usual modes of analysis for analyzing Internet discourse have proved less than optimal. Hence, this discursive medium has not, for the most part, received the kind of in-depth, extended treatment it demands, particularly concerning its role in civic society.[19]

In recent years, there have emerged alternatives to the primarily monological theories of human communication (in fact any conventional theoretical perspective, because it is based on generalizations, inclines toward monologism). These other perspectives are often referred to as "dialogical perspectives" (see, for example, Bakhtin, 1981; Bruner & Gorfain, 1984; Crapanzano, 1990; Duranti & Goodwin, 1992; Edwards & Middleton, 1986; Markovà & Foppa, 1990; Tannen, 1989), though this covering term is difficult to sustain since "dialogical" perspectives themselves tend to be somewhat unruly and difficult to classify (Linell, 1998; see also Chapter 2, this volume). Yet even dialogical analysis of Internet communication falls short if it does not acknowledge the one essential feature lacking in most such analyses: an overt incorporation of findings gleaned from the monological perspective.

What I offer is a method that encourages the analyst to keep in mind both the predictable and the unpredictable features of language. This method is ideal for examining Internet communication, particularly in the context of civic society. While the Internet, as a channel of communication, is sometimes dismissed as ordinary or mundane, depth exploration of the social worlds informing this discourse, through the lenses of monologism and dialogism, reveals its complexity as a vehicle for representing empirical experience in ways that affect civic discourse and culture.

Although dialogical analysis requires considerable analytic attention and effort, it joins other approaches in working under the assumption that Internet discourse, like all forms of communication, must be understood in both its orderly and disorderly aspects. Practitioners of the dialogic approach, while cognizant of its role as a method counter to the monologic approach (which generally relies on a coherent, orderly, unitary view of phenomena, largely unquestioned and presumed to be "the truth"), focus primarily on multiple perspectives toward phenomena, seeking reality in the degree to which human understanding embraces chaotic, disorderly, and multiple "truths." Various dialogical approaches to discussion groups and Web sites thus provide ways to unfold what at first seems opaque and thus too difficult to analyze.

In particular, I focus on the textual criticism described by the Bakhtin circle, along with dialogically inclined approaches of scholars from other disciplines. These offer analysts of Internet communication interesting and provocative perspectives that permit resolution of some of the field's most persistently troubling questions.

ABOUT THIS BOOK

The goal of this book is to describe and use the dialogic perspective to analyze Internet discourse, and to extend the insights gained through dialogic inquiry by contrasting them with features of the monologic perspective. I closely analyze utterance, especially civic discourse, as seen in EDMs and Web pages/sites. Specifically, I provide depth exploration of Internet discourse in these two public venues to investigate the process of fashioning and understanding civic discourse in a technologically mediated world.

Although the data sources I regularly consult are wide-ranging and comprehensive, I concentrate particularly on key data sources that pertain to civic discourse, manifested as assertions about racial, political, sexual, and cultural identity, as expressed and redefined through messages posted or the way in which a Web page/site is constructed. These sources of data include social activism sites ("Swastika on the Lawn" [a site devoted to exposing anti-Semitism]); campaign Web sites (presidential candidates for the 2000 United States presidential election); and public discussion of political issues (extended message threads from lists discussing Wen Ho Lee [on an Asian politics list] and radio talk show host Laura Schlessinger's opinions on lesbian adoption [on a gay/lesbian issues list]). In each case, the selected data set has been chosen because of its relevance to dialogical conceptions of the Internet, as well as to satisfy certain parameters of analytical interest (for example, the threads need to be of sufficient length and must discuss subjects in appropriate depth; the Web sites need to exhibit adequate distinction from one another in terms of language and visual presentation conventions; and the issues they address must represent diverse but important aspects of civic life).

The remainder of the book is devoted to expansion of these ideas. Chapter 2 explains three lines of development, from the standpoint of five intellectual traditions (Vico, pragmatism, phenomenology, Vygotsky, and Bakhtin), that have led to current thinking on dialogism. In outlining the history of dialogism, I also emphasize how dialogistic ideas developed through contrast and interplay with monological perspectives. Chapter 3 deals with dialogical principles, again as contrasted with and compared to monological perspectives (through the dual reading method), as discussed in Chapter 2, applied to the first of the two principal civic discourse venues, e-mail discussion messages (EDMs). The dual reading method, originally derived primarily from the recognition of language's simultaneously monological/dialogical character in the work of the Bakhtin circle, has other roots in the developmental lines explored in Chapter 2. In the initial reading, EDM threads are analyzed from a structuralist-functionalist perspective, achieving a content-based analysis of the thread's centripetal (conventional, predictable, monological) features.[20] In the alternative reading, the thread is analyzed from a centrifugal perspective (by linking thread utterances to multiplex worlds of meaning that inform them), achieving a critical-descriptive (dialogical) interpretation of the symbolic and cultural features "brought into" the thread's utterances by their composers and those who read them. To demonstrate this analytical method, I perform a detailed analysis of two discussion threads, one dealing with the case of Los Alamos engineer Wen Ho Lee, and the other dealing with radio personality Laura Schlessinger.

In Chapter 4, I apply the dual reading method to the second of the two principal Internet civic discourse venues, Web pages/sites. This dual reading approach (similar to the method used on EDMs in Chapter 3) puts more emphasis on site design than on linguistic content. This is because the central question of interest with relation to designing Web sites for civic discourse is not so much what is said (as it was for the e-mail discussion messages), but rather how standard elements of the site (including, but not limited to, text) are configured in idiosyncratic ways, resulting in greater or lesser degrees of persuasive effectiveness.

Emphasis will be placed on the interaction of orderly features of site design (for example, HTML code, image formats, design conventions, and so on), as well as the unique, unrepeatable aspects, such as how these elements are combined in unique ways.

The use of dual reading on Web pages/sites will be illustrated in two case studies of the Web site as a tool of political persuasion. In the first study, the sites of the two major 2000 U.S. presidential candidates, George W. Bush and Al Gore, will be analyzed in terms of their development during the period June 1999 to just after the U.S. presidential election in November 2000. In the second study, a social activist Web site devoted to increasing awareness of, and combating, anti-Semitism, "Swastika on the Lawn: A Year of Anti-Semitism in Massachusetts," will be examined to explore some reasons that seem to make the site effective in dealing with hate speech/crimes.

In the final chapter, attention will be focused on what has been accomplished by the dual readings in the two previous chapters. The analytical difficulties of dealing with Internet discourse will be revisited, and the advantages of the dialogical approach in analyzing civic discourse summarized, particularly concerning its use in conjunction with monological reading. Furthermore, it will be shown that various dialogical approaches, particularly those advanced by the Bakhtin circle, point toward ways to emancipate those who study computer-mediated communication from an overreliance either on the regularities of structural-functional explanations, or on idiosyncratic readings growing out of critical-cultural explanations.

Internet discourse, with its capability to cross national boundaries and reach diverse audiences easily and quickly, is transforming the face of civic and public communication. We thus stand in need of in-depth methods for analyzing public and civic discourse in computer-mediated venues, by examining the sociohistorical and cultural groundings that give rise to particular forms of Internet discourse and how such discourse shapes and structures civic society. I hope this book will contribute to the ongoing dialogue necessary to reach that goal.

NOTES

1. TCP/IP specifies the rules for transmitting data on the Internet. The TCP provides rules for transmitting data; IP routes packets of data. TCP/IP is the protocol upon which the operation of the Internet is based, and it was originally

formulated to connect dissimilar systems; it is now supported on almost all platforms (Stevens, 1994).

2. HTTP is the communications protocol used to connect to servers on the Web. HTTP establishes a connection with a Web server and transmits pages coded in HTML to the browser of the connected computer. Addresses on the Web typically begin with an http:// prefix; however, in the absence of the prefix, Web browsers typically default to HTTP (Snyder, 1997). HTML is the format for documents on the World Wide Web. HTML consists of tags in angular brackets (< >) that specify how fonts, graphic elements, links to other pages, and the general layout of the page will be displayed on the user's browser (an example of a very simple tag is <BOLD>Make this bold.</BOLD>, which renders the enclosed text in bold typeface) (Powell, 2000).

3. URL specifies the route to a file on the Web or other Internet facility. The URL consists of protocol prefix, domain name, subdirectory name(s) (if any), and the file name of a specific Web page. Thus, in the URL "http:// www.anydomain.com/data/material.html," the protocol is "HTTP," the domain is "www.anydomain.com," the subdirectory name is "data," and the name of the page is "material.html." All these elements are necessary for the user's browser to be directed to a specific page on the Web.

4. A newsreader is a "Usenet client program that enables a user to subscribe to Usenet newsgroups, read articles, post follow-ups, reply by e-mail, and post articles. Many Web browsers also provide these functions" (Microsoft Corporation, 2002, p. 365).

5. "There are also services that let users simply navigate through the news system by following links on a webpage. The former service called Deja-News, now purchased by the Web search service Google, is the best known and most complete such site" (Henderson, 2003, p. 256).

6. Usenet is a "worldwide network of UNIX systems that has a decentralized administration and is used as a bulletin board system by special-interest discussion groups. Usenet, which is considered part of the Internet (although Usenet predates it), is comprised of [sic] thousands of newsgroups, each devoted to a particular topic" (Microsoft Corporation, 2002, p. 543).

7. A BBS is "a computer system used as an information source and forum for a particular interest group" (Freedman, 2001b, p. 28., s.v. "BBS"). Freedman says that, although these were popular in the United States before the explosion in Web use, they are less so today, but are still "used throughout the world where there is much less direct Internet access" (p. 28). Still, Margolis (1999) estimates the number of BBSs in the United States alone in the "tens of thousands" (p. 67).

8. "The most common form of mail list, 'Listserv' is a registered trademark of L-Soft International" (Cooperative Extension, 2001). Replies to messages are distributed to everyone who is subscribed to the list. LISTSERV updates the list by scanning for the words "subscribe" and "unsubscribe."

9. Weinberger (2002) uses the terms *Web* and *Internet* interchangeably because, as he says, the distinction, though real in a technical sense, is not "being observed in the public consciousness" (p. 8, n. 1).

10. However, as Lessig (2002) has convincingly shown, although the basic idea of the Internet aims at openness, it must be accessed through layers that exercise increasingly stringent controls.

11. XML is a markup language that, like HTML, defines data on a Web page, using a similar tag structure. However, HTML can only define how Web page elements are displayed ; XML can define what these elements contain. A source of XML's extraordinary power lies in the fact that its tags can be defined by the user, whereas tags in HTML are predefined (Ray, 2001).

12. Whether such host sites are free is questionable, since advertisements are displayed on one's site unless one pays a fee to have them removed.

13. A flame is "an abusive or personally insulting e-mail message or newsgroup posting" (Microsoft Corporation, 2002, p. 216).

14. Of course we should not be so innocent as to think that it is actually the candidate himself who answers all these questions. Nevertheless, the visitor seeking "contact" with the candidate comes closer to making a real connection, even when she or he communicates with the campaign staff, publicly posting a reply in the name of the candidate.

15. "Founded in 1995 as Deja News, the site was initially created to archive and search Usenet discussions. In 1999, it rebranded itself as a product decision-making site with consumer opinions and reviews, and product comparisons. In 2000, eBay's Half.com acquired the consumer service, and Google acquired the Usenet archive in 2001" (Freedman, 2001a, p. 229).

16. This feature of Internet communication was dramatically demonstrated in a study by Demetriou and Silke (2003), in which a spurious Internet site promising access to illicit material was set up to determine if visitors would take advantage of it.

17. A perhaps more effective way of understanding the interdependence between monologism and dialogism is through a culturally alternative lens, such as the Chinese philosophy of Taoism (Chan, 1963). Eastern schools of thought prove somewhat better at accommodating a "both-and" rather than an "either-or" perspective. For example, something like the order implied by monologism is conceived in philosophical Taoism as the active, or yang, force, whereas the alternative to that order, which could be conceived as dialogical, is seen as the passive, yin, force. Without trying to draw too precise a comparison, we can see how Taoism unites the two "opposing" forces in the first words of the Taoist classic *Tao Te Ching*: "The *tao* [way] that can be told of is not the constant *Tao*; the name that can be named is not the eternal Name" (Chan, 1963, p. 97). In this brief epigram, the author, by tradition Lao-Tzu, admits that whatever he can say about the nature of the universe cannot be about the true universe, since the true universe is too complex to describe (a dialogic

insight). Therefore, he has to settle for the imperfect medium of verbal discourse (a monological mechanism). Yet Lao-Tzu has no trouble accommodating this paradox, and gets it out of the way in the book's very first characters.

18. A chat room is "the informal term for a data communication channel that links computers and permits users to 'converse' by sending text messages to one another in real time" (Microsoft Corporation, 2002, p. 97).

19. The exception to this generalization is that there are a considerable number of studies of the Internet and conventional political parties (see Chapter 4).

20. "Bakhtin's group acknowledged the influence of unitizing forces, conventional agreements which make it appear on its surface to be monologic (these they called 'centripetal forces'). Operating along with centripetal forces, however, they argued that there are dialogic elements which, being unique, vigorously resist unification ('centrifugal forces'). Thus, 'Every utterance participates in the "unitary language" (in its centripetal forces and tendencies) and at the same time partakes of social and historical heteroglossia (the centrifugal, stratifying forces)' (Bakhtin, 1981, p. 272; see also Morson & Emerson, 1990, p. 30). The Bakhtin group saw social language as a perpetually unsettled struggle between these two forces" (Holt, 2003a, p. 228).

Chapter 2

The Development of Dialogism: An Exploration of Major Influences

In trying to describe how dialogism has come to be a part of the modern repertoire of tools for analyzing communication, we encounter a fundamental problem. For any given perspective toward language and cognition, there are as many ways to look at that perspective as there are people to think about them. As Kuhn's work on paradigms (1996) has shown, no way of looking at the world develops as neatly and precisely as it is depicted in the accounts of those who reconstruct its history at some later date. The idea that the development of any perspective proceeds in an orderly fashion is a monological illusion that serves the convenience of scholars and other commentators looking for tidy accounts of an overwhelmingly chaotic history of intellectual development. Dialogism is a particularly apt case of this general principle: it encourages multiple perspectives and as a result its precepts are especially unruly and thus difficult to generalize about.

Moreover, ideas influencing dialogism are deliberately conceived to resist the authority of monological perspectives dominant in their time. Certainly each intellectual innovation can be seen as a case of subsequent formulations challenging previous ones. With dialogism, however, the lines of thought proceed from the assumption that monological systems—known by that or a similar name—need to be challenged. Given that dialogism embraces multiple viewpoints, compounded by the fact that every perspective develops chaotically, dialogism particularly resists narratives about its development.

Despite such difficulties, I believe dialogism's "development" can be best described in terms of three broad themes: (1) mind-world: from dualism toward unity; (2) social actor: from passivity toward activity; and (3) knowledge: from emphasizing the given to emphasizing the new. I examine how each theme is treated in five perspectives in Western philosophy: (1) the principles of language and culture described in the work of Vico; (2) pragmatism; (3) phenomenology; (4) Vygotsky and activity theory; and (5) the work of the Bakhtin circle. This is, of course, only one way to discuss how dialogism emerges in modern thought; other themes and other thinkers could also be discussed. The themes I deal with, however, are broad enough to bring out many features of dialogism without getting too entangled in a highly structured account of dialogism's "history."

As I progress through these perspectives, it should be remembered that any given dialogical insight is defined primarily by how it is different from a corresponding form of monologism. I focus on dialogism, rather than monologism, because it is the latter that is widely accepted as being true, often with little or no question as to its validity. Hence, the first task in opening up utterances is to realize the limitation of understanding them by unreflective application of only, or primarily, the monological view. Dialogism is inherently oppositional, constituting a challenge to monological knowledge that previously might have seemed unassailable. At the same time, dialogic insight does not substitute for monologic knowledge; as I will show, language and thought always has both monologic and dialogic qualities. For this reason, when I turn to analysis of Internet discourse, I will take, one at a time, the monologic then the dialogic view, and then compare their insights to generate a fuller, richer view of Internet utterance.

MIND AND BODY: FROM DUALISM TOWARD UNITY

The first idea that characterizes the growth of dialogism has to do with transcending mind-body dualism, which is the position that mind and matter are two distinct things. This dualism originates with Descartes' *Meditations on the First Philosophy* (2000), first published in 1647. Descartes argued that his essential nature must be nonmaterial, since, as a subject of conscious thought, he himself could not be merely extended matter; his mind, by its qualities (for example, indivisibility, noncorporeality), must be entirely different from the physical world. The effect of the Cartesian view on 17th-, 18th-, and 19th-century philosophy cannot be overstated. Descartes has influenced philosophers such as Locke, Hume, Liebniz, Kant, and even Husserl, though each of these thinkers grapple with mind-body dualism in very different ways.

Cartesianism, a set of philosophical and scientific principles based on Descartes, is both rationalist (it holds that knowledge is derived from reason) and Platonic (it holds that the origin of knowledge is innate ideas). Mind-body dualism held considerable sway in 17th- and 18th-century Europe, and despite criticism from many modern commentators (see, for example, Bakhurst, 1988; Rorty, 1979; Ryle, 1984; Scribner, 1985), positions based on Cartesian principles remain influential even today, perhaps because they provide relatively neat, clean answers to some of reflective philosophy's most persistent puzzles.[1] Cartesian dualism offered the possibility of applying the clear principles of mathematical and other formal reasoning to questions about mind and the world in which it functions. Moreover, as one of the first influential reflective Western philosophers, Descartes' work was a key factor in leading Western philosophy toward those mental habits—such as reflective analysis of mind and its relation to world—that would result, paradoxically, in many of the philosophical systems that inform dialogism (see, for example, pragmatism [James, 1991]).

Mind-body dualism, as formulated by the followers of Descartes, has been challenged, in different ways, by each of the five perspectives I identify as leading to dialogism. Each line of thought examined in the following discussion offers a different view of how mind encounters world, and each posits an interaction between the two that will prove useful as I examine Internet discourse.

Vico and the Move from Mind-Body Dualism

It is during the first flush of Cartesianism's influence in Europe that we encounter an articulate resistance to mind-body dualism, in the form of Vico's *New Science* (1999), first published in 1725, revised in 1730, and revised yet again in a third edition that appeared shortly after his death in 1744. *New Science* was the culmination of a number of trajectories taken by Vico in questioning Cartesianism, and it is in this book that he breaks decisively with Descartes, specifically with respect to the question of what are appropriate objects for understanding. Ignoring many of the preoccupations important to Cartesianism—for example, the quest to comprehend the natural world—Vico asserted that one understands something only if one makes it oneself, and vice versa. This principle has become famous as his well-known declaration *"verum factum"* (the true and the made are convertible). According to Vico, efforts to understand God or the natural world are futile since, not having been made by humans, they cannot be understood by humans. According to Vico, despite the range of questions and approaches taken by philosophers throughout history, they share a common problem: they wrestle with questions to which they can find no answers.

As a way to disentangle ourselves from fruitless attempts to understand things beyond our ken by pretending to grasp them according to abstract systems of thought, Vico proposed turning back to the language of ancient stories and myths created in the rough-and-tumble of real, often chaotic, living, historic cultures. For example, he venerates Homer, and is particularly impressed with how Homer used immediate, sense-based poetic language to describe the battles of *The Iliad*. Contrary to the opinions of subsequent interpreters, Vico argues, what Homer writes is not philosophically elevated prose:

> [Homer's poetry] is certainly not characteristic of a mind chastened and civilized by any sort of philosophy. Nor could the truculent and savage style in which he describes so many, such varied, and such bloody battles, so many and such extravagantly cruel kinds of butchery as make up all the sublimity of the *Iliad* [*sic*] in particular, have originated in a mind touched and humanized by any philosophy. (Vico, 1984, p. 303, para. 785)

However, the genius of Vico lay not in realizing that Homer's language was inadequate to the task of philosophizing, but in granting to visceral poetic discourse the status of being a legitimate way to describe the events. Berlin (1979a) has memorably described the distance between modern and ancient accounts:

> Vico's central point is that poetic feeling, which "must plunge deep into particulars," [624] cannot exist when men think in concepts: inspired singers, of whom Homer is the greatest, cannot coexist with philosophers. Whatever these later, milder, more rational times—the age of men—may create, namely, the arts and sciences of elaborate civilizations, they cannot give us within the same "cycle" "burning imagination" or celestial sublimity. [825] This has vanished. We can realize the splendour of this primitive poetry only by understanding the "wild, crude, and terrible" [808] world from which it springs; we

can do this only if we abandon the idea of the artistic superiority of our own "magnificent times" [123]. (p. 127)

This reorientation toward the specific over the general in describing discourse, and simultaneous elevation of sociohistorical specificity as a legitimate view, works to undermine the separation of mind and material world (body) because it removes from the critical thinker the safety of monological pretensions to understanding. We read staid 17th-century accounts of the "philosophy" of Homer, and then the bloody descriptions of battles in *The Iliad*, and we are brought up short by Vico's observation: Homer had it right in his writing, because he was immediately involved with the cultural reality of the time in which he wrote. Although no one can reconstruct the battles Homer described with complete accuracy, we stand a better chance of understanding them if we read Homer, than if we read a historian of the 17th century. Homer was, to revert to slang, "closer to the action." Ever master of the pithy philosophical epigram, Vico (1999) expresses this thought incisively: "Philosophy considers people as they should be, and hence is useful only to the very few who want to live in the republic of Plato, rather than to sink into the dregs of Romulus" (p. 78).

Despite these interesting insights, I would guess the modern reader will find quite a few problems with the approach Vico takes, both in *New Science* and elsewhere (Berlin [1979b] aptly describes him as not having "enough talent for his genius" and his ideas as "often mere sketches, inchoate, ill-formed" [p. 114][2]). Despite its weaknesses, however, Vico's unusual view of human history (which, it must be said, was more drastic in his time than it is now) moves us away from the idea that there "is" a "real" history out there to be transcribed, and toward the idea that historians inscribe history, nearly always during a time that differs greatly from the period they write about. In contrast to Descartes' precise and rather arid formulations, which some employed to try to bring the imagined substantiality of natural science to the more speculative practice of philosophy and the human sciences, Vico celebrates those aspects of society that resist classification: the odd, perplexing, mysterious, and ultimately "inappropriate" elements that cannot be fit into a set of master categories. According to Vico, one gains such insights by lessening rather than increasing the cognitive distance between oneself and the object of one's inquiry.

This shift in how we see the writing of history has important implications for the problem of mind-body dualism. It undermines the notion that the historian can assume a stance removed from the phenomena she or he describes. It encourages historians to pay more attention to the details of historical periods and not be so sanguine as to think they can achieve accuracy in historical accounts merely by explicating them in terms of a currently accepted monological perspective.

Pragmatism and the Move from Mind-Body Dualism

Another challenge to mind-body dualism comes from pragmatism. As is true of other streams of thought that feed into dialogism (for example, the broad, diverse category of "phenomenologists" and the fractious lot that were the Bakhtin circle), philosophers whose contributions come under the designation "pragmatism" are a varied and contradictory group. Briefly, pragmatism tackles philosophy on the grounds of truth: an idea is held to be true if it can be demonstrated useful to the person contemplating it. Although similar ideas crop up in the writing of other thinkers before him, Peirce is generally credited with being the founder of pragmatism, formulated in the early 1870s. However, the declaration of pragmatism as a distinctive approach to the study of philosophy was by James in an address in 1898 (Menand, 1997, p. xiii). Pragmatism was extended and elaborated in the work of Dewey (1903), Addams (1902, 1912), and Mead (1934, 1938; see also Miller, 1973). Although the heyday of pragmatism was in the early 20th century, its tenets have always been present in intellectual circles, though sometimes not by that name, and sometimes not strictly related to philosophy. Pragmatism has undergone a revival of sorts in the work of Rorty (1979, 1982), following his decision to move beyond the realm of philosophy and into a more broad-based area of inquiry that also includes literature and political science.

Without wishing to venture too far into the rich history of pragmatism, it is safe to say one of the movement's central goals is to create an intellectual environment that permits thinkers to embrace truths that do not necessarily have to be proven true a priori, but rather can be judged by another standard. With pragmatism, the standard for truth is usefulness: how useful is the philosophical idea to the person who applies it? Pragmatism realizes a situation in which philosophers are not forced to contest only over very abstract issues. James (1991) offers a sensational, though instructive, example:

Imagine, in fact, the entire contents of the world to be once for all irrevocably given. Imagine it to end this very moment, and to have no future; and then let a theist and a materialist apply their rival explanations to its history. The theist shows how a God made it; the materialist shows . . . how it resulted from blind physical forces. Then let the pragmatist be asked to choose between their theories. How can he apply his test if the world is already completed?. . . there is to be no more experience and no possible differences can now be looked for. Both theories have shown all their consequences. . . . . The pragmatist must consequently say that the two theories, in spite of their different-sounding names, mean the same thing, and the dispute is purely verbal. (p. 44)

Despite significant problems with this approach (two of its most prominent critics were the renowned philosophers G. E. Moore [1922] and Bertrand Russell [1910]), pragmatism must be viewed as a key element leading to an intellectual climate in which dialogism can be considered. This is not due entirely to pragmatism's criterion of utility, a feature that has led to considerable controversy (Rescher, 1995). Rather, the aspect most useful for dialogism is pragmatism's emphasis on what Linell (1998) has called "the gradual emergence of meaning" (p. 44). In other words, the fact that pragmatism insists on judging a philosophy based on its usefulness somewhat undermines the time-honored approach to learning self-reflection through reading philosophical classics, and then thinking about what these works have to say about the lives of oneself and others. The pragmatist argues that this approach is not as beneficial as some philosophers might have us suppose.

For many purposes of truth—and particularly those we can never corroborate, so to speak, face-to-face—it is sufficient for ideas to lead us in the direction of reality and to aid us in our dealings with it. James speaks of this process of worthwhile *leading* as one by which an idea's truth is verified. Truth is not, in other words, an ingredient in ideas from the outset but is acquired by them. Truth is what happens to an idea when it is put into the relations that confirm it. (Gunn, 2000, p. xxv)

Gunn's summary lays out what, to the pragmatist, is the more appropriate strategy: to lead one toward reality. One encounters a position as laid out in the philosophical work and then examines it to determine if its insights are useful. Far from encountering philosophical thought in some predominantly stable, seemingly unchangeable form, one is free to reformulate ideas, and then, comparing them—to one another, to one's own experience, and to dynamic changes in sociohistorical circumstances—reformulate them to suit one's own needs. This should not be taken as an extreme form of relativism in which any philosophy is as valid as any other. The tests for determining pragmatic value are, regardless of the specific approach to pragmatism one uses, far more stringent than might be expected (to see how demanding and complex this process can get, one can look to the examples in Lecture III, in James's *Pragmatism*, "Some Metaphysical Problems Pragmatically Considered" [1991, pp. 39–56]). Pragmatism opens to inspection by a fresh perspective some of the cherished, more monologically inclined, assumptions that have so strongly influenced modern philosophy. Repeated contemplation of pragmatic value means that meaning is not presented whole, but emerges incrementally through acts of cognition and expression.

One way in which pragmatism can illuminate the dialogical move from separation between mind and world lies in the idea that others in a community inevitably inform our choices about the utility of a particular philosophical idea. The inclusion of community in the determination of utility was not an overt concern of early pragmatists, perhaps because those who lived in the time when these ideas were formulated (late 19th and early 20th centuries) were not privy to some of the more developed ideas about community (for example, Anderson, 1991) that would come to prominence in the latter 20th century (although one does find in Dewey an emphasis on what Posner [2003] has called "deliberative democracy" [p. 106], which implies pooling of ideas and approaches and hence suggests the involvement of community).

A significant development of the connection between pragmatism and community came with Rorty (1979, 1982), who has popularized the notion that, since truth, as an abstract quality, cannot be determined, its pursuit should be dropped and we should concentrate on the practical aspects of living, including cultivating the ability to make choices between the kinds of lives we will lead. It is probably no surprise that the kind of life Rorty advocates is open, inclusive, freethinking, and democratic. Such inclusion undermines the individualism implied by mind-body dualism, since one must collaborate with others to reach the pragmatic evaluation.

The collaborative mode reflects what Vico calls *"sensus communis,"* that is, "an unreflecting judgment shared by an entire social order, people, nation, or even all humankind" (1999, p. 80 [142]). Even if we do not go as far as Rorty, surely it is clear that an earlier form of pragmatism such as James's strongly implies communal involvement. If not according to the standards of others with whom one lives, how would one determine utility? It could hardly be simply a matter of personal choice. If we judge two philosophies as being so materially similar to one another that there is no practical difference between them, we must refer to shared thoughts, espoused by communities of interested parties, that explain, at the very least, what those perspectives are. Then, in applying these ideas to "real life" (seemingly the goal of most of philosophy), we must weigh the sense of the communities of people to whom we apply them, leading us still further from abstraction and closer to considering ideas as the expressions of living human beings.

Pragmatism also leads away from mind-body dualism through its insistence that particular individuals have personal and potentially idiosyncratic ideas about the efficacy and success of applying philosophy to life. The result is a decrease in the status of the "expert" philosopher and a corresponding increase in the status of the pragmatic thinker who tests each idea. Again, pragmatism is by no means an anything-goes philosophy. Nonetheless, and quite in line with the view of life as an open vista of possibilities, the individual is given the opportunity to determine, nearly always in disagreement with traditional views, a position uniquely applicable to that individual's practical needs.

According to most strains of pragmatism, it is more than merely possible for the individual to assume the role of both critic and creative constructor of philosophy; instead, this is seen as part of the social actor's personal responsibility. When we view pragmatic inquiry as a kind of trade-off between the views of people who share a sense of a collectivity's moral and ethical stances, we see how the pragmatic perspective is a way of granting validity to multiple views, and indeed of reinforcing a communal bonding to embrace these divergent perspectives. This collective orientation, in which context all philosophy exists, makes idealistic Cartesian dualism between mind and material world all the more difficult to sustain. As MacIntyre, for example, has written of philosophical topics of concern, "Morality which is no particular society's morality is to be found nowhere" (1981, p. 265); the philosophy not enacted in specific circumstances literally does not exist.

Pragmatism, in its relentless pursuit of the continual reformulation of philosophy, as well as its persistent calling of philosophy to account for its usefulness, is grounded in the social character of philosophic inquiry. Its position is that the individual's mind cannot conceive of philosophy by itself alone. This fact dramatically highlights the process of the emergence, through interaction, of meaning, which led Linell (1998) to identify pragmatism as one of the sources of modern dialogic approaches to the study of human talk. As pragmatism is to philosophic knowledge, dialogism is to the study of discourse. Both perspectives question the authority of monologism by inviting us to see meaning as a process rather than as a starting point or final goal, and philosophy as a collective, not an individual, human enterprise. All this leads us further away from the idea of mind and world as separate entities.

Phenomenology and the Move from Mind-Body Dualism

The several traditions associated with the philosophical approach known as "phenomenology" also lead away from mind-body dualism,[3] primarily because of what they imply about alternative conceptions of reality. Before discussing the implications of this fact, I should dispose of some misconceptions about phenomenology. Earlier I noted that proponents of pragmatism have taken it in divergent directions. This is, if anything, even truer of phenomenological approaches. For one thing, the term *phenomenology* has been used in philosophical discourse at least since 1764, and one dictionary (Reese, 1996) offers thirteen separate uses, ranging from Kant to Sartre (pp. 570–71). One leading expert on the subject comments:

> In contemporary philosophy there is no system or school called "phenomenology," characterized by a clearly defined body of teachings. Phenomenology is neither a school nor a trend in contemporary philosophy. It is rather a movement whose proponents, for various reasons, have propelled it in many distinct directions, with the result that today it means different things to different people. (Kockelmans, 1999, p. 664)

The name most closely associated with phenomenology is Edmund Husserl (1859–1938). Husserl proposed a way for human beings to see and fix the essential features of the world, which many phenomenologists hold to be obscured, rather than revealed, by language and thought. To do this requires finding a method for eliminating contingent (that is, nonessential) aspects of experience; this process Husserl called the *"epoché"* (phenomenological reduction), or the description of mental acts without reference to theories and suppositions. This is different from the approach of, for example, psychologists, who tend to focus on such matters as the causes and consequences of mental acts. Husserl specified a starting point as the "bracketing" of existence (that is, temporary suspension of the question of existence).

We are interested in phenomenology, as an influence on dialogism, primarily because of its implication that an object of thought must be seen from different perspectives. Beginning with a deep questioning of material existence and how it is presented to our thought processes, phenomenology is one of the more radical approaches to the study of mind and world, as shown by its effects in shaping some of the more subjective approaches to sociology (Berger & Luckmann, 1966; Garfinkel, 1967; Schutz, 1970, 1971; Schutz & Luckmann, 1972; Wolff, 1978).

It is in the espousal of multiple perspectives that we find the first clue to phenomenology's role in the dialogic move away from mind-world separation. Although the idea of multiple perspectives is not peculiar to phenomenology, phenomenologists propose a more thorough critique toward traditional philosophical ways of knowing. Phenomenologists believe the reality of any object of thought must be seen in itself, experienced directly, without the interference of abstract systems circumscribing thought processes. Thus, phenomenologists argue further, there is a need to move away from abstraction and toward direct experience.

Under the traditional model of Cartesian mind-body dualism, it was thought essential that abstractions act as intercessors between mind and world. The world could not be experienced by mind directly (they were seen as separate), and the role of conscious thought was to try to find the most appropriate and effective way to mediate the mind-world relation. This led to interminable debates, not only about procedures for thought, but also about other essential features of the worldview, such as presuppositions and first causes. Under various philosophical systems that followed Descartes (of which the most evolved is probably Kant's), it was believed that humans should approach the real world through a complex system of consistently interrelated procedures and concepts. That the "real world" did not appear to directly encounter the thinker (nor the thinker it) seemed not to matter; indeed, philosophers were apparently more content with trying out and debating systems of abstractions, than contending with a directly experienced empirical world.

With phenomenology, however, most of these problems concerning the "bridge" between mind and world are either relegated to insignificance or ignored. Phenomenologists urge the thinker to go directly to the source of appearances—namely, the object itself—to understand its "reality." According to this view, the human agent (as in pragmatism) takes a more prominent role in thought and goes to the effort of dispensing with the system standing between mind and world. Again, as in pragmatism, this leads to the situation in which many interpretations of reality can be brought up for consideration. Indeed, it could even be said that in phenomenology one sees the relativistic stance of pragmatism extended much further. While there is in James, for example, a rationalist bent in examining philosophical ideas to determine their "practicality," in phenomenology such conventional thought is not required and is even disparaged.

If one takes the view that no interpretation is privileged—in fact, that *any* interpretation is suspect, merely because it *is* an interpretation—conceivably any individual's experience of the object is equally valid. This idea has had, as noted, an impact on sociology, causing some sociologists to question why it is assumed that those in their profession have a more valid view of social life than the people who live it (see, for example, Garfinkel, 1967). Again, with the breaking down of a barrier between mind and world—in the case of phenomenology, the barrier is abstraction that obscures direct experience—we have what might be called the "democratization" of knowledge. In phenomenology, and to a lesser extent in pragmatism, increasing autonomy is given the individual thinker (and communicator) to be the chief agent in formulating a personal worldview.

Phenomenology also points away from mind-body dualism through its opposition to naturalism and speculative thinking, and/or preoccupation with language. Naturalism is the view that assumes the human world should be seen according to the same kinds of perspectives and with the same methodologies as those used in the natural sciences. In a way, phenomenologists, by declaring naturalistic theories to be examples of how scholars used abstract thought to interpose irrelevancies between themselves and the empirical world, have come to Vico's critique of Cartesianism. Like Vico, some phenomenologists profoundly distrust elegant, complex configurations of concepts through which to view the natural world; such views, they say, are distracting. Phenomenologists argue that natural scientists build up complicated, but ultimately unprovable, edifices of knowledge and theory in order to avoid experiencing the empirical world directly. Subsequently, many of these scientists then devote time and energy to the maintenance of these intervening mental structures.

The problem phenomenology has with naturalistic perspectives and methods is that, while they seem to work well for natural phenomena (though not entirely, as discoveries in the realm of quantum physics have shown for what were previously regarded as ironclad "laws" of classical physics [Albert, 1992; Bell, 1987; Cushing & McMullin, 1989]), they are ill suited to the study of human beings. (Note here the similarity of phenomenological insight to Vico's conclusion regarding the unlikelihood that the physical sciences and mathematics could offer any hope for understanding the untidiness of history as it was "made" by living human beings.) According to phenomenologists, consciousness is far too complex to be described by nomothetic, empirical, predictive models based on mathematics.

In some ways the scientific method can be seen as one of the purest of monologic perspectives. It has stood not only natural sciences in good stead, but the many fields of knowledge that have tried to imitate natural science methods. So entrenched is the scientific method that scientists who support it and its accompanying methodological procedures often do not question whether it is appropriate. Thus, when an alternative appears, it is usually vehemently resisted by the majority who espouse the monologic approach, simply because, as Garfinkel (1967) demonstrated with the ethnomethodological process, all it takes to unhinge a monologic viewpoint is to put it to a test in a situation in which its taken-for-granted, yet unacknowledged, assumptions do not hold.

Phenomenologists also pursued their critique in the area of language, and it is this trajectory of inquiry that is particularly relevant to the current discussion. Phenomenologists regarded language as perhaps the ultimate means to deceive and obstruct perception. In phenomenology there is a distrust of language, not necessarily because it relays false information, but because words represent another way of invoking the specter of abstraction.

In this way, the phenomenological critique strikes at the foundation of our ways of knowing. "Of course," everyone knows we grasp the world by means of language, and "of course" this is the way we encounter the natural world. However, phenomenologists refused to accept these notions; instead, they said, language works to obscure "reality."[4] Just as the scientific method leads us to a false sense of security by luring us into believing we have a regular, predictable way of approaching unknown empirical phenomena, so does language lead us to believe that we understand the phenomena it describes, when in fact all we understand is words and other symbols—and, as Bakhtin was to convincingly demonstrate, even these we understand only very poorly.

Phenomenology's assumption of multiple, equally valid, subjective realities works to undermine our faith in the reliability of language, because reality can be represented linguistically in so many different ways. This potential for multiple representations leads to further questioning of the separation of mental and physical realms. For if the goal of conscious thought is to remove the barriers of conceptual and linguistic abstractions from between thinker and thought object, how can one espouse any view that suggests they are separate entities?

Vygotsky and the Move from Mind-Body Dualism

Vygotsky (1978, 1981, 2002), largely through the work of influential students such as Luria (1976, 1979), is credited with being the founder of sociohistorical approaches to psychology in the former Soviet Union (Wertsch, 1981) and by implication with later developments, in both the Soviet Union and in the West, that led to activity theory (Wertsch, 1981). Vygotsky's view represents a very concrete example of a move from mind-world dualism, in that he proposed an approach to child development and learning that does not presume a primarily naturalistic, monologic model of mental activity. According to the conventional view, the teacher's role, whether formal or informal, was to find a useful pedagogical method, use this to convey information about the empirical world to the student, and rely on standardized assessment procedures to determine what the student had learned (Vygotsky, 1978, p. 86). These views are similar to the perspectives taken in the natural sciences regarding the scientific method. They assume the empirical world is more or less stable and that it is possible to derive an optimal method for "conveying" information about that world to the student. The learning process is rendered in neat, clean models assumed to apply not just to single, specific children in all their diversity, but to many different "children," as an abstract, covering term.

The problem was that, as Vygotsky discovered, general learning models used to teach children failed to explain what seemed to be going on in teacher–child interactions. Information was not being conveyed in more or less uncontaminated fashion to the child and then checked by the teacher. Rather, both teacher and child seemed to construct together the meaning of what was being taught. A famous example from Vygotsky (which I paraphrase and embellish here) has since become part of the folklore of activity theory. A parent is in a room with a child. The child reaches for a cookie, but lacking depth perception, seems not to realize she cannot reach it. However, the parent does not assume the child is deficient in this elementary perceptual and motor task; rather, seeing the child raise her hand, the parent asks, "What is that you want, a cookie?" and gets it for her. What has the child learned? Certainly not that the cookie, as a desired object, can be physically reached. Rather, sociohistorical psychologists in the Vygotskyan tradition argue it is the child's incipient formulation of a gestural activity, later to be refined in other interactions, called "pointing," that will, at least at that stage of her development, get for her the cookie she wants. No meaning is assigned to the pointing gesture by either the student (the child) or the teacher (the parent), acting alone—indeed, it is not yet even a pointing gesture. Rather, there has been a collaboration in which the beginning of a symbolic meaning for a physical activity (a gesture) has been derived, by mutual cooperation, where no such gesture was previously meaningful.

This idea of a gray area between consciousnesses where meaning is creatively thought out and collaboratively developed became a key element of Vygotsky's view. It poses an alternative to classical experimental psychology, and not only because it questions the scientific method. Vygotskyan psychology, like other approaches that lead to dialogism, privileges the specific over the general, the concrete over the abstract. If one cannot know what is in the minds of interactants, or be able to predict how their interaction will modify these unknown contents, then it is very difficult to predict the outcome of laboratory experiments that form the backbone of conventional experimental psychology and pedagogy. The basis of the conventional scientific approach to mind is thrown into question, since Western psychology, because it imitates natural sciences, draws generalizations said to apply to "the mind," rather than individual minds.

This idea fits nicely into the distrust of language seen in other approaches leading to dialogism. Western psychology deliberately tries to remove circumstantial specificity from the experiments whose results comprise the greater part of its knowledge base. Moreover, it does this by assigning labels to mental acts and then quantifying these as variables through increasingly complicated systems of thought. Much like the phenomenologists, Vygotsky sought psychological knowledge to explain the direct experience of the studied individual in a given situation.

Another connection of Vygotsky's work to the question of mind-body relation has to do with his position that interaction, as a means by which children are acculturated, is a key element of human thought. The priority given the notion that ideas are shaped by human contact is one of dialogism's most characteristic features. In Vygotsky's view, monological models try to separate the human world (the body) from the abstract mental world (the mind). Vygotsky sought to remedy this by looking at their union in specific teacher–student interactions.

A particularly provocative and useful concept expressing this is Vygotsky's "zone of proximal development" (ZPD or ZOPED) (1978, pp. 84–91). According to this notion, there exists, for every educational activity, a goal state for student performance the teacher wishes to achieve and a state at which the student currently is. Vygotsky used the ZPD as a spatial metaphor to conceive of the distance between these two states. The ZPD, according to Kozulin (2002), is

> the place at which the child's empirically rich but disorganized spon-taneous concepts "meet" the systematicity and logic of adult reasoning. As the result of such a "meeting," the weaknesses of spon-taneous reasoning are compensated by the strength of scientific logic. . . . The final product of this child–adult cooperation is a solution, which, being internalized, becomes an integral part of the child's own reasoning. (p. xxxv)

By phrasing his idea as a zone of proximal development, Vygotsky reveals his view that the student acquires skill, not as a more or less straightforward transference, but as part of a mutually constructed state continuously in the process of becoming. In other words, the separation of ideal (mind) and actual (body) is "proximal," its elements neither con-tiguous nor their relations predefined. Moreover, this is "development" in that the zone, while not specifying a path for the learning process, suggests an area where collaborative learning can take place. Also, in the ZPD, there is a mutual striving toward union between actual and ideal states, requiring the participation of both teacher and student. In other words, neither the actual nor the ideal state can be precisely de-fined. Rather, modification of the perspective of both parties, via the ZPD's dynamic character, permits mutual development in each inter-actant. The "goal," when eventually achieved, will be something that cannot be predicted from the initial states of teacher and learner.

Such a view significantly undermines faith in the objectivity sug-gested by Cartesian dualism. If we accept Vygotsky's notion that there are no firmly set initial and final states in the learning process, as well as his principle that interactions between teacher and student cannot be specified monologically prior to learning, then we must assume that the consciousnesses of teacher and student are bonded to each other in future states of interaction (across the ZPD), and that these will change dynamically as sociohistorical circumstances change. Thus, in no way can these minds be considered separate from the world in which they interact.

Finally, there is in Vygotsky yet one more interesting way to undermine the notion of mind/body separation: his theory of mediated action. This revolutionary principle states that mind never acts upon an object directly. Rather, all ostensibly "mental" activity is mediated by something in the actor's environment. The significance of this idea extends far beyond its role as another facet of the learning process. Mediated action brings into analysis of teaching and learning the realities of the specific physical environments in which all learning takes place. If we try to understand the learning process or other mental activity via controlled experiments in the precisely engineered environs of the laboratory, we unfortunately render the learning process in artificial terms.

That which mediates between the actor and the (allegedly) separate object toward which that individual's activity is directed is a "tool." According to activity theorists who were later to be strongly influenced by Vygotsky (Engeström, 1987; Lave, 1988; Leont'ev, 1978), although a tool may be physical, such as a hammer or a screwdriver or a computer, the category is much broader: it can also include such tools as mental models, ideas, words, schemata, and so on (Engeström, 1987). Regardless of its type, the purpose of the tool is to mediate activity. Mediated activity is thus another way in which the actor is tied to sociohistorical specificity. From this perspective, it is impossible to see the individual mind and the physical body/environment as separate. Every time the environment is changed, linkages among elements must also change.[5] Thus, with Vygotsky and activity theory, there is more than the customarily close connection between actor and object we have seen in other approaches leading to dialogism: in Vygotsky, that link is even further cemented through the medium of physical environment, in all its unfathomable specific detail.

Bakhtin and the Move from Mind-Body Dualism

If you examine it on the surface, you might get the impression that the work of the Bakhtin circle was a key element leading to dissolution of the Cartesian boundary between internal mind and external world. In fact, the view of Bakhtin's group inclines more toward Kant, at least in regarding mind and world as fundamentally nonidentical. The Bakhtin approach to language and culture is based on otherness, that is, the realization that consciousness really is otherness. Moreover, this is not, as Holquist (1990) somewhat cryptically puts it, "a dialectical alienation on its way to a sublation that will endow it with a unifying identity in higher consciousness" (p. 18). Rather, the mind (representing an internal state) and the body (representing the empirical world) remain forever separate, though not, as in Descartes, because the mind is an object susceptible to objective contemplation through a monologically inclined set of assumptions. Rather, it is because the relentlessly heteroglossic character of the world makes it impossible for a single mind, oriented to that world from within the parameters of its unique architectonic configuration, to view the world as anything "other" than "other."

Ironically, the idea of mind and world being forever other *to* each other is in effect the most telling blow to Cartesian mind-body dualism. One of Descartes' most cherished principles was that the natural world and the empirical world could be known. This is what led him to treat the mind as separate from the world in which it functioned. However, the Bakhtin circle's work begins with the notion that the mind is forever different from all other minds, indeed all other manifestations of reality. It is in the uniqueness of the individual mind that Bakhtin grounds his theory of utterance. For, if all individuals begin from a basis of radical alterity from each other, then any attempt to represent the empirical world linguistically, hoping to have this representation understood by others, must fail. Moreover, this idea implies that minds not only differ from each other, they also differ from any empirical "reality" apprehended and represented by each individual mind.

One way the Bakhtin circle leads us from mind-body dualism is through its view of consciousness. According to Bakhtin, the capacity to have consciousness is based on otherness. In Bakhtin, consciousness does not rest on presumptive unification of disparate elements of the empirical world—such fusion is clearly impossible. Instead, since he believes there is no way to synthesize the world external to mind, Bakhtin proposes that we view the mind as involved in a struggle between what it knows will, in the end, resist synthesis, and the pretensions of systems of thought and language that lead people to think they really are synthesizing experience.

With respect to mind-body unity, Bakhtin proposes a way of "unifying" mind and world while accepting, along with Kant, that there is an "unbridgeable gap" (see Holquist, 1990, p. 17) between the two realms. Unlike Kant, however, Bakhtin does not assume there are, outside the mind, "things in themselves": "there may be things outside mind, but they are nevertheless not in themselves" (see Holquist, 1990, p. 17). The Bakhtin view directs attention away from mind-body dualism by appealing to a conception of mind as unique and by insisting that it is this uniqueness that prevents separation between individual consciousness and the sociohistorical circumstances in which it functions (this is similar to the linkage noted in the discussion of Vygotsky, though it is based on different assumptions).

The fact that mind and world are distinct in their otherness from each other also means that understanding cannot be unitary. The necessity for actors to try to unite disparate elements of the world (a process dictated by each individual's idiosyncratic configuration of mind) undermines any monological pretension that experience is unitary. Bakhtin argued that the tension involved in the opposition between shared and idiosyncratic aspects of language is what makes communication meaningful. If we choose to see language through the lens of monologism (as, for example, in structural linguistics), we agree momentarily to a unity and regularity language simply does not have. Likewise, if we assume language has no such unity, we also fail to grasp its true character, because regularity and structure are conceptual frameworks by which we think and talk about language. It is only by realizing that living, sociohistorically specific discourse has both monologic and dialogic qualities that we can even begin to try to understand it. Nor does it concern the Bakhtin group that a complete understanding of living language can never be achieved, since they began by assuming linguistic completion will forever elude the social actor.

The Bakhtin circle's work gives us another way to understand dialogism's move from mind-body dualism: its principle that understanding language arises from a differential relation between the "center" of one's consciousness and that which is not the center. It should be noted again that Bakhtin's idea of the self does not allow it to occupy a stable point of reference. Rather, the self is defined by its difference from whatever is outside it. Thus, if the self is to engage in the acts of ongoing self-definition and redefinition needed for understanding, it must continually orient toward the broader world. In this respect, the Bakhtin contribution to dialogism carries similar suggestions of instability seen in other dialogically inclined systems of thought. An aim of dialogism is to undermine faith in the monological illusion of stability. Bakhtin's work pushes this formulation perhaps to an extreme, showing the self on its own in a world of alternative, contesting representations, fashioned by minds that are, necessarily, radically different from one's own. Not only that, the task of the individual is continually to orient toward this difference, and thus forever to be adrift, as it were, in a sea of essentially inimical difference.

Summary: The Move from Mind-Body Dualism and Internet Communication

One of the most striking characteristics of Internet communication is how it renders the physical world much less substantial. Time and space are distorted. We communicate with people we may never see in the flesh, forming impressions of them based on words alone. We and these others seem disembodied, constructed of cyberutterances, and unable to connect with the physical reality that seems to have served all our lives to define existence. As a result, in cyberspace, we can try on "new" identities; we can "be" different people, or if not assuming an entirely different identity, we can at least more easily experiment with different behaviors. It is interesting that people on the Internet use the abbreviation IRL (in real life) to denote what does not occur in cyberspace. To me, this suggests that Internet communication is, to a great extent, seen as *un*real.

These qualities of the Internet bear upon evolving intellectual positions concerning mind-body dualism. Obviously, with the Internet, we are dealing with definitions of the self that are far more malleable and less substantial than in perhaps other forms of communication. The size and scope of the Internet make it impossible for anyone to comprehend even a significant part of that which goes into it. Yet in classical studies of humans and society, we have had the benefit of reference points to help us make sense of social life, defining ourselves as parts of families, members of political parties, graduates of schools, and so on. We could see the indications, in physical reality, of these concepts and use them to make sense of our lives.

With the Internet, this is less easy to do. I suspect I am not alone when, in surfing the Internet, I experience an odd sense of disconnection. Sitting at my desk, I can see, touch, hear the sensations in my environment; once I step through the portal of my browser "into" the Internet, though, what am I? Although I cannot sense the environment of cyberspace, it is "as real" as "real life" and in some ways more so. Moreover, increasingly, Internet users feel a sense of connection with the cyberworld; practices that make no sense "IRL" are essential tools for survival on the Internet, and vice versa.

This means that Cartesian dualism, whose place in philosophy has become increasingly tenuous over time, is even less useful in the context of the Internet. Dialogical modes of thought, all of which challenge dualism, are much more consonant with the qualities of a medium in which many things, including the self, can take a multiplicity of forms. The Cartesian notion of the self, comfortably contemplating its seemingly firm monological grip on the world, is of little use on the Internet, where one could communicate for years with a person and not ever realize that "person" is actually merely a living individual's carefully constructed online persona. Nor, for the reasons cited above, can mindbody dualism be of much use in conceptualizing an audience for Web pages/sites. Cartesianism sought refuge in firm categories and "clear and distinct" ideas; however, in composing pages, one must deal with an inexpressibly vast and varied audience. There can be no clear separation of the composer from the audience, simply because no one knows even approximately what that audience is.

THE SOCIAL ACTOR: FROM PASSIVITY TOWARD ACTIVITY

An implied feature in the five perspectives examined in this chapter is that to pursue dialogically inclined inquiry demands more energy and commitment than to see things according to monologically inclined views. This is not to say that seeing the world according to a prevailing monologic view is easy. For example, it requires years to master a monologic perspective such as the scientific method and the techniques of research and analysis that inform it. The same could be said of any philosophical school of thought, from Aristotelianism to symbolic logic. At the same time, even under the standards of the most demanding monologic perspective, there is a background of practice, a set of agreed-on traditions upon which any practitioner, from novice to expert, can rely. It may take time and energy to learn how a monologic perspective is practiced, but the resources to learn it are, to a greater or lesser extent, readily available.

Such frequently is not the case with approaches informed by dialogism. Because dialogism requires challenging monological perspectives, one may not rely on established knowledge and procedure.[6] Moreover, as we have seen, views informing dialogism demand the actor perform work to expand the problem space in interpreting phenomena. For example, Vico refused to rely on the accounts of history formulated in his day, recommending instead the considerably more difficult task of exploring what (to the modern mind) might seem meaningless, barbaric images from before the time of what moderns term "civilization." Since no standards had been established for analyzing such images, Vico had to knit together his own method for foregrounding sociohistorically specific material. Although everyone has to do this to some extent for every utterance, for the dialogically inclined, two unavoidable tasks are involved: first, the controlling character of the monological view must be discerned, and second, appropriate dialogical alternatives must be advanced.

In the following, I explore more specific ways in which precursors of the dialogical view place less emphasis on passive reception of the principles of previous thinkers and instead insist on more individual activity in advancing beyond restrictions of the received view. I proceed in the same order as previously, beginning with Vico.

Vico and the Move from Passivity

An important way Vico and others embrace the dialogical idea of moving from passivity in understanding is through emphasis on the *construction of meaning*. The key word in this phrase is *construction*: in dialogically inclined approaches to understanding, the human agent is given a much greater role in defining reality. The social actor is not only assumed to be more personally complex than is usual in monologic views, but is also viewed as capable of more diverse and broadly ranging activity. These expansions of potentiality, moreover, are situated in a reality allowing for myriad viewpoints that privilege subjectivity. The mind reels at the complexity of the world thus presented; indeed, one could be led to conclude that a possible reason to seek the comparatively safe shore of monologism is that the world of limitless potential offered by dialogism is too terrifying.

The first way Vico expresses the move from passivity is through his principle that the purpose of human activity is to construct cultural understanding (to "make" what becomes "true"). This means individuals are not seen as more or less passive receptors/transmitters of inherited culture, or as perceivers of such culture through the lenses of monologism. Not only are individuals responsible for actively constructing culture, there is literally no other way the transmission of culture can occur.

For Vico, only that culture which is made by social actors can be understood by them. This view leaves no room for cultural elements that do not result from human activity. Ideas thought to result from passive reception (for example, faith in divine intervention) have no place in a world where each person must, by the act of living, not only construct her or his reality, but collaborate in constructing others' reality as well.

By downplaying the importance of monological abstractions, Vico shows historical people as less likely to be influenced by monological systems of thought. Social actors seldom rely on abstractions to conduct their lives; rather, they engage life as directly as do the learners and teachers in Vygotsky's model of skill acquisition. It is the formulation, following experience, of increasingly complex systems of abstraction, all removed to some extent from direct experience, that makes people tend to passive reception. If passivity is the largely uncritical acceptance of a dominant, monological view as legitimate, then activity refers in Vico and others to the difficult task of holding up a particular idea or utterance or system of thought to inspection. This task can be extraordinarily effortful and performing it will likely lead to conflict with those espousing the received view. It is therefore the antithesis of a predominantly passive approach to understanding.

Another Vichian idea pointing toward the move from passivity has to do with Vico's broader theory of history. Vico saw individual human activity as situated within a much larger movement of historical circumstances. Individuals were not necessarily seen in Vico as being actively involved, to any significant degree, in the creation of their culture, even though he did argue that it was to their representations we must turn in order to understand history. It must be noted that Vico did not hold a particularly high opinion of ancient people, often seeing them as nearer to animals than humans. However, this, with respect to monologic versus dialogic authority, is just the point Vico is making. Why should one look to refined, sophisticated accounts, written long after events they describe, when we have valid accounts from people who lived during these past times? Why, in other words, should we privilege discourse just because it conforms to our expectations about what "legitimate" discourse should be? By insisting on this point, Vico places responsibility on the shoulders of academic interpreters of historical discourse to be more active in fashioning their interpretations. Vico's shifting of the responsibility for understanding is a call for more activity, more knowledge, and more ingenuity on the part of the historian.

"Poetic wisdom," as Vico calls it (1999, bk. 2), demands that a great deal more effort be put into composing utterances. Vico's ideas concerning the historian's responsibility for making the effort to interpret utterance also applies to the way these utterances were formulated by ancients in the first place. Ancients had the difficult task of making sense of a world where few monologic systems existed to help them, which is another way of saying they lacked the trappings of civilization, including education. Thus, despite the low opinion Vico holds of the cultures in which ancient writers came to prominence, he does give them their due as primary interpreters of a reality that must often have seemed monstrous, horrid, and fatalistic. With little "civilized thought" (largely monologic) to guide them, ancients still actively utilized poetry and other kinds of direct, visceral literary imagery—these were tools for an active enterprise that later rhetoricians would render passive by converting them into abstractions they referred to as "tropes"—to render the world in a way that made sense to them:

> All figures of speech . . . —metaphor, metonymy, synecdoche, and irony—which were previously thought to be the ingenious inventions of writers . . . became figurative only later, as the human mind developed and invented words which signified abstract forms, that is, generic categories comprising various species, or relating parts to a whole. (Vico, 1999, p. 162)

Later elaborate scholarly systems of abstractions about figures of speech represent a move toward the safety of passive acceptance of categories. Vico's work refocused recognition on the original composers, those who worked hardest at it, denying credit to practitioners of monologically inclined views of rhetoric for having "discovered" such usages.

Pragmatism and the Move from Passivity

Like Vico, pragmatists favor highly individualistic perspectives. Pragmatists go even further in arguing that an effort of will is not merely an inescapable facet of existence, but the driving force that informs the governing standard—utility—by which all ideas must be judged. One way to see the shift from passivity is in pragmatism's view that to determine the practical value of any philosophical idea demands an effort of will. Individual thinkers, in other words, may not passively accept philosophical utterances, but must actively evaluate them.

The pragmatic enterprise requires intention and correction through consciously analyzing feedback. The process challenges the presumed authority of monological perspectives, since pragmatists insist that the only value in a philosophical principle is that which it has for person who contemplates it. This means no idea can be accepted without question, since value is to be determined through application to personal experience, which varies from person to person, and changes continually even for a given individual. Linking this with Bakhtin's concept of the uniqueness of each individual's worldview, a given philosophical principle cannot mean the same thing to more than one person, or even the same thing to the same person at different times or in different circumstances.

Monological authority depends on the widespread acceptance, largely without conscious or extensive questioning, of ideas more or less passively received. Whether a given idea will affect one's view of, for example, what is ethical, moral, aesthetically pleasing, and so on, depends on principles received from others. By instantiating such guidelines into one's consciousness, one imports templates that can then be used to process sense and other data to come up with a way of seeing particular "real-life" situations. There is of course nothing wrong with this; indeed, virtually all learning, education, acculturation, and so on, is built on the active intake and modification of processes and ideas by which the often inchoate data about the empirical world can be understood.

Pragmatism, however, introduces a different kind of philosophical process.[7] Pragmatism proposes a shift in degree of individual responsibility. Rather than simply offering individual active evaluation of philosophic utterance as an alternative, pragmatists argued that such utterances should be judged by no standards other than their pragmatic implications. This means that no philosophy, no matter how monologically sanctioned, is immune to the scrutiny of the individual social actor.

Another way pragmatism presages the shift from passivity has to do with the idea of community and communal sense as a measure of the practical utility of a given perspective. This elaboration of pragmatism is (as we saw previously) primarily associated with the work of Rorty (1982). Although Rorty's approach represents a comparatively recent evolution of "classical" pragmatism, some, such as Menand

(1997), characterize Rorty's growth as a transformation from "a philosopher to an intellectual" (p. xxxiii), a metamorphosis Menand thinks responsible for a "revival" in pragmatist thought. According to Rorty, it follows naturally that knowledge of the interests of one's community offer a useful standard to evaluate one's actions. This knowledge should be considered at least a part of one's repertoire of pragmatic knowledge to be used in evaluating philosophical utterances.

Rorty's argument implies that the social actor must go outward to determine the sense of the community. In pragmatism, passive acceptance of another view is impossible—the sense of the community (unless through unacceptably monologic means) will not be presented to the social actor for passive acceptance. Because the worldviews of social actors are inherently incompatible (see the previous discussion of Bakhtin), and it is these actors who comprise communities, it takes a great deal of effort to determine what principles they might share as a group. Moreover, the sense of the community, once determined, still must, by dint of considerable individual effort, be conjoined to the contents of personal experience to determine the practical value of a particular point of view.

Phenomenology and the Move from Passivity

To begin to look at the various ways phenomenology helps us comprehend the move from passivity, I turn first to its bedrock principle: nothing in the world of appearances may be accepted at face value. In this respect, phenomenology goes far beyond pragmatism, where the central idea was that we should suspect *ways of knowing*—according to phenomenology, we should suspect all appearances, all language, all systems of knowledge.

Phenomenology's stance on epistemology is similar to that of pragmatism. Individual consciousness is the only means for getting to the essence of phenomena. Just as with pragmatism, it is not enough to accept theoretically defined, linguistically described representations of phenomena. The individual must actively probe for himself or herself the link among mind, perception, phenomena, and so on. This critical examination of course demands a great deal of effort, as it aims at the core of meaning, questions it, and reemerges with sharper awareness and a higher level of knowledge.

The relentless questioning of appearances proves of great benefit in the development of dialogism. For dialogism to evolve, for alternative interpretations of discourse and phenomena to be considered, there must first be a distrust of extant representations. Alternative interpretations of phenomena cannot be given credence so long as one is under the sway of accepted representations as "reality."

A particularly useful phenomenological concept to elaborate the move from passivity is the notion of the "lifeworld." The lifeworld *(Lebenswelt)* is associated with the later writings of Husserl (1970, 1975). According to Husserl, the world in which we live contains the material from which scientific and mathematical representations are abstracted— indeed, the word *abstraction* suggests removing from phenomena essential qualities that result in a representation less complete than the phenomena themselves. Husserl saw the Lebenswelt as having its own appearance and its own standards for evidence and truth. However, science went astray when it started to view itself as distinct from these phenomena, focusing on elements disjunct from the lifeworld. The task of science, Husserl argued, should not be to separate but rather bring together scientific truth and the intuitive, directly experienced truth of the Lebenswelt.

With respect to dialogism, the lifeworld validates subjective experience as distinct from the so-called objective truth of the scientific (or other monological) method. This has great implications for the activity involved in judging phenomena and appearance. The ambitious goals Husserl proposes demand of the individual a number of strenuous activities. The thinker must evaluate the nature of scientific inquiry, questioning its foundations. Scientific method is built on the—very monological—idea that one can work from a vantage point uncontaminated by the vagaries of subjectivism, and indeed, in its more extreme formulations, is thought to guarantee objective truth. By questioning this ostensibly bedrock principle, one obviously invites a great deal of conflict, and assumes a responsibility that will require considerable, active exertion.

Another phenomenological distinction useful in seeing the move toward activity is the distinction between *direct* and *indirect* knowledge. As noted, one of the chief goals of phenomenology is to lessen distinctions between reality and mental representations of reality. Humans get sidetracked from direct experience primarily through abstract thought and language. Therefore, in making the distinction between direct (unmediated) knowledge and indirect (mediated) knowledge, phenomenologists call into question the grounds of knowing on which monological views are based. This, too, requires arduous activity: in inquiring about direct and indirect knowledge, phenomenology extends its questioning beyond the range of knowledge included in conventional science (as with the lifeworld) and expands it to all human thought.

Indeed, the fact that individuals see fit to distinguish between direct and indirect knowledge presupposes they have come to the conclusion that their perspective on "reality" has become somewhat tenuous. Moreover, to deliberately question monological views and turn to intuitive forms of understanding suggests a decision to refocus one's energies toward a search for essential truth, as difficult, time-consuming, and frustrating as this quest may be. Having faith in monologic perspectives is inertial; one follows the comparatively less difficult path of assuming the predominant, received view is true, since it is already widely accepted and entrenched. To challenge these set ideas, one must swim against the current and by so doing contribute to the evolution of one's consciousness. Phenomenology's great strength is that its precepts demand a confrontation of all facets of life with a questioning, open, intuitive mind. The true advocate of the phenomenological perspective is forever in the active mode, always "on."

Vygotsky and the Move from Passivity

In elaborating the dialogical move from passivity, the work of Vygotsky plays a critical role. While other perspectives have the individual wrestling with poetry and history, or philosophical utterance, or the shakiness of thought and language, Vygotsky focuses on the reality of human-to-human interaction. One way to see this is in his assertion that culture is not an entity transmitted in toto and unchanged from teacher to student. Rather, Vygotsky holds that the learning experience is collaboratively constructed through interaction. This position calls into question many learning models, which reify culture as something that can be "transmitted." Some anthropologists, for example, have called into question what was originally the prevailing monologic view, the "culture as object" metaphor (see, for example, Benedict, 1934). Nevertheless, a surprising amount of learning practice still regards knowledge as somehow "in" the mind of the teacher and "something" to be placed "in" the mind of the student. This is the so-called transmission model of teaching, which assumes that knowledge is best broken down into discrete elements or building blocks relayed, in more or less immutable form independent of circumstance, from teacher to student. The transmission model assumes we can know reality through knowing its constituent elements.

As is often the case with monological perspectives, it is more comfortable to take refuge in the transmission model (especially if one is to judge by the prevalence of the lecture method in formal education). However, Vygotsky, by experience and reasoning, knew the model could not realistically describe learning. Observing teachers and students, he saw they were collaboratively fashioning a situation that had not previously existed. In other words, through their interaction teacher and student are not passing along culture, but going to a great deal of trouble to create it.

The Vygotskyan metaphor of the zone of proximal development is also useful in explaining the shift from passivity. If we accept the idea of a ZPD, it is difficult to assume knowledge goes "from" the teacher "to" the student. Instead, the ZPD is a "hot zone" in which activities can take different trajectories, depending on what comprises the consciousnesses of teacher and student, as well as the sociohistorical features of the learning environment. What happens in the ZPD is collaboratively constructed, and therefore the "results" or learning outcomes cannot be accurately forecast in advance. If one views the learning process this way, one is obliged to see teacher and student as having to exert much more effort than would seem to be involved in the transmission model.

Bakhtin and the Move from Passivity

As noted in discussing mind-body dualism, the Bakhtin idea of human consciousness presupposes an enormously arduous, never-ending adjustment to the fact that one's mind differs from all others. Thus, of all perspectives leading to dialogism, the Bakhtinian view depicts the greatest demands on the social actor. Bakhtin does not even grant the social actor the comfort of being able to assume a unity in cognition and language, insisting from the outset that difference is a fact of life and that the act of living demands one must learn to deal with it.

An implication of this idea is that, although the self cannot stop in space and time, for it to be an object of perception, it must do these very things. This means the self remains invisible to itself, and the pursuit of consciousness remains forever frustrating. Nevertheless, because the self ceaselessly presses outward, searching for material to use in trying to understand, individuals are forever active. (Notice how far removed this idea is from the scenario of the mind comfortably contemplating itself, objectively, in Descartes' meditations.) In place of the monological stability assumed by many philosophies of mind, Bakhtin emphasizes how little the mind can depend on anything in its search for understanding. Indeed, in Bakhtin, the quest for self-understanding, as that concept was previously formulated, is completely relegated to the background, and in place of the *passive* reception of thought, there is the relentlessly *active* demand to be wholly involved in a search that will never end.

The degree of activity involved in this process can seem over-whelming. Not only must we forever seek what is outside the self, but due to the inherent difference in the perceptual configurations of all humans, we only dimly understand what we find. It is as if we were looking for clues to a puzzle in a dark basement, using a flashlight that flickers sporadically on and off, illuminating the territory only inter-mittently, but leaving us most of the time in the dark. Moreover, we are doomed to pursue this frustrating task forever.

Finally, an added dimension in Bakhtinian thought implying increased activity is that the process of understanding must take place through the mediation of language. The self, in addition to trying to understand its relation to others and the world at large, tries to unite abstractions inherent in language with lived experience, which is never abstract but intensely particular. Language is the way one expresses one's perception of the world; yet language is built on the presumption of regularity. Nevertheless, despite our awareness of its deficiencies, and our knowledge that we must work to make language yield meaning, language is still the best means we have of expressing our relation to the world, even though we know it is the infinite particularity of that world that resists any classification. Thus, Bakhtinian thought implies yet another form of activity, in place of passivity: we are responsible for uniting abstraction and particularity. In this respect, Bakhtin proves the toughest taskmaster preparing us for the dialogical move from passivity.

Summary: The Move from Passivity and Internet Communication

In large part because of the scope of the Internet, communicators in the medium have had to become more active to use it. This activity is demanded regardless of whether the communicator is the utterer or the perceiver of Internet utterance. If the former, she or he must learn not only the mechanics but also cultural rules for this vast system of communication. Using EDMs, the communicator must engage in writing, which (even by modest EDM standards) is still more demanding than talking. Composing Web pages/sites takes even more work, necessitating the learning of a vocabulary and technical processes, as well as creativity in combining elements to achieve a desired effect (and, once "up," the page/site must be maintained and kept current).

Nor is the perceiver of Internet utterance spared effort in actualizing communication. With EDMs, one must put effort into composing responses, and in so doing, not simply answering points from single posters one by one, but often combining the points made by others to achieve a "sense of the list." With Web pages/sites, the so-called surfer (the metaphor suggests skimming the surface), to experience the site/page utterance, has to exert energy: to read, to decide, to navigate, to assess, to penetrate deeper or leave the site, to provide information and/or feedback, and so on. Apart from that, one who analyzes the site (for whatever reason, as scholar, user, or composer) is faced with an enormously effortful task, involving all the kinds of understanding needed to make the page/site, and more.

Despite its popular reputation as the domain of passive receivers of electronic signals, Internet communication takes work, and it is, moreover, *mindful* work, that is, it involves effort that for the most part cannot be performed, as it were, on "autopilot." To use Internet communication, you have to participate; and unlike other forms of communication at which we become adept through socialization (such as conversation), with Internet communication one can seldom proceed with a limited degree of conscious attention. To be sure, there are conventions used in both EDMs and Web pages/sites that are expected, and are used as conveniences, probably without much conscious thought (abbreviations such as LOL [laughing out loud] might be examples of these). However, Internet communication is the one form of one-to-one communication in which a number of hardware and software elements have to intercombine for communication to occur. As anyone who has failed to gain access to a server, or had a computer crash, can testify, there are many points in the process at which the electronic and physical parameters can break down, and it takes effort to maintain them in working order.

KNOWLEDGE: FROM EMPHASIZING THE GIVEN TOWARD THE NEW

Previously we saw how contemplating five precursors of the dialogic view gradually erodes faith in monologism, shifting attention toward mind-world union and activity. The third theme is closely related to the two already covered, but involves how we see knowledge, a key component of mental functioning. In monologism, while previous knowledge (the "given") is privileged, in dialogism, more significance is accorded to original or creative knowledge (the "new").

In discussing this third line of development, I will discuss some ways the new is given an enhanced status. In all of these approaches, the key to understanding the potential for alternative interpretation of utterance has to do with generating alternatives, and more importantly, with whether these interpretations can be considered as valid as those formulated from monologic views. In the following, I look at how each line of thought leading to dialogism has found it necessary to counterpose the given (that is, the received view, generally carrying the stamp of monological authority) and the new (that is, alternatives to such views, often explicitly and purposefully diverging from the monologic perspective). As previously, I turn first to Vico.

Vico and the Move from Emphasizing the Given

We have seen how Vico reformulated the contentious notion of culture, rendering it more dynamic than it is in many monological perspectives. Some quite influential work in anthropology has seen "culture" as a reified entity, "transmitted" from generation to generation, much as a valued heirloom might be passed on from ancestor to descendant. However, to Vico, the *verum factum* formula means culture is manufactured continually. His scholarly contemporaries, in trying to understand the past in terms of the present, imposed accepted (given) systems of thought, accompanied by highly complex vocabularies and concepts. The approach Vico advocated, turning back to the ever-fresh (if crude or incomprehensible) insights of an earlier time, was resisted largely because viewing history as dynamic and continually shifting (new) proves too onerous for most conventional theories. In monologism, the given is embraced and the new is regarded with suspicion.

According to Vico, and other dialogically inclined thinkers who acknowledge a debt to him (such as Dilthey, 1988; for more on Dilthey, see Ermarth, 1981]) culture is negotiated through the act of living. Through this process, Vico said, ancient people made sense of life, primarily without benefit of comprehensive monologic systems of thought used by later commentators to simplify an infinitely variegated world into coherent patterns. In other words, ancient people engaged the world as it was presented to them, and formulated their views unaware of systems of thought and practice we know as "civilization." To Vico, this meant that the ancients, in their own way, were far more accurate and creative in dealing with the dynamic flux of life than scholars who tried, retrospectively, to understand what historical actors "must have meant."

Vico thought the world described by ancient poets such as Homer was terrifying, the more so because monologic perspectives—science, religion, history—that reassure modern people that the world is not as chaotic as it seems were not available to ancient people. Ancients had to reinvent their world unendingly, and often in response to natural events, such as environmental catastrophes, over which they had little or no control. Lacking the refuge of monological abstractions, for example, they were unable to generalize about what "should be done" from situation to situation, and had to fall back on inventing explanations for the natural phenomena they encountered. In such circumstances, the new must always predominate over the given.

Another Vichian idea useful in understanding the shift from prioritizing the given is Vico's position that culture does not come from the self. Since self and world interact, what changes "in" the world causes changes "in" one's self (and vice versa—the made and the true are convertible). To grasp the implications of this concept, the "external" world should be viewed as a configuration of elements that never ceases changing. Since the so-called internal and external worlds are inextricably interrelated, the dynamism of the external world transfers its limitless changeability to the internal consciousness of each social actor. Social actors, then, whether they find it comfortable or not, reflect on and contribute to the dynamism of life, and thereby develop an appreciation for the "new," in addition to the given.

Pragmatism and the Move from Emphasizing the Given

The contribution of pragmatism to the shift from prioritizing the given is best seen in its central principle: nothing in philosophical thought can be accepted as monological (given) without question. Instead, the pragmatist philosopher must always seek to offer new interpretations by testing philosophical utterance according to the standard of utility.

One important way pragmatism actualizes this insight is through rejecting certainty as an intellectual goal. Certainty is a quality assigned to an idea that is already, or is destined to be, given knowledge. But some pragmatists, particularly the later ones (for example, Rorty, 1982), argue that philosophical disputes ultimately come down to differences in vocabulary, and therefore urge moving beyond the quest for certainty altogether.

Of all ideas put forward in pragmatism, the position that much of analytical philosophy is futile has, as one would expect, proved to be one of the most contentious. Pragmatism is seen by some philosophers (mistaken, in my view) as questioning the validity of all philosophical knowledge. To some extent, it is possible to see every philosophical utterance as an attempt to impose on the relentless disorder of the world a systematic perspective (a given view) whose purpose is to render the world less uncertain. The difficulty, some pragmatists would argue, is that there are some questions and issues at the core of most philosophies that have not been, and probably cannot be, resolved (Rorty, 1982). If pursuit of certainty is fraught with so much uncertainty, as it were, it cannot be a principal project of philosophy.

Certainty is tied to assumptions that world and mind are stable, though the five predialogic perspectives clearly show they are not. Since, in pragmatism, the individual is advised to disregard both stability and certainty, it then becomes one's responsibility to continually revise one's point of view to accommodate the ever-changing flux of life. The given cannot be unreflectingly assigned priority over the specificity of existence, either in living, or (as in philosophy) in accounting for living.

Perhaps the final blow delivered by pragmatist philosophers to the tradition of prioritizing the given is that utility, the master measuring instrument of pragmatism, is itself constantly changing. In other words, what each person means by "utility" changes all the time, leading to changes in what is regarded as "pragmatic." This ongoing revision is inevitably based on the individual's experience, as well as the activity of thinking through that experience according to the standards of one's unique, nonreplicable consciousness. Unlike Kant, who proposed a transcendental synthesis (that is, a synthesis that transcends the limits of empirical inquiry), in pragmatism, conception and experience are mutually reinforcing. Events that occur as a result of a unique process of living (the new) result in the formation of consciousness, which leads in turn to revised perspectives that inevitably cast subsequent experiences in a different light.

Phenomenology and the Move from Emphasizing the Given

We have seen how phenomenology assumes that all representations of reality are in some sense misrepresentations. Through the process of thought, not to mention variations that come from expressing thought in language, phenomenologists champion a return to grasping the essential qualities of phenomena. In essence, phenomenology calls into question all of what is regarded as given.

One way this is done is by broaching the possibility of more than one "reality" (or, rather, the possibility that more than one description of reality can be valid, or, still more accurately, that all representations are equally invalid in departing from the essence of phenomena they describe). This implies that each engagement of phenomena by individual consciousness brings the possibility that new representational "realities" can be created. However, we should remember that it is the descriptions of "reality" that are multiplied, not versions of "reality"— the phenomenological position is that none of these representations can adequately reflect the richness of phenomena. To phenomenologists, the essence, the "real," exists at a point beyond thought and words. Nevertheless, in performing the actual work of the intellect, one must rely on thought and words. Though imperfect, these representations, by their very imperfection, generate alternative views of the essential reality they attempt to express, but never can.

Phenomenology also helps us understand the shift to prioritizing the new through its emphasis on direct experience, of oneself and of others. In social life, this leads to the fascinating idea that each person's experience of phenomena results in views of reality unique to that individual alone. Thus, any consciousness we encounter must present us with a different view of a given phenomenon, and more importantly, we must acknowledge the validity of each such viewpoint, at least in comparison to other views, if not to the essential reality of the represented phenomenon. This means the view taken on a specific issue by an individual person cannot be coincident with a widespread monological rendering of how one "should think" (that is, the given view) regarding that issue. If each person's construction of a monological ("given") principle is equally valid (or invalid) then the uncritical acceptance of such a sanctioned principle is untenable. In place of the unitary given, one must deal with the multiple perspectives, each reflecting variations on the new.

Vygotsky and the Move from Emphasizing the Given

In the work of Vygotsky and the activity theorists he inspired, the new could almost be characterized as a sacred quest. Vygotsky and his adherents profoundly distrusted models that presupposed predictable outcomes from static configurations of elements in the learning situation. Vygotsky, as we have seen, was one of the first to point out that learning is mediated, that is, a process in which the participant acts, not directly toward an object, but through some mediating instrument or tool, whether physical or conceptual. Since learning must take place in some specific sociocultural environment, this means it is difficult, perhaps impossible, to formulate a general theory of learning that applies across situations. The almost limitless variability in environment, physical and cultural, is in effect the "wild card" in the learning process. Even if one could define an optimal teaching strategy for one situation, it might not apply in another situation, because conditions in the new situation will inevitably be different, and what is given can no longer be relied on.

Vygotsky's work explicates the shift from prioritizing the given through his principle that the meaning of language, concepts, gestures, and so on, are manufactured in the process of social interaction. A highly useful feature of dialogism is that it highlights the importance of social context in modifying cognition and communication. In Vygotsky, social interaction is given a different reading than it is in monological approaches. In the latter, elements of social interaction are often variables, whereas in Vygotsky they are viewed as a constituting force that affects outcomes unpredictably. Social interaction in dialogism is not set, but is dynamic both in interacting with other elements of sociohistorical understanding and in changing in response to the flux of life.

Bakhtin and the Move from Emphasizing the Given

The Bakhtin circle asserts that, through language, the given and the new are inextricably linked. A highly provisional analogy to the Bakhtinian view of "given–new" is the dichotomy between centripetal and centrifugal (see Chapter 1). *Centripetality* (a term from physics) refers to the fact that language has elements that are predictable and standardized (roughly, given) while *centrifugality* refers to the fact that language also has qualities that are unpredictable and unique (roughly, new). In the

Bakhtinian view, language and consciousness require the interaction of both forces, as well as the realization that their reconciliation is forever impossible.

A fascinating idea to emerge from this line of thinking is that, for Bakhtin, the perceptual horizon of the self must remain eternally open and unfinished (Holquist, 1990, p. 22; Holt, 2003a). As it encounters the world, the self perceives itself to be the center and all else arrayed in such a way as to conform to the perceiver's perceptual configuration (architectonics). This view of the horizon of potential is, for the self that sees it, infused with infinite possibilities—it is forever and completely open. However, to see one's own potential as open automatically means one must see the perceptual horizons of others as closed and finished: the "selves" of others are consigned to being neutral and homogenized with the world as one sees it. Because the self has no choice but to try to reconcile its limited self-awareness with the (almost entirely unknown) perceptions of others, the Bakhtin group seems to be painting a very bleak picture of individual potential, where the individual forever tries to complete the Sisyphean task of melding itself to an onslaught of the new, that which cannot be understood, far less synthesized. Nevertheless, this picture is for the Bakhtin group a cause, not for pessimism, but rather the infinitely hopeful opening of possibilities for expansion. Dealing with this predicament offers a way for the individual to accommodate both the inevitably predictable (given) and the unexpectedly idiosyncratic (new) qualities of language and thought, both of which constantly confront every social actor.

One other way the Bakhtin group contributes to the move toward prioritizing the new is in its principle that understanding living language requires effort in completing one's own utterances and thoughts. This activity is unpredictable, requiring ongoing adjustment to recognize new, as against given, understandings. In joining oneself to existence, one can rely on very little given information. One must depend instead on incomplete information obtained by trying to "fill in" what one takes to be the perceptions of others, and to use these in fashioning a definition of the self. Through this unceasing process, the self is forever hungry for information, sensation, thought, language—anything that will help it in its quest for understanding. This means that everything sought by the self to aid its understanding will, in a number of different ways, be "new." By venturing forth to find evidence in the alien realms of others' perceptions, the self is always dealing with new—often radically new—information.

Summary: The Move from Emphasizing the Given and Internet Communication

A popular conception of the Internet is that it is an entirely new form of communication. While I tend to doubt this, I do believe that the Internet is, at least for the moment, one area of communication in which newness is likely to be embraced. This is of course the case with any relatively new communication technology. However, the new has an even greater role in the Internet because of the acceleration of technological advance, which touches all aspects of Internet communication. We have already seen the effects of this acceleration in the incomprehensible size and reach of the Internet, which make it seem even more mysterious. In addition, in contrast to other media in which technological improvement is accelerating, in Internet communication, improvements affect the user not simply as a receiver but as a composer of messages.

There is also a sense of impermanence that pervades the Internet, leading users to rely less on given knowledge. An example, one I have confronted often while writing this book, is the method for citing Internet communication. Along with the location of Internet material, one is required in many cases to state when one accessed the material, if one expects the page content to be changed. One does not need to search the Web too long before encountering the frustration of failing to find a page that has moved or no longer exists.

Finally, the features comprising the "reality" of cyberspace just seem essentially more evanescent than "brick-and-mortar" reality. In cyberspace, for example, creation of new human "organizations," often out of little more than electronic signals, is common. A comparatively recent example is the dot-com stock explosion in the 1990s, which saw companies with almost no physical assets "forming" into entities to trade stock at inflated prices (Cassidy, 2002). Although the survival rate is not high, it is still possible to create an entire company in cyberspace and moreover make it profitable (for example, the highly profitable Amazon.com began simply as an intermediary between customers and booksellers [Cassidy, 2002, pp. 142–143]). As a result, and because so much of what is on the Internet cannot be confirmed, popular sentiment embraces a strong bias against Internet information, a standing warning to "let the buyer beware."

These and other qualities lead to an environment for communication that relies far less on precedent and convention than any other kind. Monological knowledge gets to be monological precisely because of presumed verification. People believe they can depend on monological perspectives because the principles and knowledge upon which they are based seem to have been repeatedly confirmed by others. Given the nature of the Internet, such certainty is impossible (in fact, certainty is also impossible for seemingly firm monological perspectives as well, but as we have seen, it can be difficult for people to perceive this). It is not that we should abandon regularity in our search for meaning in Internet utterances—that such utterances depend on computers, and especially the iron predictability of programming, prevent this—but that we must give an equal, perhaps greater, degree of priority to the new than we would be prepared to do were we to take a primarily monological perspective interpreting utterances in e-mail discussion messages and Web pages/sites.

CONCLUSION

This chapter has covered a great deal of territory, examining and comparing thinkers from disparate traditions, from the thoroughgoing humanism of Vico through the relentless practicality of pragmatism, the radical questioning of the grounds of knowledge in phenomenology, and the situated explanations of learning in Vygotsky, to Bakhtin's picture of the word alone on its own in the rough-and-tumble world of alternative representation.

I began this chapter wishing to show dialogism as an alternative way of looking at language and consciousness by pointing out qualities that make it attractive as a perspective through which to examine Internet communication. Internet discourse, perhaps more than other forms, has the qualities of rebellion, antiauthoritarianism, centrifugality, disunion, and all the rest that we have seen, to a greater or less extent, in the five predialogic perspectives. Indeed, by looking closely at these perspectives as they have contributed to dialogism, we see revealed a wealth of ideas to help us understand the two predominant forms of Internet communication examined in the next two chapters. Exploring each perspective yields ideas that help us comprehend how, through a dialogically inclined set of assumptions, we are offered the opportunity to, for a time, shift our view of what language "means," from mind-body dualism, passivity, and prioritizing the given to mind-body union, activity, and prioritizing the "new."

In Vico, this can result from seeking the meaning of linguistic expression in the sociohistorical circumstances in which they are originally propagated. For Vico, meaning must not be accepted merely because it conforms to a dominant (monologic) perspective that forces sociohistorical specificity into the confines of a widely accepted set of categories, ideas, and systems of classification. Proceeding from this insight, we will later see how the creation and perception of Internet discourse depends more on a process of looking to worlds of meaning outside the raw material of the utterance (that is, the words and symbols that go into its linguistic construction). In Chapters 3 and 4, I will look at these as instances of what are called "other meaning" and see how they are an essential part of fashioning and understanding EDMs and Web pages/sites.

In pragmatism, we saw that the human mind is most appropriately seen as an entity that does not encounter "reality" presented whole and "just as it is" but rather as one outcome of a prolonged encounter in which the "external" world is modified, emerging in successive acts of understanding that involve the continuing development of the one who understands. This will prove useful in revealing the incremental emergence of meaning in Internet discourse, where utterances are presented largely devoid of the richness of detail that characterizes other kinds of communication. Often the first encounter of what "is in" the Internet-based utterance yields very limited understanding, because there seems so little, on the surface, for the perceiver to work with. Instead, through linking the message to other systems of meaning, the perceiver eventually comes to actively fortify and enrich the utterance, "filling in" details that are missing from the words and other symbols, in and of themselves. This process also involves the highly important ethical component of pragmatism, the responsibility of the individual to assess the utility of philosophical utterances. In understanding Internet utterances, this is analogous to assuming the responsibility for "making meaning," that is, unearthing the meaning of the message by intentionally performing work, instead of assuming that this meaning is presented monologically through systems of signification involved at the surface level in constructing the message.

From phenomenology, we learned that reality is far more malleable than it appears in many monological systems of thought. Phenomenology recognizes the validity of alternative approaches to the perception of meaning. Indeed, in phenomenology's principles, we find a deep distrust not only of language, but of systems of abstraction of any kind that prevent human beings from directly encountering the empirical world. While this radical insight may be less overtly useful in analyzing Internet communication, we may take from phenomenology the idea that perception of what an Internet utterance "means" depends on the perspective from which it is viewed. The idiosyncratic qualities of each person's perception are particularly important, because it is these features that provide the resources to be used in interpreting the utterance. As I will show in the next two chapters, each individual perspective leads to the importation of different systems of meaning that change how a given Internet utterance is viewed from individual to individual. This of course challenges any received view of Internet utterance that might be propagated as a "standard" way to read an EDM or a Web page/site. However, as I will also show, to fully understand an Internet utterance, we need to look both at the conventional way the utterance is "supposed to be" understood, as a backdrop to how this utterance inevitably will be understood, based on the unique architectonics of each individual who encounters it.

The work of Vygotsky, and the activity theorists who followed him, besides taking us into the realms of learning and education, also elaborates a key aspect of dialogism: the idea of a territory in which a dynamic interaction takes place between the propagator of an utterance (in much of Vygotsky's work, the teacher) and its perceiver (the student). Although Vygotsky's research related to psychology and education (Moll, 1990), the description of his zone of proximal development provides a very useful metaphor to visualize the negotiation of meaning between the composers and the perceivers of Internet utterances. In particular, we can usefully see the meaning of an utterance on the Internet (and elsewhere) as not even truly existing until its meaning is coconstructed by interactants. This is another way of saying it is not possible to see an Internet utterance solely through a monological lens, even though I will employ a monological perspective as part of the actual analysis. Furthermore, by looking at the development of meaning as a dynamic process, we also allow for such development to alter over time.

Finally, in the eclectic and provocative work of the Bakhtin circle, we see the synthesis of all of these insights in the well-known, though widely misunderstood, idea of heteroglossia. By considering Internet utterance as heteroglossic, we highlight its vulnerable qualities. Like all utterance, it is cast adrift in a sea of alternative representations that, due to unavoidable idiosyncrasies in the worldview of the consciousness of each individual who encounters it, will inevitably conflict (often dramatically) with the intent of its creator as well as all others who perceive it. Thus, the utterance's meaning is closely connected to sociohistorical circumstance (as in Vico); this meaning results from an encounter by the communicant with sociohistorical circumstance and under the aegis of individual responsibility (as in pragmatism), prone to alternative representations (as in phenomenology), and resident in an area of contested and coconstructed middle ground that cannot be forecast (as in Vygotsky). As I will show in the next two chapters, it is the Bakhtin circle whose summary of the various facets of dialogism (an idea perhaps more closely associated with the name of Bakhtin than perhaps any other single thinker) provides the most complete and useful approach to dialogistic analysis of Internet communication. However, Bakhtin stands, as the saying goes, on the shoulders of giants, courageous thinkers who stood against the tide of conventional opinion to knit together a perspective that will permit us to—finally—probe the mysteries of Internet discourse.

Although in this chapter I have explored influences on dialogism, it should be emphasized that these influences result from the constant interplay between monologic and dialogic perspectives. Dialogism is defined by its contrast with monologism, and as has been noted repeatedly, both perspectives are essential to understand living language. One critically important implication of this is that one gains dialogic insight only against the backdrop of the monologic perspective, and vice versa. As I turn to the examination of EDMs and Web pages/sites in the next two chapters, I will make full use of this idea, consciously applying, first the monologic view then the dialogic view to samples of Internet discourse, and then comparing the two readings to generate further levels of insight. It is important to realize that the conscious assumption of either the monologic or the dialogic perspective results in an impressive expansion of the problem space concerning a given sample of discourse. In effect, using each perspective strengthens the other, because the realization that utterance is both monologic and dialogic frees the analyst from habits that arise from concentrating on either perspective over the other.

NOTES

1. For example, Eccles (1989) conceives of mind as nonmaterial entity, and Popper (1972) proposes a material/ideational dualism.

2. It is of course possible to see Berlin's criticisms about Vico's lack of coherence as itself an example of a monologically inclined scholar trying, unsuccessfully, to fit a dialogically inclined approach into a conventional format.

3. To see phenomenology as leading away from mind-body dualism, one must acknowledge that originally the "founder" of the phenomenological movement, Edmund Husserl, pursued a goal very much akin to Descartes'. Like Descartes (and Kant, for that matter) Husserl's aims were to place philosophy on a sound footing by going to the root of assumptions about existence, and thereby to lead to a resolution of the squabbles between philosophers. Yet, unlike Descartes, Husserl argued the thinking self must itself be an object of examination. Husserl's original method (the so-called *epoché*, or bracketing of experience) was rejected by others associated with phenomenology, principally Heidegger and Sartre. Hence, when I speak of phenomenology's effect on dialogism, I refer to the broader realm of disparate phenomenological approaches, rather than to Husserl's classic method. It is interesting, though, to see this as yet another confirmation of Descartes' profound impact on philosophy.

4. It should be noted that, despite the inability of language to adequately describe experience, phenomenologists must rely on language to bring forth understanding of experience. Because language intellectualizes experience, and yet is the chief way we have to communicate about experience, phenomenologists often have to evoke experience through the skillful use of language. The key lies in understanding the tenuous connection between language and experience and not falling prey to the assumption that language fully represents experience.

5. This point is convincingly made by the Finnish work theorist Yrjö Engeström in his discussion of "activity triangles," in his seminal work on activity theory, *Learning by Expanding* (1987).

6. This is why, in discussions of dialogism, paradoxes abound. Because dialogically inclined perspectives rely on language and conventional modes of expression, they seem to have to make "a deal with the devil" in accommodating monological views. Vico's theory of cycles of history is perhaps the grandest of all "grand theories"; pragmatism cannot claim status as a philosophy based on anything other than its own utility (so anyone who judges it as not useful is free to reject it); phenomenologists must rely on the very words and abstractions they castigate; Vygotsky's sociohistorical circumstances must include mediating tools defined by the generalistic approach to education he disapproves of; and in order to discuss "radical alterity," Bakhtin reifies

authorial voice as either primarily monologic or dialogic. As will be clear, though, these paradoxes, though fun to confound others with (for they truly reveal the underlying instability of monologic views), are not part of the dialogic enterprise. Dialogism does not offer final answers to settle paradoxes; it aims at expanding consciousness to be more comfortable with paradox.

7. "Introduces" may not be quite the right word. As James himself notes, "There is absolutely nothing new in the pragmatic method. Socrates was an adept at it. Aristotle used it methodically. Locke, Berkeley, and Hume made momentous contributions to truth by its means" (James, 1991, p. 25).

Chapter 3

E-Mail Discussion Messages: A Means for Constructing Civic Identity

Over the years, as I have done various presentations on analyzing e-mail discussion messages, a question I am inevitably asked (with varying degrees of subtlety) is, Why bother? Since the number of EDMs is probably unfathomable, and they are hardly the products of careful composition and editing, they would seem to be unworthy of the attention of the serious scholar of communication. Perhaps my attraction to EDMs comes from my background in the analysis of talk (Holt, 1989, 2003a), but I tend to regard all communication as consequential, simply because it reflects the infinite complexity of sociohistorical circumstance. Moreover, I think EDMs are particularly worthy of attention. Briefly, I conclude that EDMs have an image problem, owing largely to the fact that we fail to see them as utterance; in the next section, I explain the dialogic conception of utterance in greater detail.

If one looks at EDMs as people usually do, as merely collections of words and other symbols, one finds very little material to work with in making sense of them. EDMs are indeed among the barest, sparsest of human utterances. Unlike some other utterances, EDMs have, for example, almost no immediately visible contextual cues to elaborate and extend the language that comprises them. They have no accompanying nonverbal cues; little or no inflection (except crudities such as capitalization, the online equivalent of shouting, or cumbersome marks of emphasis such as asterisks or underlined characters before and after text); no paralinguistic cues such as pauses, tones, and vocalizations; no gaze behavior; no kinesic synchronization; indeed, no immediate, real-time responses at all.

This leaves the investigator with an apparently depleted analytical repertoire to work with. The data one might use in analyzing other kinds of utterance, data that can be approached using established techniques, is largely excluded from the e-mail discussion message. An alternative approach, however, lies in examining the process of mutual construction of meaning for EDMs. This approach involves looking beyond the message itself, to the social context of EDMs, for clues as to what aspects of social knowledge are being employed to lend meaning to the EDM utterance. As we know from the principles of dialogism, the context in which the communication takes place enriches the utterance and this in turn expands conception of what it "means."

Another problem with getting people to pay attention to EDMs is that they contain features that on their surface may make them seem trivial, particularly when compared to conventional notions of what constitutes "good writing," the standards for which are often the result of primarily monological perspectives. EDMs are often (though not always) expressed in the vulgar register, with slang, abbreviations, and profanity, and their composers frequently seem to delight in disregarding traditional "rules" such as those governing syntax, conventional logic, evidence, and idea development. This perception is compounded by the image of EDMs as the result of rapid composition, often seeming more dashed-off drafts than polished, edited final products. Dialogically inclined thinkers such as Bakhtin argue that messages pick up the idiosyncratic qualities of the medium in which they are expressed; EDMs absorb the quickness, discontinuity, compressed linguistic formulations, and so on, that epitomize the Internet. In some ways, EDMs are more like talk than writing. Thus it is no accident that the most abbreviated form of cybertalk, the exchange in real time of messages via Internet Relay Chat is described by a name usually applied to quick, rather superficial, face-to-face conversation: chatting. Such qualities as these make it easy to dismiss EDMs or take them less seriously than other, more "weighty" forms of writing.

One reason some communication scholars give EDMs such short shrift as communication artifacts is that we tend to see them in monological terms (indeed, if convinced they are not worthy of attention, why would analysts even want to go to the effort of generating dialogical alternatives?[1]). Yet we know from the arguments advanced in Chapter 2 that all communication is given meaning by an infinitely varied environment of social circumstance. If we connect the EDM to this vast network of meaning, does it assume greater significance than if we look at it primarily through the monological perspective?

I would argue it does. If we can add to the conventional view of discourse—which in part holds that the EDM's meaning is firmly settled by its linguistic features—we can come to see it as a collaboration and the person who first utters it as merely one among a vast pool of potential partners in constructing its meaning.[2] The meaning of any utterance, but especially the EDM, cannot be settled in monological terms alone, since it must change when it is perceived by another who will apprehend it according to his or her unique view of the world. Understanding is thus achieved in struggle over meaning between the utterer and anyone who perceives his or her utterance. This fact is particularly relevant to EDMs, because the reach of the Internet is global, perhaps more extensive than any other communication medium. Since meaning is inescapably social, most of the vast community of Internet users must be included among those who fashion the EDM's meaning.[3]

As we grapple with ways to better interpret EDM messages, we also need to pay attention to the EDM thread, a sequence of messages with a common subject (or topic). The study of EDM threads, one of the oldest and most widely used forms of computer-mediated civic discourse, has not as yet benefited from the widely shared templates for interpretation available for sequences of conventional communication (for example, formal academic or political debating). Indeed, to outsiders not previously involved in, or observing, a group's e-mail discussion, upon first encounter EDM threads can seem extraordinarily opaque. Not even taking into account what lies beneath the surface of EDM thread exchanges, a great deal of work is required merely to understand what seems to be going on. Approaching EDM threads monologically, we understand their centripetal ("holding together") aspects (see Chapter 2), but not their centrifugal ("flying apart") aspects. For this reason, monological understanding, though essential, should be seen as preparatory to using both monological and dialogical methods to achieve a deeper understanding.   .

Furthermore, it is necessary to look at EDMs in a different way, because of the increasing importance of e-mail, not just in our daily lives, but as an element of civic discourse. E-mail continues to rapidly gain ground as the preferred method for correspondence. E-mail's advantages in speed and flexibility have led to it supplanting conventional postal deliveries in a number of contexts; beyond that, e-mail also has features—such as the capacity to attach documents and other kinds of computer files; quote all or part of a message in writing a reply; and, most significantly, include hyperlinks to any page or site on the vast World Wide Web—that make of it a much more complex and powerful form of written communication. Though some might prefer otherwise, the lowly e-mail message is increasingly the communication channel of choice because of its convenience, efficiency, and connections to other communication channels. Given this sea change in public perception and use of e-mail, we cannot afford to treat e-mail messages as unworthy of attention, particularly as concerns their use in the public sphere.

Finally, specifically with respect to civic discourse, e-mail discussion groups have been, and continue to be, some of the most widely used and effective forums for discussing civic issues. This has been the case since the earliest days of the Internet, before newsgroups under the vast umbrella of Usenet became the predominant arena for communication by EDMs, when the most common type of group was the bulletin board system maintained on individual computers. Today, EDM threads remain one of the most active, vital, and relevant forms of civic discourse, representing one of the last venues of public communication where one can say what one wants about any civic issue. It is because EDMs are so important in both a general and a civic sense that we need to pay closer attention to them and seek a more appropriate means to understand them. In the next section I show how this can be accomplished by considering the EDM as utterance.

DIALOGISM AND E-MAIL DISCUSSION MESSAGES

By this point in the discussion, I have used the term *utterance* numerous times, both in its usual sense (a written or oral statement) and its technical sense, as sociohistorically specific speech. Now I turn to a further definition of utterance, which may help us penetrate behind the monologic veil by viewing the EDM as utterance, that is, not according to monological standards, but according to the specifics of context:

> For speech can exist in reality only in the form of concrete utterances of individual speaking people, speech subjects. Speech is always cast in the form of an utterance belonging to a particular speaking subject, and outside this form it cannot exist. (Bakhtin, 1986a, p. 71)[4]

Bakhtin provides further details about the utterance, stating that its beginning and end are defined by a change in the person who speaks (or writes). Thus, an utterance can be as short as an exasperated sigh in the midst of a heated argument or as long as *Remembrance of Things Past*. The important thing is that it is defined as belonging to a real person:

> Any utterance . . . has, so to speak, an absolute beginning and an absolute end: its beginning is preceded by the utterances of others (or, although it may be silent, others' active understanding, or, finally, a responsive action based on this understanding). The speaker ends his utterance in order to relinquish the floor to the other or to make room for the other's active responsive understanding. The utterance is not a conventional unit, but a real unit, clearly delimited by the change of speaking subjects. (Bakhtin, 1986a, pp. 71–72)

In these two passages, Bakhtin lays out two key features of utterance: its specificity and its complexity. All generalizations about language (these arise from primarily monological approaches) are simplifications, in that, to achieve an abstract description of language one must, first, see it as something communicated by people in general (not specific people) and, second, look at it as being separate from the social life in which it takes place. That these two acts are part of nearly all conventional approaches to rhetoric is precisely Bakhtin's point: conventional approaches, because they declare ways of expression as correct or not, are primarily monologic. Utterance in social discourse partakes of the infinite complexity of social life, in all its rich detail, resisting generalization. Specificity about the details of social life thus leads to complexity in the ways in which utterance can manifest itself.

Yet, if one is to understand EDMs, one needs more information from the complex sociohistorical environment in which EDMs are uttered. Because EDMs carry the aspects of the situations in which they are used, monological explanations fail to capture the richness of circumstance that communicators use to endow them with meaning. That obvious limitation aside, though, EDMs, like most human communication, have been studied almost exclusively from primarily monological perspectives, that is, with their constituent elements parceled to preformulated categories (see, for example, Baym, 1995a, 1995b; Kollock & Smith, 1996; McLaughlin, Osborne, & Smith, 1995; Mehta & Plaza, 1997; Sproull & Faraj, 1997; Watson, 1997; Willard, 1997).[5]

Just as with other forms of utterance, we are conditioned to understand EDMs according to elements that are defined primarily in monological terms. To see this, we need only reflect on the generalizing terms we use to talk about them. I suggest that the monologic view inheres in these ideas because they generalize about the specificity of discourse in EDMs, as indeed do generalizing terms about all forms of social discourse. Not only is the idea of the "post"[6] itself an arbitrary, monological, and thus artificial notion, the post comprises other arbitrarily defined elements. For example, posted messages have headers, including a line specifying the subject (either assigned by the initial poster, or duplicating a previous subject line); date and time; name (or alias) of the poster and e-mail address from which the message originates; (sometimes) the organization or group the poster represents; in the case of some Usenet posts, various other newsgroups to which the message has been simultaneously posted; and so on. Similarly, the end, monologically speaking, of EDMs can often be denoted by the arbitrary unit "signature," which is the poster's name/alias, and perhaps some message of symbolic importance, such as a slogan or quotation or even a crude drawing made of typographic characters.

The message body (the idea of a "body" is itself an arbitrary abstraction) typically contains other similar units: quotations; emoticons;[7] abbreviations (for example, IMHO for "in my humble opinion"); and so on. In EDM exchanges, the body often has at least two other artificially defined elements, directly related to the act of replying to another message: (1) quoted material from the message one replies to (depending on the preferences in one's e-mail software, this can be automatically generated when the "reply" function is used); and (2) original material (composed by the poster to comment on quoted material). These two types of utterance (essential to the back-and-forth of EDM exchanges) can be marked (again, by browser preference) in the post: lines of quoted material frequently begin with some typographical mark (such as ">" or "*"), while lines of original material are not automatically designated in this way.

While there is no question that monological perspectives, based on seeing EDMs in terms of categories such as those I have just identified, have allowed us to understand a great deal about e-mail discussions, they do lead one to think less about those fertile features of language that lend it vitality. To render language amenable to study by monological perspectives, scholars who analyze communication must force it into theoretical categories. By so doing they take the life out of language and perform analyses, not on living language, but on dead abstractions. Communication is structural and predictable (that is, centripetal), but it is also vibrant, thriving on its contradictions and inconsistencies, and resisting classification (that is, centrifugal). It is the centrifugal features of all utterances that make of them unique moments of communication, never to be repeated.

Nevertheless, to abandon monologism, even if it could be done (and it can't) would be a mistake on a level with ignoring dialogical alternatives. What I will show here, and extend in analyzing EDMs in this chapter and Web pages/sites in Chapter 4, is that it is necessary to use both monological and dialogical insights to understand Internet utterance. In fact, this is an ideal approach for looking at any utterance, on the Internet or not; however, Internet discourse, because of its idiosyncratic qualities, makes it a particularly appealing target for initial application of these dual methods.

As I will show, we can use the monologism of threaded EDMs as a backdrop against which to superimpose various dialogically inspired alternatives, based on the sociohistorical context in which EDMs are formulated and understood. This involves expanding one's view to see EDM as utterance. This shift will require advancing beyond artificial units and toward seeing how each EDM is linked to broader sociohistorical circumstances that frame the meaning of its constituent, monologically expressed, linguistic units. The method of dual reading I introduce in this chapter advocates fusing the monological and dialogical approaches to analyzing the EDM, both individually and as part of discussion threads.

As I probe EDM utterance through using the dialogic perspective, I will show how little it sometimes takes to dislodge the monologic grip, once our minds are made aware of how much it governs how we look at language and thought. Then, by coupling these dialogical insights with the regularity and stability of the monologic perspective on "the same" discourse, we can approach a more encompassing understanding of EDMs and all other utterances, realizing that full understanding will continue to be impossible.

ANALYTICAL FRAMEWORK

A good way to approach Internet utterances is to regard them from both primarily monological and dialogical perspectives ("primarily," since a perspective can never be purely one or the other). Using both kinds of reading takes advantage of the inherent dualism in language and perception and allows analysts to avail themselves of unique insights generated by each perspective. This is not only strategically useful, but it recognizes the inseparability of the two forces in living discourse.

In the following, I present the dual reading method, derived principally from the work of the Bakhtin circle (but also finding elaboration in other dialogically inclined thinkers). In the initial reading (the *standard reading*), I analyze the thread from a structuralist-functionalist perspective, achieving a content-based analysis of the thread's centripetal (conventional, predictable) features. In the second, alternative, reading (the *utterance reading*), I look at the thread from a centrifugal perspective (by linking its EDMs to the less easily categorized worlds of meaning that inform them), achieving a critical-descriptive interpretation of the thread's symbolic and cultural features, expressed as alternatives to the standard reading. Before analyzing the EDM threads, some further exploration of the standard and utterance readings will be helpful.

Standard Reading

The first perspective I use to analyze EDMs is the standard reading, that is, a conventional parsing and classification of EDM features according to categories (such as message sequence, number, length, topic, and so on). The primary goal of the standard reading is to clarify how the thread develops and to orient the analyst toward a system of abstractions that will be useful in understanding that development. As noted earlier, it can often be somewhat confusing for someone who has not observed or participated in an EDM exchange to understand, even on the surface, what is going on.

The standard reading consists of such activities as counting and classifying messages, noting arbitrarily and artificially defined linguistic units (headers, signature files, key ideas, quoted material, and so on), identifying those who posted and replied and their inferred relationships, deriving key messages ("core posts") around which other messages are arrayed, identifying themes and categories used to organize the thread, and so on. This reading yields considerable insight into the contents and structure of the thread and the background of those who contribute to it.

The multitude of abstract (monologically inclined) categories by which we understand EDMs makes it possible for us to grasp the relentlessly unique and idiosyncratic features highlighted by the dialogic perspective. Indeed, without such categories, it would be very difficult, perhaps impossible, to understand and talk about e-mail messages. We might see in them a forbiddingly confusing body of utterances and yet be unable to coherently explain e-mail discussion threads.

However, explanations based on shared perceptions about centripetal features of EDMs are purchased at significant cost to our understanding of the message's centrifugal features. What is gained analytically by the standard (centripetal) reading comes only when we construct abstractions based on summaries of information about specific EDMs, which leads to a tendency to ignore insights based on contemplating their sociohistorical specificity. When one generalizes about classes of messages by concentrating, centripetally, on abstraction and categorization, one sacrifices the detail by which each message can be distinguished from others in the "same" category.

Utterance Reading

An alternative way of reading EDMs is based primarily on the centrifugal (unique, unrepeatable) features of language; this is what I refer to as the "utterance reading." Utterance is an idea that comes into play when we look at language as communication, rather than simply as language alone. Utterance is performed in social life, and it is therefore the epitome of the dialogic back-and-forth activity characteristic of living language. Utterances are very different from abstract linguistic units such as sentences, phrases, paragraphs, and so on. Utterances can be viewed in terms of their extensive extralinguistic features; metaphorically, one might say that these features are what gets "picked up" by the utterance as it traverses through social life (as all language must).

Utterances are grounded in the "real," sociohistorically specific world in which they are performed. It is these connections to the "real" world that make utterances different from such linguistic conceptions as sentences. The very features of centrifugality—those idiosyncratic, "messy," hard-to-classify elements that make of each utterance a unique, unrepeatable act—which must be filtered out of the standard reading, are given special status in the utterance reading.

How, then, does one bring into view the insights into the nature of EDMs that are gained by the utterance reading? Unfortunately, there is no completely satisfactory answer to this question, since the unrestrained variance in the details of sociohistorical circumstances make a complete grasp of dialogic potential impossible. A logical place to begin, however, is with the features of the social milieu, identifiable in the language of EDMs, which specify how real aspects of social life give meaning to, or "flesh out," the language. Of a perhaps infinite number of features of social life that could be used to illuminate the centrifugal qualities of utterance, four specific features prove particularly useful in both the composition and the understanding of EDM utterances: (1) OTHER MEANING, or meaning that a poster must enlist to make a point; (2) OTHER CONCEPTION, or how the poster apparently conceives of others (particularly the person to whom the poster addresses herself or himself); (3) EFFORT AT SHARING, or how posters try to conflate views between themselves and others; and (4) CONTESTING OWNERSHIP, or how posters fight for control of a particular version of the world.[8]

I derived these four categories primarily from considering what appear to be the processes involved in advancing arguments and defining relationship between communicators in the thousands of EDMs I have analyzed, particularly as these relate to the work of the Bakhtin circle. OTHER MEANING and OTHER CONCEPTION are based on two basic processes in rhetoric and public address: OTHER MEANING corresponds to the use of evidence to support an argument, whereas OTHER CONCEPTION relates to the use of information about people. EFFORT AT SHARING and CONTESTING OWNERSHIP refer primarily to two opposing forces in interaction; the former refers to finding commonality between oneself and another and the latter to finding ways to distinguish between oneself and another.

These four elements represent principal ways of bringing the world into a post. OTHER MEANING occurs when discussions compel posters to marshal evidence and other support for points they make, thus "bringing into" the post meaning systems of others (for example, statements about how people of various nations and cultures think and act, quotations from newspapers and magazines, and so on). For instance (this and the other examples are taken from an EDM thread, concerning Wen Ho Lee, that I explore in detail later), "Taiwan2547" says, "Jobs do not fall out of the sky for nothing" thereby stating commonly accepted wisdom that getting a job requires effort, an understanding with its origins in systems of OTHER MEANING.

OTHER CONCEPTION occurs when posters indicate how they conceive of others; as we saw in Chapter 2, this infinite multitude of conceptions about others in fact serves as the basis for how the social world is collaboratively constructed. While OTHER MEANING has to do with importing ideas, concepts, or systems of meaning, OTHER CONCEPTION has to do with performing evaluations by referring to information about people (for example, expressed stereotypes about cultures and professions, attributions about others' thought processes or interpretations of experience, and so on). When Wen Ho Lee thread poster Jerry Chen writes, "You are right, if I thought it through, I should have not even applied," he casts the person he is responding to in a certain way (claiming he is "right"), an example of OTHER CONCEPTION. Since Chen is replying to an earlier challenge by his interlocutor, the sociohistorical context causes Chen to redefine their relationship; he recasts his "opponent" as someone who agrees with him. Here the dialogical mode inclines us to view their relationship as dynamic rather than static.

EFFORT AT SHARING occurs when posters attempt to find middle ground between their position and other, sometimes opposing, views, thereby bringing in the world of sociohistorical circumstance through fusing at least two systems of meaning—that of the poster and of the other he or she is trying to accommodate (for example, posters trying to reconcile what others have identified as contradictions, use of qualifiers to moderate apparently extreme positions, and so on). When Jimmy Wang tells others on the Wen Ho Lee thread, "I really don't want to get into personal assaults," he not only summarizes the message he responds to as having gone too far, but also ameliorates earlier statements he fears might have been taken as too harsh.

Conversely, CONTESTING OWNERSHIP occurs when posts show a struggle over who has the right to claim a particular version of the world as "correct," thus invoking not only the poster's world, but opposing worldview(s) of others with whom the poster disagrees (for example, taking an argumentative tone, directly challenging another's position, and so on). When poster Morton MacAllister interjects into the Wen Ho Lee thread the question, "What happens if the nuclear technology you stole from the US is used to arm warheads detonated over . . . your own hometown?" he directly confronts a Chinese poster who said earlier he would have no problem spying on the United States for any Chinese country.

After I identify these four elements in the EDM messages, the next step involves writing an interpretive summary of the thread in which ideas gleaned from the utterance reading are enhanced and elaborated. After conducting both standard and utterance readings, I use insights from both to combine and extend my interpretation of the thread. The use of dual reading will be illustrated in the analysis of two e-mail discussion threads of moderate length (that is, about 50 to 75 messages): (1) a thread discussing the case of Wen Ho Lee; and (2) a thread on the controversy over public utterances on the subject of lesbian adoption by radio talk show host Laura Schlessinger).

Obviously, these "snapshots" of EDM discourse represent only the tiniest portion of the unfathomably large universe of such utterances. However, the results of the analysis will demonstrate convincingly that the dual reading method opens EDM discourse to being perceived in a vastly different way. Through this process, I propose to show the value of the dialogical view, particularly when used in conjunction with the more conventional and widely practiced monological perspective, in gradually bringing out the various meanings of EDM utterance. Through this procedure, I will eventually demonstrate that an appropriate use of dialogism is an important factor in achieving a more integrated and fuller utilization of Internet communication (both EDM utterances and Web pages/sites) for civic discourse.

TWO CASE STUDIES

As I analyze the two EDM threads in this section, I would ask the reader to hold in mind two thoughts. First, both the type of thread analyzed, and the processes by which post composers and their audiences bring meaning into the EDM, are common in e-mail discussions. Although the subject matter of EDMs is very diverse, in that just about anything imaginable, and even unimaginable, is discussed in EDM forums, my experience is that the patterns of human interaction tend to be repeated often, just as they are IRL. Second, notice the central role *identity* plays in the discussions, not only in defining the posters and their relationships to one another, but the figures being talked about: for these two threads, Dr. Wen Ho Lee and "Dr." Laura Schlessinger.[9]

Discussion of Wen Ho Lee on a Political Issues Group

In the first case study, I draw together EDMs and the world, as they manifest on one thread in an Asian political discussion group debating the impact of the Wen Ho Lee spy scandal. The ostensible topic of discussion in this thread of nearly 50 messages is the case of Wen Ho Lee, a naturalized American engineer born in Taiwan and at one time employed at the Los Alamos National Laboratory. Lee was fired on suspicion of having engaged in activities damaging to security; some in the U.S. government and elsewhere charged that Lee spied for China and called for his arrest, particularly in light of discoveries that Lee may have done more extensive damage to security protecting classified nuclear weapons secrets than was previously realized.

In 1998, a grand jury in New Mexico indicted Lee on 59 counts of removing highly classified material from the Los Alamos weapons laboratory. After a controversial investigation, in 2000, the U.S. government dropped virtually its entire case against Lee. In his book, *My Country versus Me* (2001), Lee says he was incarcerated in December 1999, and released from jail on September 13, 2000, after "278 days of solitary confinement without benefit of a trial" (p. 1). According to the same account, the judge in the case, James Parker, finally admitted, "I have been misled by our government" (p. 1). From the first hint of trouble on December 23, 1998, to his release, the government's denial of Lee's right to due process became a cause célèbre among civil rights organizations and Asian American interest groups. The thread I examine took place on a newsgroup concerned, among other things, with Asian American issues. The thread's messages were posted during the period March 15–March 19, 1999; thus, these EDMs were posted between the time Lee was indicted and when he was jailed.

Standard Reading

The Wen Ho Lee thread has 48 messages, posted by 22 different individuals. Some posters appear to be Chinese[10] (R. V. Chang,[11] Jerry Chen, M. C. Chou, Eddie Kang, Jonathan Ko, "Kuo," Alan Lin, "Malaysianer," "Taiwan2547," Jimmy Wang, "wINdlee," and Lynne Wu), some non-Chinese (Hugh Bonney, R. M. Cabron, "Jaws" Tim Landis, Morton MacAllister, and Ed Nelson), some of indeterminate ethnic/national background ("2475 C99," "Bewildered," "DDL," and "Unknown"), and a group (which may include both Chinese and non-Chinese) that also hosts a satirical Web site advising Westerners on how to behave when doing business in China ("American Tigers"). The most frequent poster (11 messages) is Jerry Chen; half the posters ("2475 C99," Bonney, Cabron, Chang, Chou, Kang, "Kuo," Lin, "Malaysianer," "Unknown," and Wu) post only once. The remaining participants post either two times ("Bewildered," "DDL," Ko, MacAllister, Nelson, and "wINdlee"), three times ("American Tigers," "Taiwan2547," and Wang), or five times ("Jaws" Tim Landis).

The subject line of 40 of the posts is "Chinese alarm over spy sacking"; 7 messages ([10], [17]–[19], and [31]–[33]) have the slightly different, "IMPORTANT: Chinese alarm over spy sacking." Possibly the word *IMPORTANT* was inserted at [10] by "wINdlee" and the revised header carried over in the six replies to his or her message. There is also one subject line in the header of message [39], of seemingly peripheral relevance to the Wen Ho Lee case: "China Spies, but India is still our enemy?" Since this post gets no responses for the remainder of the thread, the unusual subject line is not repeated. Perhaps the poster, using the reply function to respond to the thread's main heading, personalized the message by typing something different in the subject field.

In most EDM threads, a small number of core messages (sometimes only one) provoke the lion's share of comments and responses. Core messages are primary stimuli—they "get things going." "Wen Ho Lee" has three core posts around which the rest of the messages agglomerate, two from Jerry Chen, and one from "wINdlee." These are core posts, first, because they generate more (and often more lengthy) responses than other posts, and second, because they represent thematic focal points in the discussion. For these reasons, it can be said that these three posts "drive" most of the rest of the thread.

In the first core message, [6], Jerry Chen lays out the controversial position he takes on spying for Chinese countries (either China or Taiwan). Though born in Taiwan and a naturalized U.S. citizen, Chen claims not to have taken a job in the public sector because he could not guarantee that, if approached, he would not reveal U.S. secrets to some Chinese government "as long as it benefits my fellow Chinese" [6]. Chen offers this position in sympathy to the dilemma faced by Chinese such as Wen Ho Lee—also a naturalized U.S. citizen born in Taiwan—who may have felt conflict between allegiance to the American government and to their fellow Chinese. In addition to Chen's 11 messages, "Wen Ho Lee" has another 11 posts that either answer Chen directly, or answer responses Chen makes about himself to other posters. This means that, based solely on number of posts, issues raised by Chen account for 44% of the messages.

A second pivotal post occurs at [10], the first time an entire article in *Newsweek* magazine is quoted by "wINdlee." This article is quoted in whole or in part in messages throughout the thread. Message [10] is a core message not only because of the number of responses it generates (nine posts, or about 19% of the total), but also because it serves as a bridge between the case of Wen Ho Lee and the views of Jerry Chen. "wINdlee" claims to be Chinese, and the article she or he quotes argues that much of what Lee did, such as having unreported interactions while visiting China, is done by Chinese all the time. As the article puts it, "Often the 'recruits' who do help out are unaware they're being asked to spy. U.S. intelligence officials who work 'Case-200s'—alleged incidents of Chinese espionage—say they are astonished that suspected Chinese spies often confess immediately when confronted and seem genuinely unaware that they may have done something wrong" [10]. On the issue of Dr. Lee, "wINdlee" is passionate: "This punishment of a person based on ZERO EVIDENCE sets dangerous precident [*sic*] for McCarthy-like abuses of Chinese-Americans." Both the article and "wINdlee"'s analysis become merged with list discussion of Jerry Chen, who gradually assumes more prominence as a topic of discussion, just as Wen Ho Lee himself recedes in importance.

The third core message is Chen's second post, [45], near thread's end, where we learn how he came to his provocative views on national loyalty. Through a complex process of education, Chen claims to have been converted from a "timid TIer" (one who favors Taiwan's independence), to what he calls a "reunificationist," meaning he favors (or at least does not oppose) the idea of a "Big China," the unification of Chinese countries into a single superstate. Message [6] may be the true core of the thread, since the most revealing post, [45], is necessitated by how posters react to [6]. Although late in the thread, [45] generates the remaining three messages (about 6% of the total). However, [45]'s impact is far greater than the number of responses it provokes; Chen's explanation of his intellectual evolution brings into focus many questions about him—and thus Wen Ho Lee—from previous thread messages.

Although the thread I analyze is supposed to be about Wen Ho Lee, it becomes principally (though never entirely) a discussion of Jerry Chen, who, I contend, turns out to be a surrogate for Lee. Early in the thread, posters discuss a variety of issues related to Lee's case: loyalty to one's ethnicity versus national loyalty, the role of mass media in extralegal "prosecution" of accused wrongdoers, possible Chinese naïveté about America's legal system, and how America bullies less powerful nations. As the thread progresses, these issues are given less attention, as posters shift their focus from an abstract figure they hardly know, Wen Ho Lee, to the rebel on their list, Jerry Chen.

A central theme in the standard reading of the Wen Ho Lee thread is the question, Who is Jerry Chen, and how does he relate to Wen Ho Lee? As noted, Chen is the author of most of the posts (11 of 48). Moreover, his posts are longer and more elaborate, and it is he who most frequently engages in direct exchanges with others. Finally, the key post

[45], tying up the various questions and answers, has as its central focus how Jerry came to his idiosyncratic view of Sino-American relations.

Through the three pivotal posts, and others they stimulate, the mystery of Jerry Chen finally is addressed in [45], where Chen, who describes himself as an "ultranationalist Chinese" and a "capitalistic libertarian," claims to have reached his current views by diligent scholarship. Yet even at the point of this revelation, Chen is contradictory. His messages are marked by a signature file that includes dramatic statements such as, "World free trade NOW!!!!", and "Long live Republic of China!!!!"[12] Taken out of context (that is, considered as included in an abstract category), this signature file sounds like a pro-Taiwan, anti-PRC (People's Republic of China, or Mainland China) rant that might lead one to classify the Taiwan-born Chen as an anti-Communist, pro-capitalist advocate of Taiwan's independence.

After being challenged by other posters, Jerry admits having applied for several governmental jobs but says he balked when they told him he would have to sign a loyalty oath; as a result, he chose to go into equity trading in the private sector: "When confronted with the prospect of having to working [sic] within [sic] potentially sensitive information which I knew I would happily give to PRC and ROC, I decided that I cannot take that job" [27]. Still later, we learn Jerry plans to retire and move to Hunan, a province of China, he hopes while still in his forties (at the time of this thread, Chen claims to be 26). He also stipulates he "reserve[s] the right to be racist/nationalist" with his choice of wife who must be "Chinese and culturally Chinese" and that his children must be raised as Chinese.

So far, this standard reading presents a very puzzling picture of the thread's central "character." Chen is Taiwanese, seemingly enamored of free market economy and against economic management such as is practiced in the PRC, yet who wants to pursue an aggressive program of capital accumulation so he can retire to Hunan and raise a "pure" Chinese family. Based on some of Chen's early posts, one might be tempted to think he is really a Mainland Chinese spreading propaganda in favor of reunification of Taiwan with the PRC. For example, at one point, he says his "ultimate loyalty [sic] must be toward the greater Chinese state which is currently split between the PRC and ROC regimes" [24]. Since a "Greater Chinese state" seems unlikely to result from Taiwan engulfing China, most Taiwanese would take Chen's meaning to be that China would "swallow" Taiwan, a situation many of them fear. This depiction seems to be confirmed by Chen's repeated characterizations of himself as "Chinese ultranationalist" and his insistence on having a wife and children who are "pure" Chinese.

Contradictions in this picture are manifold. Chen wants to settle in Hunan, where his radical free-market economic ideology can hardly gain him favor with the Chinese government (or any other government, for that matter). Indeed, even as he thinks of moving to a province of China, whose capitalistic experiments remain limited and controlled, he closes every post with a call for the abolition of all taxes and tariffs, and free trade worldwide. It would be difficult to imagine a stance more incompatible with China's economic principles, a fact pointed out tactfully and with restraint at thread's end by Arnold Bingham: "Everyone I know of who has moved to the PRC after growing up somewhere else has found life different from their expectations and difficult" [48]. In other posts (for example, in a couple of satirical sendups by the "American Tigers"), list members poke fun at Jerry, suggesting he is naïve and overly optimistic about what awaits him in Hunan. The "Tigers" are particularly cruel, closing one of their posts with this jibe: "Let us American Tigers be the first to say that we are extremely impressed with your youthful optimism and creativity. Good luck in Hunan!" [22].

Superimposed on this picture is the crux of Jerry's motivation, revealed in [45] where he tells us he is extraordinarily idealistic, having arrived at his views of China, Taiwan, and the greater Chinese community by a long and rather tortuous self-(re)education. He started with a study of European history in high school, which led him eventually to study Chinese history "in the contect [sic] of the development of Europe." Exposed to a "huge amount of Chinese political material" at a major research university, he began to question the China/Taiwan division. At that point, during a visit to China, Jerry claims he found much he did not like and wanted to change, and that therefore his "position as a Chinese ultranationalist was complete" [45].

In several posts in the middle to late part of the thread, Chen seems almost frantic to justify himself, to convince both those in favor of Taiwan's independence and those who want Taiwan to reunify with China that he is on their side. Thus, beginning with his controversial statement about being willing to spy on the United States, he spends the rest of the thread performing face work, emerging at the end as a dedicated and idealistic (if perhaps unrealistic) student of both Chinese and Western history. Given what we can glean from the standard reading, it is possible Jerry Chen is precisely what he claims to be—a diligent scholar in the traditional Chinese mode, bravely pursuing his vision of a greater China against criticism by Chinese and others. On the other hand, he could be an agent provocateur constructing elaborate rationalizations to conceal his real motive: undermining Taiwan's efforts to achieve independence from China.

The advantage of this standard reading is that it takes elements of various posts and summarizes them in an understandable fashion. Although the standard reading focuses principally on Jerry Chen, it does so because that is one way of orienting the analyst toward central idea(s) of the thread and providing a map to follow the discussion (something that can be difficult if one tries simply to read the posts as a collection of separate messages). It is not that other posters are insignificant, but rather that they consistently orient toward the question of who Jerry Chen is. Jerry Chen is the focal person about whom the rest of the thread's "story" revolves.

I should note two things about the standard reading. First, it is only one of a large number of conventional approaches that could have been used to describe the thread. In addition to numerous linguistic or literary analytic methods, one could approach the thread using other points of focus, choosing different central people and messages, and different classification systems for the various posts. Second, any standard reading will probably choose to treat the primary unit of discourse as the post. In other words, when we want to describe the development of the thread, we speak of individual, separate messages, occurring before or after one another, and of key ideas as being "contained in" the various posts (a tendency of the English language Reddy [1979] has called the "conduit metaphor"). Perhaps unconsciously, then, those conducting most standard readings assume that threads are to be understood as posts or their component units, not as utterances.

The standard reading can take us to the point of understanding some issues and themes, and perhaps of making tentative deductions about motivation, but not much further. That which really informs the post—the entire universe of referents that infuses each and every post with such rich meaning—cannot be seen so long as we view the post, only as a post. We must also look at the EDM threads as various specific types of utterances.

Utterance Reading

For the utterance reading, I reanalyzed the thread, this time examining the four principal ways posters bring the world into their posts: (1) OTHER MEANING, (2) OTHER CONCEPTION, (3) EFFORT AT

SHARING, and (4) CONTESTING OWNERSHIP. This reading offered a different kind of insight into the reality of the discussion, compelling a focus on how posters actively formulate utterances, assembled as it were from the meaning systems of themselves and others. This stage of the utterance reading should not be seen as coding preparatory to performing a content analysis (Holsti, 1969). Rather, it is a way to get a sense of how the four elements of the utterance recast the meaning of the thread's posts in a more complex and textured fashion. This analysis permits one to extend and enrich, but not supplant, results obtained through the standard reading.

Earlier I suggested that, as the discussion evolves, Jerry Chen becomes a surrogate for Wen Ho Lee. By both frequency and length, posts about Jerry Chen tend to "drive out" posts about Wen Ho Lee the longer the thread goes on. There may be several reasons for this. First, posters do not know what Wen Ho Lee did (at this point, reports were contradictory, and even the government had not told the whole story). In contrast, posters have abundant evidence of what Jerry Chen claims to have thought, felt, and done.

Second, Chen's stated background is strikingly similar to Lee's. Both were born in Taiwan, both have contacts in the PRC, both are naturalized U.S. citizens, both are white-collar U.S. professionals, and both have what seems to be an idiosyncratic view of national loyalty. Thus, posters may see the opportunity to question Chen as if he were Lee, writ smaller.

Third, because of his celebrity, Wen Ho Lee is a distant, somewhat abstracted figure providing little in the way of real, vivid, detailed information as grist for the discussion mill (at this time there was even less information, since Lee had gone silent in the face of impending legal proceedings). Jerry Chen, on the other hand, is only too ready to explain himself at length and to engage others in direct debate. Therefore, Jerry brings details that other posters can grapple with directly, rather than having to remain frustrated as they make guesses about the enigmatic Wen Ho Lee. Posters seem to have to settle for engaging Chen in the absence of any opportunity to engage Wen Ho Lee.

For the utterance reading, we need a different view of Jerry Chen's identity. One way to achieve this is to see it as a creation formed out of what exists in the posts—a coconstruction comprising many fragments of the discourse of Jerry and others. Because of what Chen posts, other discussants bring up important facts and questions about his "identity." The information he places into the stream of discourse—as well as the replies it provokes, responses to these replies, and so on—tell us not so much about the "real" Jerry Chen (who could be called "Jerry$_1$") but an entity we might call "Jerry$_2$"—and Jerry$_2$ has an identity of "his" own, given life by utterance. Jerry$_2$ is in a sense a mirror (albeit one that both reflects and transforms images) into which other thread participants may look to see the effects of their own attempts to infuse their observations about the Wen Ho Lee case with worlds of meaning.

An utterance, Bakhtin scholar Holquist (1990) writes, "is shaped by speakers who assume that the values of their particular community are shared, and thus do not need to be spelled out in what they say" (p. 61). When posters comment on Jerry Chen, they do so knowing some posters will understand and agree (or disagree) with them. This means the portrait of Chen is fleshed out, not just by what is written in posts, but by what is not written. The number of intersections of worlds of meaning resulting from the cross-fertilization of ideas about Jerry Chen, even within a single post, would be breathtaking; the number resulting from intersections with all other utterances in the thread is literally unimaginable.

Thus, the evolution of the Wen Ho Lee thread is the evolution of the portrait of Jerry$_2$, and by extension, a reflection of the views of posters on the case of Wen Ho Lee. However, utterances do not, as monologism would have it, passively reflect empirical situations existing outside verbal description. Instead, utterances demand that whoever formulates and understands them must work hard to create a summary of worlds of meaning. Given the amount of data and number of possible systems of meaning that could be marshaled to fill in the picture of Jerry Chen, the fact that so many posters put their energy into formulations about his identity is admirable; moreover, because each utterance can only be an answer, never an original statement constructed, as it were, in a sociohistorical vacuum, to enact utterance is to take initiative, involving work not only to formulate one's "own" statement, but to summarize what has been said by others.

In this and other analyses, I will demonstrate the general analytical process on a chosen subset of utterances. These utterances in "Wen Ho Lee" concern the elaboration of Chen's identity, occurring before and after the third core post, the crucial message at [45]. According to the standard reading, [45] represents the "real" Jerry Chen—the analysis showed how that message resulted from questions posed by others. One conventional explanation for the creation of [45] is that it is a reframing message virtually wrung from Mr. Chen to protect his "face" against the doubt, suspicion, sarcasm, and old-fashioned leg-pulling one sees in various messages responding to his earlier remarks [6] about spying.

However, message [45] makes sense as a reframing of previous messages only if there is a way to demonstrate that what preceded it was either true- or false-to-fact, and there is no way to do this. As Bakhtin remarked, "Of the real author [of the utterance], as he exists outside the utterance, we can know absolutely nothing at all" (1984a, p. 184) On the other hand, read as utterance, [45] really is a reframing message, but not because it alone is so, or is so among a few other messages. Message [45] reframes earlier messages because every utterance does.

A key aspect of utterance often overlooked by those eager to embrace Bakhtin is that there is no such thing as an original utterance—utterance always answers another utterance. An utterance cannot be constructed out of nothing: it instantiates meaning already in place, including meaning invoked by previous utterers and meaning that helps all utterers understand and express ideas about the world around them.

If utterance must rely on previously uttered material, the utterances in [45] cannot be a departure from previous utterances, both in the thread and out of it—they cannot, that is, tell us who Jerry Chen "really" is. Instead, they must be viewed as Chen's active, effortful, creative reformulations of the various utterances and meaning systems given rise to (in part) by his utterance at [6]. In [6], Chen gives the group seed material that germinates in various ways and various directions, until he is compelled in [45] to clarify the responses and counter-responses, the abundance of which has led to a great deal of confusion. Throughout this discussion, though, please remember that all these posts, from [6] through [45] and beyond, involve an enormously active process in which the identity of Jerry Chen is coconstructed, possibly in order to serve as surrogate for Wen Ho Lee. Posters are not just batting back and forth opinions of Jerry Chen; with each utterance, they reformulate Jerry$_2$'s identity, and it is these reformulations, more than anything else, that compel Chen to (apparently) reveal himself at [45].

Throughout the back-and-forth about Jerry Chen, one sees the interplay of OTHER MEANING, OTHER CONCEPTION, EFFORT AT SHARING, and CONTESTING OWNERSHIP. For example, when Chen begins at [6], he says he was approached for government jobs, but had to turn them down, because "if I worked for the USA government and a PRC or ROC agents [*sic*] approached me and told me that my services were needed to help my fellow Chinese, I would do it for free and give them everything I know." Chen's utterance is a reframing of previous list discussion of Wen Ho Lee, and specifically the question of whether individual Chinese should be loyal to an adopted homeland or their fellow Chinese. Obviously, this is a controversial point (particularly among Chinese) and it is given substance through Chen's importation and recasting of OTHER MEANING. I see this as OTHER MEANING because it invokes numerous forms of knowledge about comparative governments and nationality in the long and complex history of China–Taiwan relations. This does not dampen but rather stimulates the controversy, in that Chen's reformulation sets the stage for, and in fact provokes, subsequent utterances.

The first of these answers is at [5] (although listed in the thread earlier, [5] is a reply to [6]), where Alan Lin, reformulating Chen's position through several revealing instances of CONTESTING OWNERSHIP with him, pounces on what his utterance chooses to construe as Chen's logical flaw: if Chen were willing to spy for a Chinese state, it would make sense for him to get more, not less, involved in public sector jobs: "If I were you I would definitely want to be in the US government positions," Lin says. "If I could be the president imagine what I could do for Chinese" [5]. This is CONTESTING OWNERSHIP because Lin directly confronts Chen, suggesting the latter's reasoning compels him to take a different course than the one he seems to advocate. That Lin contests Chen is significant in defining thread interactions later on, as Lin is merely one of the first to challenge Chen, thereby leading to alignments among the members over whether Chen is legitimate in making his claims (most participants seem to think he is not).

In [8], "Taiwan2547" makes a more aggressive reformulation of the OTHER MEANING. The OTHER MEANING involved here arises through the invocation of such diverse systems of knowledge as citizenship and the workings of the executive branch of the U.S. government. "Taiwan2547," after invoking these and other forms of OTHER MEANING, adds this negative evaluation (OTHER CONCEPTION): "Jerry, are you a US citizen? If you are not, then you are not telling the truth for [sic] claiming Dept. of Energy and Dept. of Defense gave you offers." Here we observe a pattern that becomes more prominent as posters and Jerry$_1$ collaborate on the picture of Jerry$_2$ to which the thread will gradually orient itself. Chen's remarks, which are more provocative initially than later on, cause posters to confront him, and from these instances, principally showing OTHER CONCEPTION and CONTESTING OWNERSHIP, Chen chooses a strategy of rapprochement more like EFFORT AT SHARING. Primarily at and after [45] Chen obviously tries to modify his earlier, rather extreme, formulations to be more in line (capable of being shared) with others on the list, invoking systems of OTHER MEANING that will be more inclusive of others, and in contrast to the abrasive and controversial (nonsharing) stance he took earlier in the thread. First, Chen said he would spy for China, a disclosure that obviously did not lead to sharing. Therefore, in responding to how others depict him (OTHER CONCEPTION) and challenge him (CONTESTING OWNERSHIP), Chen's main task is to ameliorate discord and fashion mutual understanding (EFFORT AT SHARING).

In [9], Jimmy Wang takes up the attack, relying on what does not have to be said to question Chen's truthfulness: "BTW, how to become US citizen? I would love to be one. If you can tell you [sic], I promise I would not pick on you again." At [12], Jonathan Ko says, "Somewhere in Langley, Virginia, a man wearing a dark suit is quietly labeling a file folder for Jerry Chen." Both these two humorous comments rely on OTHER MEANING; for example, Jimmy's message makes sense only if one knows about U.S. citizenship, and Jonathan's only to those who know that CIA headquarters is in Langley, Virginia. Even lighthearted kidding is undergirded by shared knowledge.

From [13] to [16], posters (not explicitly referring to Chen) debate various points about Chinese loyalty (at this point utterances about Chen do not yet dominate utterances about Lee). Then in [17] "Jaws" Tim Landis, in a multilayered example of OTHER CONCEPTION, asks a question apparently referring to Chen, to Wen Ho Lee, and the Chinese graduate students mentioned in the *Newsweek* article at [10]: "Are we to believe that PhD's and Masters [sic] student [sic] have no idea that taking something that doesn't belong to them is wrong?" Here, Landis invokes, in quick succession, thumbnail characterizations of two types of graduate students (master's and Ph.D. candidates) as well as of those who are honest. In addition to striking at the core of Wen Ho Lee's defense (by questioning how it is possible for educated people such as Lee to be so oblivious to the fact that they are breaching security), Landis's strategy plants the seeds for numerous reactions that will help define relationships as the thread develops.

Message [22], from the "American Tigers," drips with sarcasm and is one of the most telling attacks yet on Chen's self-portrayal. By this point the various responses to Chen's utterances are clearly interanimating one another. From a mere whisper of gentle criticism in [5], the aggressiveness goes up through [12], moderates a bit (through indirectness) at [17], and then increases dramatically with the frontal assault of [22]. However, utterances following [6] are being driven, not just by [6], but also by responses to it. "Utterances," Bakhtin (1986a) tells us, "are not indifferent to one another, and are not self-sufficient; they are aware of and mutually reflect one another" (p. 91). This mutual awareness permits the "American Tigers" to provide this incredulous account of previous utterances: "In summary, you are saying that while you would be happy to spy for China, you would not do so if you had to break your loyalty to your employer, plus you would not spy anyways [sic] since you don't want to be faced with the decision of which China to give the information to, and besides the money is not very good. Did we get it all correct?" [22].

Jerry Chen apparently feels they did not "get it all correct," because he throws himself into answering nearly all his questioners in the next seven posts ([23] through [29]). In a barrage of reformulations, Chen tentatively recasts himself by responding to Alan Lin [23], Arnold Bingham [24], the "American Tigers" [25], "Jaws" Tim Landis [26], "Taiwan2547" [27], Jimmy Wang [28], and Jonathan Ko [29]. Chen's responses, however, are surprisingly tentative; in at least four of the seven messages, he limits himself to rephrasing or clarifying what he has said before. These reformulations are important, because in repeating earlier thoughts, they are uttered in circumstances considerably different from those when they first were uttered. There is some vital new information, however. In a conciliatory move calculated not to offend antireunification Taiwanese, we learn Chen's loyalty "pecking order": "more loyal to ROC over PRC, more loyal to PRC over any other government" [26]. Moreover, in [27] Chen reveals that the U.S. government jobs he rejected were not ones he sought eagerly; rather, he says, two offers came after he did résumé "carpet bombing" and it was the loyalty oath the jobs required that led him to reject them.

These seven messages, as utterances, fill in the portrait of Jerry Chen. Chen's response-utterances certainly involve effort. His post at [6] generates so much criticism that he feels compelled to write in quick succession seven separate EDMs, in all of which he must, first, summarize the OTHER MEANING of the poster; second, frame messages in such a way as to convey his OTHER CONCEPTION of his critics (polite with Arnold Bingham, wearily frustrated with "Taiwan2547," snappish with the "American Tigers," and so on); third, make preliminary overtures through EFFORT AT SHARING (toning down of some of his earlier positions) that will later lead to more fully fledged attempts at

rapprochement with his critics; and fourth, continue, through CON-
TESTING OWNERSHIP, to claim his vision of a Chinese superstate as a
valid and desirable goal. From all these utterances, we learn at least two
important things about Jerry Chen. First, he seems sincere about wanting other posters to approve of him, and second, despite his desire for
approval, he has no intention of abandoning his original position.

After one more intermediate set of utterances, the stage is set for
message [45]. In two successive, comparatively belligerent, posts ([34]
and [35]), the "American Tigers" dog Chen, calling "Taiwan2547" an
"idiot" [34] for supporting Chen, and implying he converted to Com-
munism between sending out his résumé and getting job offers [34].
In [35], the "American Tigers" become even more confrontational, challenging Chen to give up his U.S. citizenship and work for China or
Taiwan: "This is what a China ultranationalist should do if you are
really one" [35]. Here and elsewhere, the "American Tigers" rely on
OTHER CONCEPTION (principally of Chen, but also of more peripheral figures such as "Taiwan2547") to formulate sarcastic utterances
about Chen and his idealistic goals. The relentless skepticism of the
"American Tigers" can be viewed as a foil based on OTHER MEAN-
ING in that it invokes, by means of factual refutation, a geopolitical
picture different from the one Chen propounds; both this alternative
picture and the depiction it challenges encompass numerous systems
of OTHER MEANING. The "American Tigers" set the position against
which Jerry Chen must pit himself. It is their utterances that, (1) make
it clear that more toned-down criticism (of the sort Arnold Bingham offers) will not be developed into a haven for Chen, and (2) that Chen's
tentative attempts at reconciliation from [23] through [29] will not be
sufficient to gain credibility for his controversial views. Were it not for
the combative posts (verging on "flame") of the "American Tigers,"
Chen's placatory efforts might have been sufficient. People who make
utterances do so expecting they will be answered, though seldom do
they get the answer they anticipate or want.

In [43], Jerry Chen provides brief answers to some points raised
by the "American Tigers," and in [45] he tells how he was reeducated
as a "Chinese ultranationalist" (as discussed in the standard reading).
Although [45] is still a crucial post in the utterance reading, it is crucial in a different way. In the standard reading, I argued that the
purpose of [45] was to provide a strategic adjustment of disparate
views of the "real" Jerry, Jerry$_1$; in the utterance reading, [45] is compelled by an accumulation of utterances that converge on the portrait

of Jerry$_2$. Thus, through the lens of the standard reading—seeing EDMs as separate artificial linguistic units—we fall short of understanding Chen, the focal character of "Wen Ho Lee." Through the lens of the utterance reading, we see the collective construction of Jerry Chen (Jerry$_2$) as an entity of far more significance to the issues of justice and civil rights raised as posters discuss Wen Ho Lee.

Comparison of Standard and Utterance Readings

My purpose, as I have stated repeatedly, is not to recommend that utterance readings supplant standard readings of EDMs. The categorization and classification of messages and message subunits is essential to understanding the often confusing stream of discourse in a discussion thread. Furthermore, classification and categorization are most useful to the analyst when the thread is seen as standard arbitrarily defined units.

Many times, though, using standard readings, one comes eventually to a point where conventional categories no longer help. Such is the case with "Wen Ho Lee." Not only was it impossible to penetrate the mystery of the puzzling Mr. Lee, but also early in the thread, we encountered the even more enigmatic Jerry Chen, whose circumstances are similar enough to Lee's that he becomes a surrogate. We are thus presented with another puzzle the standard reading could not solve: is Jerry Chen a Chinese agent provocateur, a sincere scholar devoted to a "Greater China," both, or something else entirely?

Through the utterance reading, we can recast the question, Who is Jerry Chen and what does he have to do with Wen Ho Lee? to Who does Jerry Chen seem to be trying to be, how do he and the others use post discourse to mutually construct an identity, through the thread, that will make sense to the list community and thereby help them understand the Wen Ho Lee case? Through answering this latter, more complex, question, we finally discover why Jerry Chen becomes important: not simply because he dominates the standard reading statistics, such as number, length, and detail in his posts and responses to them, but because his thread identity—"Jerry$_2$"—is a careful and calculated knitting together of often contradictory representations, an EDM quilting party of sorts, involving all the thread posters and many more people besides. All this results in a richly varied and colorful portrait of a relevant figure that posters have placed a great deal more effort into constructing than they could ever have done had they dealt only with the remote Wen Ho Lee. The utterance reading tells us that Jerry Chen is a construction posters can hold on to, grapple with, refashion, discard, and reappropriate in endless cycles of utterance and response and reutterance. They and Jerry$_1$ worked hard to create Jerry$_2$, and it is clear that "he" has been and will continue to be useful in helping them understand the complex issues of the case of Wen Ho Lee.

EDM threads are not merely closed, linear, and restrictive, but also open, multiplex, and inviting. These qualities of EDM threads make them an ideal channel for the propagation of ideological messages through civic discourse. If approached with sufficient appreciation for their complexity, they allow us to understand vox populi, in its purest sense, what participants in a democratic, freely available forum have to say about the issues of the day.

In the next section, I demonstrate dual reading on a different EDM thread, this one focusing on a well-known radio talk show host who steps on the toes of a particularly erudite and contentious online minority activist group. In the analysis, we will see some of the same processes (such as list member surrogacy) as we did in "Wen Ho Lee," as well as some surprising new ways to formulate civic identity through the medium of Internet discourse.

Discussion of Laura ("Dr. Laura") Schlessinger on a Gay/Lesbian Issues Group

The thread examined in this section is "Laura at the Carnival" ("Carnival" for short), and its focus is the radio program *The Dr. Laura Schlessinger Show*, at one time aired on more than 450 radio stations with a weekly audience estimated at 18 to 20 million (Bane, 1999, p. 228).[13] Her audience figures have at times placed Schlessinger in the lead among radio talk hosts, ahead of Howard Stern and equal to and in some markets surpassing her previous closest competitor, Rush Limbaugh (Schrof, 1998). Schlessinger provides guidance to callers (as many as 50,000 can call during a typical three-hour program [Schrof, 1997][14]) that is direct, confrontative, and largely devoid of softness or support. Rather, Schlessinger challenges callers: "Like a mythological creature who is equal parts therapist, rabbi, and drill sergeant, Schlessinger chides, cajoles, and sometimes condemns her callers. . . . She's been hailed for reviving public discourse on character and deeded for her gruff approach toward callers whose actions don't meet her standards" ("Dr. Laura," 1998, p. 29).

However, as Schlessinger's audience has grown, so has the controversy surrounding her. Information about possible past indiscretions and anomalies that contradict her strongly moralistic public persona has come to light. First, it has been asserted in several

sources (see, for example, Bane, 1999, esp. pp. 63–73) that Schlessinger
had a long-term romantic affair with her radio mentor Bill Ballance
while still married to her first husband.[15] Much later, in 1998, Ballance is
said to have sold photographs he had taken of Schlessinger cavorting in
the nude (Seligmann, Reddick, & Pappas, 1998) to Internet Entertainment Group, a Seattle-based firm specializing in Internet pornography.
In 1998, an article by Leslie Bennetts appeared in *Vanity Fair* alleging,
among other things, that Schlessinger had dated her second husband,
Lew Bishop, while he was still married. Despite her on-air advice to
prioritize traditional family values, Schlessinger remains estranged
from her sister (Bane, 1999, p. 101) as well as her mother (Goodman &
Griffiths, 1994). Although Schlessinger was also estranged for a time
from her father, one source (Hill, n.d.) reports that they reconciled in
1988, shortly before his death in 1990. Schlessinger's mother, however,
recently died in isolation, apparently without ever having reconciled
with her daughter.

   Moreover, Schlessinger's abrasive and confrontational personality
has led to public clashes with many groups, including feminists over
her advice to mothers that they quit their jobs and stay at home with
their children, when Schlessinger herself, despite having a minor child,
hosts a nationally syndicated radio program, performs speaking en-
gagements, and is the author of several best-selling books. She has also
tangled with the American Library Association over the issue of allowing unfettered access to the Internet by children in libraries (Oder &
Rogers, 1999), and gays and lesbians over numerous public statements
perceived as antigay, including at least once referring to homosexuality
as "deviant" and a "biological error" (Elber, 2001).[16]

   "Carnival" is taken from one of the oldest newsgroups devoted to
gay and lesbian issues. "Carnival" is actually a subthread of a much
longer thread, "Trials of Dr. Laura" (Holt, 2003c). "Trials" was initiated
by a listener complaint that Schlessinger called a lesbian couple that
adopted an infant "despicable." In response, 75 messages were posted
by 31 different list subscribers over a five-day period between June 25
and June 30, 1999.

   The reason for calling the subthread "Carnival" is that the way
Laura Schlessinger is treated resembles a process described by Bakhtin
(1984b) as "carnivalization," a technique he found used by some nov-
elists, especially Rabelais. Carnivalization reverses the normal order of
things so that what is elevated in society is brought low and what is
lowly is elevated. Bakhtin observed that this process, which he found

parodized in Rabelais, reflected a common social configuration in the Middle Ages, where occasions (such as certain holidays) were provided for rulers to "legitimately" be made fun of, and commoners allowed to be, for a proscribed time, released from authority. Others (see, for example, Stallybrass & White, 1986) have observed that carnival can be seen as a master metaphor for various sorts of rebellion throughout history. Whatever its form, carnivalization is a reversal of the positions between those in authority and those they control. Moreover, one key feature of carnivalization is humor, occurring as parody, exaggeration, and so on. In other words, status is reversed by subordinates making fun of superiors.

This is what appears to happen in "Carnival." Posters to this thread, via a relatively mundane and perhaps seemingly inconsequential discursive process, work to lower the status of Laura Schlessinger, while simultaneously elevating their own. This is accomplished through several topic sequences: in the chief topic, discussants argue about whether Schlessinger has the right to call herself by the title "Doctor"; in another line, they propose that, if Schlessinger can be considered a legitimate counselor, particularly on sexual matters, then they can too.

In the terms used throughout this book, the authorities lampooned through carnivalization represent *monologism*. They endorse specific forms of expression, backed ultimately by the threat of violence, that define the terms under which others must live. Similarly, contesting voices through which carnivalization is accomplished represent *dialogism*: they endorse rebellious, nonconformist discourse that questions the legitimacy of the monological view. Thus, in carnivalization we see the eternal struggle of the seamless, enforced view of reality against resistance by those who feel they have the right to challenge it. The fact that the Internet makes such challenges readily accessible is one factor that renders this mode of communication such an appropriate tool for civic discourse. With these ideas in mind, let us turn to the dual reading of "Carnival."

Standard Reading

"Laura at the Carnival" comprises 51 posts by 24 list members, a subthread of a more comprehensive thread posted over a five-day period. The majority of the posts (19 messages, about 37% of the total) originate with four people: Brad Kranze posts six times[17]; Vince Majors posts five times; and James Land Jones and EST each post four times.

However, this simple count (a monological method) presents a false picture of posters' relative contribution. Three messages posted by EST are extremely short, as are three of the six messages posted by Brad Kranze. Vince Majors and James Land Jones, on the other hand, not only post comparatively long messages, but also introduce creative elaborations concerning "Dr." Laura's qualifications. These elaborations, along with the enthusiasm others display in taking them up, leads to most of the carnivalization in the thread.

To set the stage for the standard reading, and to adequately describe the thread's carnivalization, as well as the monologic/dialogic tension underlying it, I should distinguish among the several discussions going on. In an active group, there is almost never a point-by-point progression from one message to another, even among messages that "share" a common header (in this case, the header of every message is "Dr. Laura's Credentials"). Some monologic views would have it that to "define" a thread one merely aggregates messages with a common header. Once a message header changes, that message is no longer part of the thread (this is how the Google "groups" search engine, which I used to compile both "Trials" and "Carnival," works).

Obviously, though, this is not what occurs in most threads (see, for example, "Wen Ho Lee"). Rather, messages in the "same" thread often diverge from one another, some directly elaborating the point identified in the header, and others only tenuously "on topic." Conversely, what is encountered in a "different" thread is often "on topic" with respect to "another" thread. In "Carnival," one can see at least six or seven subsets of messages dealing with specific topics that relate, closely or not, to Schlessinger's qualifications.[18] We see this unpredictable amalgamation of message trajectories not only in Bakhtin's version of carnivalization, but in other sources identified as influencing dialogism (Vico, for example, acknowledges the value of "illogical" modes of expression in the writings of ancient peoples). Communicating in the spirit of dialogism, one does not need permission to depart from the topic. In e-mail discussion, divergence from conventional topicality seems more the rule than the exception, which may be why EDM threads yield so readily to dialogical analysis.

In "Carnival," as in "Wen Ho Lee," there are three core posts. The first is the initial message in which Les Anders posts Laura Schlessinger's professional qualifications and says he "expects an apology" [1]. This post initiates discussion of the aspects of the debate over qualifications. By providing Schlessinger's credentials in detail, Anders gives less combative participants the opportunity to discuss, for the most part reasonably, various qualifications one needs to counsel others. On the other hand, by saying he "expects an apology," Anders offers himself as a target for merciless teasing. This interesting duality makes of this initial message a doubly effective core post.

A second core post occurs in direct response to Anders's initial message. This message, [4], is by James Land Jones and it gives Jones entrée to dispute whether Schlessinger, since she is not an M.D., has the right to call herself "Dr. Laura," and also to recount his mother's qualifications as a counselor. He also takes the opportunity to introduce, almost offhandedly, a theme that will provide the impetus for the carnivalization process: "Sorry, Dr. James is every bit as good a Dr. as Dr. Laura, and when I go on the air and start yapping I want respect" [4]. This post stimulates list discussion in which, as I will show in the utterance reading, Schlessinger's status is lowered vis-à-vis that of contributors to "Carnival."

The third core post is comparatively late in the thread (number [39] out of 51 messages) and is by Vince Majors. I should note that, although Majors is identified as posting only a single core post, it is really his elaboration [9] of James Jones's core post at [4], and responses to others' elaborations on this topic (at [26] and the first part of [39], whose latter part makes [39] a core post), that sustains more than one subsequent thread trajectory. Jones and Majors work in tandem to produce, sustain, and direct much of the remainder of the thread. This is the way core posts usually function; they do not necessarily make an impact in and of themselves, but only affect the list through the collaboration they stimulate with other posters, a point explored in greater detail (as it was with "Wen Ho Lee") in the utterance reading. A post can be as well phrased as possible, and yet have no effect on thread development if no one responds to it. On the other hand, an off-the-cuff remark can define the focus of an EDM, provided other posters develop it.

The latter part of [39] introduces, seemingly almost accidentally, discussion of the British television program, *Two Fat Ladies Cooking* (produced for the BBC, but also aired on American networks, such as The Food Network and ABC), which energizes a discussion of lesbian stereotypes in the latter portion of the thread. Responding to a remark about caring for penises (one of the rambunctious "topics" proposed for discussion by the faux "Doctors" clamoring for the same opportunities Schlessinger has had), Majors states, "Gardening and pet shows are very popular in the UK right now," an offhand remark that leads Brad Kranze to declare *Two Fat Ladies Cooking* as his "absolute favourite" [42].

These three core posts, then, define the chief points of focus impelling discussion in "Carnival." To presage the utterance reading, only the first two would seem, on the surface, to be related to the main topic, ostensibly defined by the official (monologic) subject header, which refers to Schlessinger's qualifications. Indeed, if we take a sufficiently monological perspective toward the thread, only those messages responding to the factual content of [1] (that is, Laura Schlessinger's work and educational experience, objectively related, as on a résumé) would be considered "topical." Certainly, it would seem to be difficult, under even the most open-minded monologically inspired interpretation scheme, to construe discussion of a popular British television cooking show as relevant to the credentials of "Dr. Laura". However, as we will see in the utterance reading, nothing could be further from the truth.

Utterance Reading

Just as "Wen Ho Lee" was driven by questions about the identity of Jerry Chen and how he is a surrogate for Dr. Lee, "Carnival" is driven by a different kind of question about the "true" identity of a famous figure: a question of whether Laura Schlessinger is qualified to give advice, especially under the name "Dr. Laura." In a relatively brief thread, the question of Schlessinger's credentials diverges into other discussions about qualifications (not necessarily Schlessinger's). These strands include elements that appear irrelevant to the main topic, but turn out to be highly germane when considered in dialogical contexts.

I begin with the first core post of "Carnival" (see standard reading) by Les Anders [1]. This message, containing a complete listing of Laura Schlessinger's professional qualifications, is an example of multiplex OTHER MEANING. Résumés as a whole and each of their constituent items invoke different systems of OTHER MEANING. To understand the ways in which Schlessinger is certified to practice counseling, one would have to know what certification means; to make judgments about specific qualifications, one would have to know about systems of meaning that inform them. For example, Emma Elston explains what is needed to be a marriage, family, and child counselor (MFCC), in response to an answer by Dan Roth [10], who was in turn responding to a question by Kevin Barrett Browne [8]: "There is an internship program, usually in the context of a master's degree in counseling or social work" [14]. To understand Emma's post, one must be familiar with meaning systems informing concepts related to higher education—"internship" and "master's degree"—as well as the helping professions—"social work" and "counseling."

In the initial post of "Carnival," Les Anders, apparently believing his data will elevate the tone of discussion (in "Carnival," as in the longer thread from which it is taken, Anders's tone is relentlessly, even painfully, polite), simply states Schlessinger's professional qualifications. Discussants posting prior to "Carnival" are almost unanimous in thinking Schlessinger is unqualified to give advice to those who call her for counseling. Their chief objection appears to be the confusion attached to the title "Doctor." Schlessinger holds a doctorate in physiology, thus technically (to some) entitling her to call herself "Doctor" (for example, Wen Ho Lee, holder of a doctorate in physics, is customarily referred to as "Dr. Lee"). However, in the context of her radio talk show, where she gives what many (not Schlessinger herself, it should be noted[19]) regard as counseling, the term *Doctor* might suggest Schlessinger is trying to foist on the unwary the idea that she is in fact a psychiatrist, that is, a medical doctor. This is a good example of what phenomenologists refer to as the tendency of language to misrepresent reality. Schlessinger's detractors think it is wrong to assume the title "doctor," since this may give the impression, at least in the context of giving advice, that one's degree is in psychology or a related field. That Schlessinger does not, at least overtly, specify that her doctoral degree is in physiology—nor even that "doctor" does not refer to a medical degree—provides the cue to the alternative representations that drives discussion throughout the thread.

That Anders chooses to interpret the dispute as a need for more information is very revealing. Although he does seem to enact the pragmatist's principle that one ought to judge utterance by the standard of practical utility (hence, he apparently thinks the pragmatic way to settle the dispute is to bring in information from Schlessinger's résumé), his strategy also shows he does not quite agree with others that the "real" dispute is over the title "Doctor," and not other information about Schlessinger's background. Instead he offers what many would consider a legitimate answer to any question about qualifications—a résumé. Having recited objective facts about Schlessinger's education and work experience, Anders feels the issue is resolved, so much so that he declares he is entitled to an "apology," presumably because list members doubted him and hence the validity of his evidence. Here, Anders also seems to be following the pragmatist principle that the freedom to interpret an utterance lies in the power of the individual consciousness that encounters it.

But the reaction to the invocation by Anders and others of OTHER MEANING reveals the power of dialogical, centrifugal forces summoned by other participants. They do not want to let go of the "Doctor" issue. As phenomenology might have it, the discursive label *doctor* generates multiple meanings that are not, in themselves, attached to what is described. It is this susceptibility of the term *doctor* to multiple interpretations that leads to the dispute: not meaning just one thing, it means many things. Like other words, *doctor* has a great range of connotative meaning, and it is each individual's meaning that is brought to the perception of the message in which the word is used, not some general definition such as that found in a dictionary. Hence, each participant in the discussion will invoke his or her own meaning in the debate over whether Schlessinger "really is" a "doctor," which is another way of saying that multiple OTHER MEANINGS are invoked by different people.

Indeed, one might say that most of the rest of the messages derive their energy from resisting what obviously appears to Anders as a complete, seamless, authoritative, and hence monologically based answer to a straightforward question. To almost everyone else, the issue is equally straightforward: if Schlessinger is to claim the title "Doctor," then that claim is going to be made fun of—carnivalized. That carnivalization comes to dominate the thread is dramatically shown by the fact that, in the wake of responses to his post, Anders retires from the discussion, at least for the next five days.

Although importing knowledge to help understand professional qualifications is an example of OTHER MEANING, it is intimately connected to OTHER CONCEPTION. Anders tries to fortify Schlessinger's standing by citing facts about her background, a positive form of OTHER CONCEPTION. The resulting responses, however, almost exclusively are negative examples of OTHER CONCEPTION, directed not only toward Schlessinger, but also Anders. A particularly telling characterization (also involving OTHER MEANING) is one by Richard Wilson [16]. While agreeing with an earlier poster, Maria Chandler [13], Wilson lambastes Schlessinger as not being up to what he thinks are the already low standards set by talk radio:

> Even by call in [*sic*] standards it's ridiculous and formulaic. Her entire schtick [*sic*] is basically hummed to "name that tune". If her guests get

more than 4 words in before she cuts them off and reads their beads, she loses. She never does. [16]

Apart from the specialized media terminology—*shtick* and *name that tune*—needed to interpret this statement, Wilson also invokes some general impressions about talk radio. This form of OTHER MEANING assumes not only what one might call "objective data" about talk radio, but common stereotypes: talk radio (that which Wilson refers to as "call in") is "ridiculous" and "formulaic." Here too we see an overlap of OTHER MEANING and OTHER CONCEPTION, in that Wilson obviously has very specific, negative ideas about participants in talk radio that he wishes to advance.

Wilson's response, however, carries significantly monologic overtones in the guise of OTHER MEANING. His post is overtly declarative, expressed so as to close discussion of the issue: he uses the word *is* and ends by declaring, "she never does." Moreover, most of the other contributors, to a greater or lesser extent, appear to agree with Wilson. That being the case, why does the thread continue?

I think it is because list members have to satisfy needs other than the need for information. Just as Vygotsky, considering the multitude of goals and tools available to the social actor, held the educational experience to be different each time it is performed, so the EDM thread can be taken in different directions, depending on the information that is brought in, and more importantly, who participates. For example, think how differently this thread might have evolved had Les Anders chosen (like Jerry Chen in "Wen Ho Lee") to respond directly to his critics, instead of retiring from the discussion. People do not join lists simply to exchange information. The Net is more fun, as these list members prove. Even though members may agree with Wilson that there is no mystery about Schlessinger's qualifications and her approach to giving advice, the thread has to keep going for contributors to get other things off their chests. This is the ribald, unconventional, free-form discursive experimentation that imparts to this group, and the Internet in general, its unique flavor. Even when the quest for information is satisfied, the party has often just begun.

A fascinating feature of "Carnival" is the degree to which opinions expressed on it are polarized. Schlessinger has a lone defender (Anders), with most of the rest of the contributors strongly of the opinion that she has no business dispensing advice. Rarely is evaluation of Schlessinger's qualifications measured or restrained. An exception is this less censorious example of OTHER CONCEPTION in [13], from Maria Chandler, who somewhat incongruously signs herself "Mean-MaliciousMaria." Chandler replies to the criticism of Les Anders by Andy Kennicott [6]: "To be quite honest, the standards to be a 'counselor' are often way too lax for my decidedly biased tastes. This woman sounds in no way qualified to be dishing out the advice she is giving."

If only as a contrast to the untrammeled vituperative tone in the rest of "Carnival," this OTHER CONCEPTION of Laura (and by extension, of Anders) is worthy of attention. Chandler refers to her own tastes as "decidedly biased," and prefaces her points with the lower key introduction (indicating possible uncertainty) "to be quite honest." She does not state unequivocally that Schlessinger is not qualified, but that she "sounds like" she is not qualified. These differences make Chandler's post a marked contrast with negative remarks about Anders in posts by Elena [15] and Dennis Felson [18]. Finally, Maria Chandler is one of the few posters to distinguish between Schlessinger's qualifications and her advice. Chandler does not say Schlessinger should be forbidden to give any advice (as is suggested by Vince Majors and others), but that it *sounds to her* as if Schlessinger is not qualified to give the advice she is "dishing out."

This OTHER CONCEPTION introduces an alternative view of the list members. Along with the ribaldry, the celebration of the bawdy and the outrageous we see in the posts of, for example, Vince Majors, there are more staid contributions by a core of contributors who appear to be mental health professionals. Strangely, one of these is Les Anders (Anders represents the extreme of conventional professionality, in that he does not seem to "get" the predominantly derisive tone of the discussion), though there are others. These are the posters who can be counted on to lower the level of rancor when it becomes too high. Maria Chandler's post is an example of an attempt, through OTHER CONCEPTION, to downplay what might have been taken as an overly negative question directed to Les Anders (to Anders, Andy Kennicott had asked, incredulously, "how on earth can you be a social worker?" [6]). The numerous "one-down" markers (Millar & Rogers, 1976) in Chandler's post show that she, at least, is not ready to join in the fun through uninhibitedly "piling on" Les Anders. In fact, she is one of the few posters who does not conflate bad feelings about "Dr. Laura" with similar feelings about Schlessinger's defender, Les Anders. She replies to Andy Kennicott's direct confrontation of Anders but pointedly never mentions Anders himself. In this way, Chandler accomplishes, dialogically, a number of goals simultaneously. She is, so to say, selective about her carnivalization: she allies herself with most list members regarding Schlessinger, thereby adding to the move toward carnivalizing her, but does not go so far as to carnivalize Anders, as do most of the others. Chandler's voice is added to the comparative minority of "Carnival" discussants who try to balance the extravagant characterizations with a more measured, professional approach. Through this subtle "toning down" mechanism, Maria's OTHER CONCEPTION thus serves to counteract the elements of OTHER CONCEPTION that seem so unrelenting in their scathing portrayals of Schlessinger and Anders.

A more seriously critical instance of OTHER CONCEPTION occurs in [15], where Elena takes Les Anders to task for failing to truthfully explain his motivations. Replying to Andy Kennicott's rather amazed question about how Anders could be involved in social work and not know what was necessary to hold the MFCC, Elena writes:

> Rather than boggle your mind at the idea that someone who appears to be so ignorant could be a social worker, isn't it simpler to apply Occam's razor and consider that perhaps he *aspires* to be a social worker, but in fact knows nothing about the field? That theory would certainly fit in with his articles to [this list]. [15]

The relentless criticism of Anders perhaps needs some further explanation. Anders and Schlessinger must be seen as the principal targets of OTHER CONCEPTION in the "Carnival" thread. As noted earlier, throughout the larger "Trials" thread from which "Carnival" is taken, Anders emerges as the lone defender of Laura Schlessinger. Since nearly everyone else is against Schlessinger, even Anders's tentatively polite reframing of issues in the debate is, for the most part, greeted with undiluted scorn. Moreover, members (perhaps even Anders himself) seem quite comfortable with this mode of expression.

This previous contentious history is one reason why nearly every instance of OTHER CONCEPTION in "Carnival" is negative, and concerns either Les Anders or Laura Schlessinger (or both). The merging of these two targets is hardly coincidence, and may be another example of the phenomenon we encountered in "Wen Ho Lee," where "Jerry Chen," taking unpopular positions onlist, became a surrogate for Wen Ho Lee himself. Possibly Anders performs the same function in "Carnival": denied access to the "true" target of their ire (Schlessinger), list members must be content with the substitute (Anders).

Still, responses like Elena's seem excessive. Unless they have some previous history of animosity, her response is out of proportion to Anders's initiation of the topic, which involved, after all, merely reciting certain facts and requesting an apology. However, if we see Anders and "Dr. Laura" as conflated in the minds of Elena and others, we open an interesting field of conjecture. What is being said about Anders is also being said about Schlessinger. This may mean that what Elena is severely criticizing in Anders is what she probably also thinks about Schlessinger. Yet clearly Schlessinger's qualifications are superior to those of Anders. It is interesting that Anders himself suggests this possibility by his almost reverential presentation of Schlessinger's credentials, as if these alone are a more-than-adequate refutation of any objections. Thus, the conflation of Anders/Schlessinger may offer an advantage to Elena herself; it is almost as if, by venturing his opinion about Schlessinger in a forum where it is almost certain to be ridiculed, Anders declares himself to be the only person who would think Schlessinger is qualified. By questioning Anders's qualifications, list members indict the only person on Schlessinger's side, leaving her (essentially) with no defenders. These uses of OTHER CONCEPTION thus provide a verification of the multiple trajectories followed by utterances introduced into social life: individual utterances in "Carnival" accomplish a number of goals in casting both Anders and Schlessinger as illegitimate.

Another revealing example of OTHER CONCEPTION further extends criticism of Les Anders, and also reinforces the possibility that he has a history of contentious interaction on this list. At [18], Dennis Felson, replying to an earlier charge that Anders is an "illiterate twit" (post [3], by Jason Edward Houghton), states:

> Well, why are you surprised? This is the man who looked up "a great deal" in the dictionary and read what it said there as indicating that his incorrect usage of it was correct. The man can't read. And he obviously doesn't understand the conventional and widely understood meaning of the term "medical degree." That is, he thinks that the phrase "She holds no medical degree" is false because he doesn't know that "medical degree" does not refer to any doctorate or any degree in a medical field, but to an actual M.D. And the man claims to be a social worker. With employees like him, it's no wonder the system doesn't work. [18]

Here we see criticism not only of Anders's own qualifications and experience, but "the system" as a whole. This is as good a point as any to note that perhaps it is the absence of any response from Anders that permits these increasingly acrimonious statements about him. In Felson's message, one senses the criticism has gone too far and Felson is questioning things about Anders that no one could be in a position to judge (for example, Anders "doesn't know" that "medical degree" and "doctorate" are not the same thing).

This OTHER CONCEPTION also situates Les Anders in the discursive history of the list. This is done in a way that initially seems odd, but in fact may not be. What seems odd about Felson's "bill of particulars" is how specific it is: he refers to very precise utterances Anders has previously made and what is wrong with them. What may not be odd is that Felson expects other members to know, without too much explanation, what he is talking about. When advancing such a robust negative evaluation, one ought to use the best evidence. Therefore, it is likely that the acts of which Anders is accused—such as misinterpreting the phrase "a great deal"—are well enough known to list members to need no further explanation.[20] Simultaneously, this portrayal reveals not only that Anders's past history with the list is less than harmonious (also indicated in Elena's post), but also confirms the strong sense of collective consciousness, in that members seldom feel the need to explain things to outsiders.

OTHER CONCEPTION, along with CONTESTING OWNERSHIP, is also strongly featured as list members use ridicule to carnivalize Schlessinger, leading to some interesting subthreads involving other media productions. A particularly relevant subthread has to do with what is required to be a talk show host on a level with Schlessinger. These should be seen carnivalizing sequences, involving the upending of authority and official culture. Bakhtin (1984a, 1984b) viewed these occasions, often characterized by irreverent, ribald humor of the kind we see in "Carnival," as a rejection of the ideology of the church and other powerful medieval institutions. Just as the lowly participant in the medieval festival was permitted, for a time, to indulge in the forbidden and laugh at the sacred, these list members, in addition to arguing about the "facts" of Schlessinger's qualifications, use scatological humor and outrageous comparisons to elevate themselves and bring down Laura Schlessinger.

It is fairly easy to see how OTHER CONCEPTION is involved in this process, but less easy to see the role of CONTESTING OWNERSHIP. CONTESTING OWNERSHIP comes in with the espousal of an alternate reading of sociohistorical circumstance; one could view the inversion of "high" and "low" culture as a contest for ownership of representation. This approach is hinted at in the negative evaluation (an alternate, contesting, reading) of "call ins" by Richard Wilson ([16], previously discussed), but actually manifests overtly, albeit indirectly, a bit earlier, in [4], with James Jones's offhand remark, responding to the citation by Les Anders of Schlessinger's doctorate in physiology [1], already cited but repeated here for convenience: "Sorry, Dr. James is every bit as good a Dr. as Dr. Laura, and when I go on the air and start yapping I want respect." Jones, it turns out, has a doctorate in mathematics, and true to the spirit of carnivalization, takes this as a warrant to claim a status equal or superior to that of "Dr. Laura." Jones's point is that the "Doctor" title is the key: the field of endeavor in which it was achieved is irrelevant. To Jones, the ownership of the title "doctor" is thus open to question and eligible to be contested.

This short utterance by Jones provides the entrée for most, if not all, the carnivalization that will define the thread. I previously noted the role of Vince Majors, in message [9], in expanding on Jones's basic idea (Majors's elaboration is quoted below). However, Majors actually replies to an utterance by Duane Charles Deland in [7]: "Hey, when I finish my PhD [sic], can I be a guest doctor on your show?" Taking up the sequence, Majors says:

> Join the queue. Dr. Terry Winston is already booked for a guest slot discussing the emotional needs of the menopause, I'm down for a discussion of clitoral massage, Dr. Andy Kennicott is slated for a show on female sexuality in the 21st century, Dr [sic] Brad Kranze is doing bigamy from the wifely perspective (so to speak), Dr. Barney Wroczy will be hosting a call-in on the use of sex-toys as an instrument [sic] of female emancipation and Dr. Maria Chandler will be talking about how to get your man into bed and keep him there. [9]

Majors's rather elaborate list, apparently embodying list culture, forges past and future connections among list members through a multiplex EFFORT AT SHARING (as well as multiple strands of OTHER MEANING and OTHER CONCEPTION).

This specific, noticeably centrifugal, EFFORT AT SHARING seems to have other purposes as well. First, there is the pairing of list member names with the title "Dr." (although, perhaps because Majors appears to be British and thus also unfamiliar with American talk radio, he does not get it quite right, pairing the title "Doctor" with both the given and the family names). This is EFFORT AT SHARING because Majors attempts to imitate what previous posters have had to say about "doctors" and the topics they discuss on talk radio. Though none appear to be M.D.s, some contributors to "Carnival" do have doctorates; others, such as Duane Deland, say they are in the process of working on their doctoral degrees; and still others seem to have no college degree at all. However, in dialogical processes such as carnivalization, the actual, that is, the official or monologic, content of a title is not particularly important. What is important is that one be able to claim the title "Doctor" to assume the guise of expert on some exotic subject. Majors's post suggests that anyone interested in any area could be a "doctor," and anyone he identifies in his list is as qualified to speak on those subjects as "Dr. Laura" is on the subjects she discusses.

Another, more subtle, way opinions are melded in this EFFORT AT SHARING is through OTHER MEANING, for the "topics" for each "host" share something else in common: each topic can, without too much effort, be related to Laura Schlessinger herself. The "emotional needs of menopause" (Terry Winston's topic) calls to mind mood swings sometimes suffered by women of Schlessinger's approximate age during menopause; perhaps Majors is circumspectly offering this as an explanation of Schlessinger's acrimonious interactions with others. Likewise, such topics as "bigamy from the wifely perspective," "sex-toys as an instrument of female emancipation," and "how to get your man into bed and keep him there" could also be taken as thinly veiled references to the scandalous stories about Schlessinger's alleged amorous exploits. To understand the implications suggested by these references involves the instantiation of multiple systems of OTHER MEANING. Majors's post seems too carefully crafted to have been conceived to accomplish only a single, dominant, monologic goal; consideration of the post as EFFORT AT SHARING, coupled with OTHER MEANING, permits a more dialogical unfolding of alternative explanations.

Through CONTESTING OWNERSHIP, authority to say what the "doctor" title "really" means is thrown open to question and is taken by various posters in still other directions. Message [25] is a post by Jake Dowling. Dowling is replying to James Jones, who states in [17], "Yes, but none of this ABD crap.[21] I'll want to see your diploma, signed, sealed and in your hot little hand." This responds to an utterance by Duane Charles Deland about wanting to be on the "Dr. James Show" [7]. Dowling offers the following example of extreme carnivalization when he takes the discussion out of the realm of "legitimate" academic achievement altogether: "I'm not a doctor, but I sometimes operate the fax machine for one. Is that close enough?" [17]. This can be taken as an example of CONTESTING OWNERSHIP because, although there is no direct confrontation between Dowling and Jones (though there is between Jones and Deland), Dowling's offering of such a wildly variant interpretation of the topic makes it clear that his view of the world is, at least ostensibly, placed in opposition to that of both of the two previous posters.

An important feature of this CONTESTING OWNERSHIP is how it illustrates the acceleration and unrestrained growth, once begun, of the dialogical mode of analysis. Once a point of view has been challenged, a wedge is driven into the supposedly seamless architecture of the monological underpinning that supports it. After the first breach, we see a growth in the number of alternative interpretations of resistance to the authority of the term *doctor*, from the question about whether being on the verge of becoming a doctor is enough to a declaration that it is not to the utterance I focus on now, the ridiculing of any discussion. This is one reason the dialogical perspective is so useful in analyzing EDM discourse: it is ideal for teasing out the growth of alternative viewpoints, viewpoints whose relevance to conventional topic structure can, monologically considered, be obscure or even invisible.

One certain indicator of dialogue on the Internet is the suddenness with which topics crop up in EDM threads. Such is the case with *Two Fat Ladies Cooking*, the popular British television series that featured two women preparing frequently unremarkable British food with cheerful abandon. A revealing exposition of the program begins innocently enough; in [39] Vince Majors mentions that "cookery shows" are popular in Britain, and in [42] Brad Kranze identifies "Two Fat Ladies" as his favorite. Following this staid introduction, Brad Kranze revisits the topic through an unusual elaboration, in [48] making the link between the program and stereotypes about lesbians:

> I'm no expert in British regional or classist accents, but the Two Fat Ladies seem to have a certain disaffected aristocratic manner of speech. Likewise, I don't have strongly developed lesdar, but something about those two triggers recognition. Perhaps their motorcycle-and-sidecar transport?

Kranze uses the term *lesdar*, seemingly a variant of *gaydar*, slang for the purported ability of gay people to identify other gays (that is, as if using "radar"). Here, Kranze invokes numerous references to OTHER MEANING—British accents, "class," "motorcycle-and-sidecar transport," aristocracy, and so on—to come up with a not overly subtle suggestion that the "Two Fat Ladies" are lesbians. Oddly, there seems little justification for the intensity of this reaction (which works to further inflame subsequent responders, including Vince Majors, who uses it as a springboard to formulate a violent fantasy about the two women); no justification, that is, except for the (very important) fact that Mr. Kranze's unique architectonics seem to have interacted, as predicted by Bakhtin, in a particularly volatile way to produce the utterance containing his response.

This invocation of multiple systems of OTHER MEANING confirms both the breadth of knowledge of these list members and their ability to communicate in "high-context" fashion.[22] Indeed, it could even be said that only a true member of this, one of the most respected of gay/lesbian newsgroups, could get away with stating such stereotypes; were someone not sharing the community's principles to stereotype lesbians this way, she or he would be—indeed has been—cruelly reprimanded onlist. Within this community, however, such contentiousness is not only allowed, but encouraged.

Beyond that, however, this invocation of OTHER MEANING features the linking of three traits that deserve our attention: being female, being lesbian, and being a media icon. To understand the possible significance of these points, it is worth noting where this post occurs in the thread: it is in response to a post by Stan Simpson concerning his plans to get a "Two Fat Ladies" cookbook as a present for another list member,[23] "Victor" [47]: "His birthday is coming up, so he may get the third cookbook as a present. Maybe." Given the odd connection, we are obliged to ask ourselves why would a reference to a birthday gift lead to a discussion of lesbian stereotypes?

One explanation is that Kranze is trying to say something else here and seizes upon the introduction of the "Two Fat Ladies" to make what at first might seem to be an unconnected elaboration. Dialogical inquiry permits us to consider whether there is in the connection female-lesbian-media icon a comparison of the "Two Fat Ladies" and Laura Schlessinger.

Before rejecting this as too outlandish, consider the culture of the list in which we find this thread. Most, perhaps all, of the contributors can be seen as involved in an ongoing EFFORT AT SHARING, since they appear to be gay or lesbian;[24] moreover, by revealing at least some information about themselves on an Internet group, they could be considered "out" (a subgroup that shares a select set of behaviors), that is, their sexual orientation is, to some extent, known. Then there are the issues they have been talking about. OTHER MEANING is brought in through issues about "Dr." Laura raised in other places concerning homophobia (ascribed to Schlessinger as the result of public statements taken to be antigay/lesbian). In "Carnival," issues are discussed that involve OTHER CONCEPTION (that Schlessinger calls herself "Doctor" traps the unwary caller), as well as the OTHER MEANING necessary to interpret the references to sexuality (the numerous sexual references suggested as topics for imaginary radio programs at, for instance, [9], [26], [36], and [39]).

If one combines all these representations in various ways then perhaps one can see the image of "Two Fat Ladies" offered in [48] as the culmination of various carnivalization trajectories, intercombining utterances linked to the four utterance elements, that have continued to develop throughout the thread. For example, significant OTHER CONCEPTION (both of Schlessinger and her critics) is involved: like many gays and lesbians who, prior to "coming out," must deceive others to escape oppression, Laura Schlessinger is perhaps accused of having lived a number of deceptions. Schlessinger, while publicly advocating the sanctity of marriage, is reported to have both cheated on her husband and participated as the "other woman" when the man she was with cheated on his spouse. These various representations of events in Schlessinger's life obviously conflict with each other, and here (as well as in other media venues), we see many examples of CONTESTING OWNERSHIP over whether charges about Schlessinger are true or false. It is difficult to comprehend how gays and lesbians, particularly such as those on this list, who are very vocal about gay/lesbian concerns, would not be sensitive to issues regarding deception of others concerning one's sexual activities. In this way, their criticism of Schlessinger is a highly unusual form of EFFORT AT SHARING, in that they challenge her to be less exclusive in her moral judgments. Because it is also CONTESTING OWNERSHIP of Schlessinger's carefully constructed public persona, these utterances work together to form a classic carnivalization inversion: what begins with the counselor giving the moral lesson, ends with her being the student rather than the teacher.

Considering these possibilities, then, gives us an alternative lens for examining Kranze's suggestions. He mentions—quite deliberately, one suspects—strange, even ridiculous, data to confirm the "Ladies" are lesbians (and we can infer this is his intent because he uses the term *lesdar*): their accents, and the fact that they ride together on a motor-cycle. Note how this invocation of OTHER MEANING stands out precisely because it is so unusual. Underlying his depiction is the suggestion that we need to focus on this strange data because otherwise one would not be able to discern that the two are lesbians. Therefore, and perhaps this connection does not even occur at the conscious level, we can legitimately ask: is the same thing being said about Laura Schlessinger, also a woman, also in the media, and also a practitioner of some behaviors stereotypically associated with lesbianism (an "unfeminine" aggressiveness, the "soul of a drill sergeant," and so on)?

I do not think list members, through direct and indirect OTHER CONCEPTION, are suggesting (as some do with the "Ladies") that Schlessinger is a lesbian. Rather, they may be performing another variation of carnivalization, through invoking OTHER MEANING, by equalizing the status between themselves and Schlessinger. First, by CONTESTING OWNERSHIP, they question Schlessinger's claims of professional status, and then, by some very circuitous routes, they question her claims to moral status. They say to her, in essence, "If you think you can look down on us, guess again." This is a highly effective confirmation of the dialogical quality of Internet discourse: a predominant, largely unquestioned view, presented to a diverse group, is challenged in several interesting ways to yield not just one, but a number of alternative interpretations.

Confirmation of the vitality of *Two Fat Ladies Cooking* as a carnivalizing mechanism is the seriousness with which Kranze's post is taken immediately by Vince Majors. Majors, in a fascinating example of CONTESTING OWNERSHIP, offers an unrestrained and rather shocking reaction to the "Two Fat Ladies":

> [T]he food they prepare is uniformally [*sic*] revolting, their affectations irritating to the point of infuriating, and their show invariably makes me long for the presence of both ladies and a 2 by 4 with a big nail through it. [49]

This utterance, a response to the post by Brad Kranze ([48], quoted previously), is phrased so as to establish an important list cultural principle. Kranze's post referred to qualities of the "Two Fat Ladies" that might lead others to see them as lesbians. Kranze had previously identified this program as his "absolute favourite" [42]; however, Majors is apparently unwilling to let either this evaluation, or Kranze's remarks about "lesdar," go unchallenged. This uncharacteristically violent opinion on this list is interesting, not simply as an example of how two posters can contest ownership of a representation, but also as an indication—much to be expected in dialogically inclined exchanges—that even those who appear to be engaged in an EFFORT AT SHARING on "one" issue (dislike of Laura Schlessinger) can be involved in CONTESTING OWNERSHIP on other matters. This provides dramatic confirmation of the multiple meanings of social discourse; while accomplishing one goal, the utterance accomplishes what might seem (from a monological perspective) an opposing goal.

It is the interplay among Kranze and Majors, and James Jones, capable of being perceived analytically through the four kinds of utterance elements, that actualizes the spirit of carnivalization in this thread. However, true to the individualism in many EDM sequences, people can agree on some things, but vociferously disagree on others. In [49], Vince Majors's extravagant threat scenarios concerning the "Two Fat Ladies" (later in the message he re-creates a picture of them as victims of mutual erotic asphyxiation) must be seen in a context broader than his dislike of the program. Majors appears to be quite angry, perhaps because of what could be taken as Kranze's inappropriate mention of negative stereotypes about lesbians.[25]

Comparison of Standard and Utterance Readings

Considered only or principally according to the monological perspective, "Carnival" appears to be chaotic, a disorganized mess of spontaneous responses and counterresponses loosely clustered around a debate about whether Laura Schlessinger is qualified to give advice to those who call her radio program. From the perspective of the communication analyst, exchanges on this list, one of the oldest and most well-established on the Internet, are high-context, that is, the posters have extensive knowledge of each other and are intimately familiar with the free-form process of carnivalization that seems to be an important part of the contributors' discursive repertoire. I would also guess list members are well aware of the value of the pithy witticism that might someday be immortalized on the list's Web page of notable quotations. These posters have fun, even when they seem to be insulting each other.

Carnivalization (which is one of several metaphors Bakhtin used to clarify the concept of heteroglossia), however, permits the analyst to even more clearly conceptualize the effect of the four utterance reading indicators. Carnivalization functions as a kind of umbrella concept, tying

OTHER MEANING, OTHER CONCEPTION, EFFORT AT SHARING, and CONTESTING OWNERSHIP together. Upon taking the dialogical perspective, we saw that the posters are making penetrating and deadly serious points about Schlessinger and the problems that widely known public figures like her cause when they make intemperate statements about gays and lesbians.[26] The communication style on the list enables participants to formulate messages that help them subject Schlessinger (and others) to the inversions that characterize carnivalization: they use, to take just a few examples, shorthand references to popular culture (OTHER MEANING); extensive evaluation of others (OTHER CON-CEPTION); bonding with each other, as in response to a common irritant, Les Anders (EFFORT AT SHARING); and frequent disputes (CON-TESTING OWNERSHIP). This is done by bringing in information that reflects varying degrees of the obvious (such as the references to *Two Fat Ladies Cooking*) and the subtle (such as the bringing together of sexual orientation, reputation, and profession, applied—perhaps—to Laura Schlessinger). To discover how these qualities manifested themselves on the list, we were required to consider a large and varied group of media and other cultural influences, which in the standard reading appears unconnected and even random.

It is worth noting again that these utterances, infinitely varied in terms of what they mean to individual social actors, take place against a backdrop of regular patterns of linguistic organization, governed not only by the monologic frameworks by which computers function, but by shared understandings about the nature of social interaction. The point to remember about both "Wen Ho Lee" and "Carnival" is that human communication, no matter how disorganized it appears on the surface, results from the efforts of people who live their lives according to a more or less consistent set of social understandings, and as such displays regularity and pattern (Sacks, 1992; Sacks, Schegloff, & Jefferson, 1974; Schegloff, 1968). This is one reason why it is impossible to dismiss mono-logical perspectives, and to depend exclusively on dialogical insight. It is up to the analyst to discover the patterns, and in the realm of EDMs (and Web pages/sites, as I will show in Chapter 4), analysts can apply dual reading to obtain significant and insightful results.

CONCLUSION

Both the monological and the dialogical perspectives are essential to realizing the potential for EDMs to improve civic discourse. The monological framework is needed to organize the written discourse into a more or less coherent pattern; the dialogical framework is needed to generate awareness of alternative forms of expression. Even though subthreads seem to fly off in all sorts of unrelated directions, we have seen through the dual reading method that there are several underlying patterns tying the messages together, and that these are not necessarily immediately evident to the casual observer.

At the same time, discursive exchanges, to be considered valuable in the public/civic sphere, must usually display variety and quality—in classic democracy, consideration of alternatives is held to be the best guarantor that optimal solutions to problems will be achieved. To accomplish this, numerous ideas and forms of knowledge, the conceptions of others, particularly their disputes and collaborations, must be brought into discussions. In many ways, the range of options available to EDM posters (such as linkage to Web sites, capability for use of graphics and sounds, and so on), not to mention the reach of the Internet and the freedom of expression granted by comparative anonymity, make the seemingly lowly EDM a powerful tool for bringing in far more of the world than is perhaps possible with other message forms.

As we search for new ways to look at communication and the realm of civic discourse, we would do well to take account of the perspectives offered to us by the rich and varied history of dialogism. Too often, scholars, like the philosophers and historians of Vico's time, treat the elements of civic discourse principally as abstractions endorsed by widely accepted, principally monologic systems of thought, as if terms such as *freedom, justice, social responsibility*, and *human dignity* had any existence apart from the lived experience of people in the most mundane and lowly of circumstances. The elements of civic life, and discourse, can be discussed in global terms, but they are experienced at the level of daily human activity. Therefore, to fully understand civic discourse, we would do well to explore the manifold ways ideas are agreed upon and fought over in human interaction. It is there that we discover, sometimes in the homeliest of venues, that human beings have worked hard to make sense of their world and that if we can but see this, we will have gained a window on even the most intractably difficult of concepts and ideas.

In both the EDM threads analyzed in this chapter, we have seen ways in which people come to grips with the complexities of civic life. Confronted with someone who arouses controversy—whether an accused spy or an acerbic radio talk show host—the people on a list, both individually and as group members, must perform difficult and demanding cognitive and linguistic work (of the kind discussed in Chapter 2 with respect to the moves from passivity and given knowledge) to formulate their impressions of these people, and more broadly, what these individuals have to say about civic identity. Once this is done, they then must make their perceptions fit the circumstances of their own lives. They have to experiment with various formulations of utterances, and as they encounter people who think differently, adjust how they see situations, a quality reflected in the divergence among their utterances. Yet the end result of this process is that, collectively, they fashion a linguistic product that represents, if not a "real" person, at least how they understand that person, particularly with respect to views of the world that the person propagates.

The resulting images of the "real people" about whom discourse is fashioned are actualized in various ways, seemingly consistent with the needs of the people who post to EDM discussions. Wen Ho Lee is and will forever remain an enigma. But although Lee may be a cipher, issues about human rights and responsibilities that his case brings into public discourse are only too clear, relevant, and pressing. These include the legal rights of immigrants, questions of patriotism and loyalty, cultural identity, the role of media in democratic and nondemocratic societies, and many other important concerns.

Likewise, the image that emerges of Laura Schlessinger is of a media creation who has attained prominence because of her proclivity to make alienating statements that drive wedges between people, rather than uniting them. Whether one sees this as an unpleasant but necessary palliative to a pervasive laxity in moral standards (as do Schlessinger's supporters), or an unreasonable attempt by a morally flawed media exploiter who capitalizes on fear and hatred to advance her career (as do her detractors), those of both camps can use the medium of the EDM thread to bring in ideas from "outside" the list to construct their respective representations. As in the case of Wen Ho Lee, it is the creativity of those who construct utterances, as well as their willingness to continue to engage (or withdraw) that ultimately work to coconstruct a representation that shows the best efforts of a number of people to come to grips with a problem of civic identity.

In both cases, we learn the same thing about civic discourse and civic identity. If we are to understand the issues addressed in EDM threads, as the people understand them, to know them in terms of how they fit into the civic identities of real, living individuals, then we can profitably begin by immersing ourselves in communication used by the people. A very good way to do this is to start by grasping "the world in a post."

NOTES

1. In their early years, this problem was also faced by conversation analysts who could not convince the rest of the academic community that there was any benefit to be had from microanalysis of mundane conversation.

2. The notion of "first" utterance is also rendered somewhat more uncertain in dialogism. Dialogism throws into doubt the idea that utterance is cut off from what precedes and follows it.

3. "Most" is an appropriate modifier, since not everyone has access to all e-mail discussion groups. However, both groups I look at in this chapter, and many others besides, can be accessed through public search engine archives such as Google and do not require membership, even though one group is moderated and the other is not.

4. When Bakhtin uses the word *speech*, he refers to both written and oral communication.

5. For the much less numerous dialogically oriented studies of EDMs, see, for example, Argyle, 1996; Mitra, 1997; and Stivale, 1997.

6. Or, for that matter, EDM.

7. "On the Internet in e-mail, chatting, and posted messages, an emoticon (sometimes referred to as a 'smiley') is a short sequence of keyboard letters and symbols, usually emulating a facial expression, expressing a feeling that supplements the message. Most of these emoticons use several symbols to create a small face with an expression such as a smile, wink, or turned-down mouth" (Thing, 2002, p. 234).

8. In this and subsequent discussion I capitalize the four utterance elements to call attention to them.

9. The analysis of the thread will reveal the reason for using quotation marks around Schlessinger's title.

10. As will become clear, the presumed ethnicity and nationality of the posters is very important in interpreting the messages.

11. The names of these individuals have been changed, but are similar in structure to the names used to identify the posters to the thread.

12. This is a reference to the controversial designation of Taiwan as "Taiwan, Republic of China," or more commonly, "Taiwan, ROC." This label reflects the view that Taiwan is part of China (a "republic"), not an independent political entity, and is thus objectionable to many people in Taiwan.

13. More recently, however, Schlessinger has suffered some setbacks in building her media presence. Her television show (which taped its last episode in March 2001) was dropped, or placed in poor slots (such as the middle of the

night) by several major markets. Schlessinger attributed this to activist campaigns by gay/lesbian groups (Elber, 2001). Her radio show was also dropped by stations in some markets (such as Milwaukee [Cuprisin, 2002]) or else moved out of desirable slots (such as Los Angeles [Ho, 2002]). As of April 2002, the number of radio stations carrying her program had slipped to fewer than 350 (Ho, 2002).

14. Only about 18 of these callers will get to talk to Schlessinger on-air during any given program (Bane, 1999, p. 231).

15. I should emphasize that I am making no judgment concerning whether these allegations are true, any more than I could confirm or deny the utterances in "Wen Ho Lee." However, as part of the public discourse about Schlessinger, these allegations, whether provable or not, play a part in the discussion in "Laura at the Carnival."

16. According to Hill (n.d.), Schlessinger "was formerly tolerant of homosexuality, but over time her views on the subject slowly became more in line with the conservative religious elements of society. Finally, on her show airing August 6, 1998, Laura proclaimed that "homosexuality is destructive." She also said that her former tolerance regarding gays was "inappropriate" (sect. 4.16).

17. As with "Wen Ho Lee," pseudonyms similar to the structure of the real name, are used to identify posters.

18. Whether a response is "relevant" or "on-topic" depends on a primarily monologic view of topicality.

19. In an interview with Donna Petrozzello for *Broadcasting & Cable* (June 10, 1996), Schlessinger said, "It's not an advice show. It's a morality show" ("Schlessinger, Laura," 1997, p. 40).

20. This list is remarkable in that it sponsors a meticulously maintained Web site that contains not only notable posts, but information about members, alive and deceased, including birthdates, and even a page that sorts members by astrological sign. This dedication of site maintainers in recording elements of list culture is like nothing else I have encountered on the Internet.

21. ABD means that the person thus described has completed everything required to get a doctoral degree, except for the last, most difficult part: writing and defending the dissertation.

22. In high-context communication (Hall, 1983), most of the meaning of a message is in the context not the language of the message itself. Hence, those communicating in high-context fashion seldom need to "spell out" what they mean, since it is usually understood without explanation. Lists that have many members and have existed for a long time (such as this one) often feature a considerable amount of high-context communication.

23. The identity of the gift recipient is confirmed in a list of people responsible for notable quotations, recorded on a Web page maintained by the list managers. "Victor" does not contribute to "Carnival."

24. Both direct and indirect information about the sexual orientation of list members is available from a variety of sources on the site that maintains the

list. The list itself is part of the site, and its moderators make it clear that one does not have to be gay or lesbian to participate in discussions. Nevertheless, the participants in "Carnival" appear for the most part to be gay or lesbian, even if this is not obvious in the posts in "Carnival."

25. Of course it is also possible that Majors, as a Briton, is reacting to Kranze's remarks about "classist" British accents.

26. I call some of these statements "intemperate" largely because Schlessinger later repudiated them.

Chapter 4

Web Sites as Means for Propagating Civic, Political, and Ideological Concepts

In the previous chapter, e-mail discussion messages were examined as channels to propagate utterances about ideology (I use "ideology," here, as in Chapter 1, in the Bakhtin sense, that is, as a gloss of the Russian *ideologija*, which Bakhtin uses to refer to the sum total of a view of the world [1981, pp. 331–333]) that might not find a place in other communication venues. In this chapter, I turn to the other widely used way of propagating utterances about ideology, Web pages/sites.

As with EDMs, Web pages/sites can be designed to express ideology and they can be read to discover circumstances that led to them being composed as they have been. These circumstances reveal the traces of civic life that reflect the ideology of composers of Web pages/sites (and those who employ them), as well as how designers see visitors who will read these pages/sites.

Although in some respects similar in how they are composed and read, Web pages/sites differ from EDMs, chiefly in the degree of skill and amount of effort needed to create and revise them. Despite their greater complexity, however, Web pages/sites are not much less accessible than e-mail, either to site visitors or designers. The Web page is created and changed through the medium of coding, principally via markup languages such as HTML (by far the most common), XML, and so on (see Chapter 1). Beyond these widely available resources, the basic page can benefit from higher level coding such as Java or JavaScript.[1] However, to get a basic Web page with minimal advanced features, or even a site (a coordinated, interlinked set of pages) on the Web requires only slightly more effort and knowledge than composing e-mail.

Moreover, composing Web pages/sites is becoming yet easier, owing to the increasing availability of resources. For example, there are several locations where one can construct a Web site by following very simple step-by-step instructions using preformatted templates.[2] With minimal training, one can also construct sites using software, such as Dreamweaver, widely available through companies and educational institutions; Dreamweaver, like other software, is available in a trial version, which can be downloaded for free and used for a limited period. Web pages can even be made with browser software (available for free), such as Netscape Composer. Finally, increasingly, curricular programs at the university level, or earlier, teach students how to make their own Web pages. Focusing on the implications for political Internet discourse, Graham (1999) summarizes the accessibility of the new technology:

> Anyone anywhere at anytime, even with relatively limited means, can put things on and take things off the web [sic]. More importantly, in a way, as greater and greater amounts of software become available, both for purchase from commercial providers and freely donated by enthusiasts, the ordinary citizen can deploy impressive forms of presentation while lacking the skills, not just of engineers, but of artists, typographers and experts. (p. 69)

The resources I have cited comprise just a few of the indications that, as access to and use of the Internet increases, and as computers become more powerful, sophisticated, and available, construction of Web pages may someday be nearly as common a feature of online life as e-mail. Those who think this unlikely might reflect that not too long ago e-mail was considered comparatively exotic, and certainly very few could have predicted how much a part of our lives it would become.

Although we have seen how EDMs can be useful in propagating ideological messages, the Web page/site obviously has even more potential for this purpose. The information that can be included in an EDM, though more than simply text (for example, most e-mail programs permit users to attach graphic material and sound files, change size or color of font, and so on), still registers well below the impact of a well-designed Web site. The skillful designer of sites is able to lead visitors through numerous presentations of information via a unique conceptual path (Horton, 2000; Siegel, 1997), which is impossible within the confines of the straightforward e-mail message. Moreover, unlike EDMs, coordination of individual pages within a site permits one to think conceptually in terms of an array of utterances, linked to each other in interesting and potentially persuasive ways (Horton, 2000).[3]

Considering such qualities, the Web page/site seems ideal for civic discourse. It is a mass medium, but unlike other mass media (such as television or film), one does not need expensive equipment (other than the computer) or exhaustive technical training to compose effective utterances. Of course, despite the fact that Web pages/sites can be viewed by as many visitors as they can attract, Web pages/sites have their limitations. One such limitation constraining use of Web pages/sites as a tool of civic discourse—and there is no denying its seriousness—is that access to computers, servers, and similar technology is by no means universal (Sparks, 2001). This means that not everyone can put up a page reflecting a point of view, and the audience for one's page/site utterances will also be limited to those with Internet access. Nevertheless, these conditions continue to change with the steadily increasing access to computers.

With our current understanding of Web pages/sites, it would be easy to envision them as conforming to a linear or transmission (primarily monologic) model of communication, in that the Internet is conceived of as a space (cyberspace) where there exist communication artifacts such as Web pages/sites and to see the visitor as rather like a prospector who goes to these "locations" to "dig out" what is available. Yet the fluidity and dynamism of Internet communication, especially according to the principles of dialogism, persuade us that, just as is more obviously the case with EDMs (see Chapter 3), the communication between Web page/site designers and those who encounter their utterances is likewise, to some extent, multivocalic, heteroglossic, and open-ended.

Confirmation that the Internet expands the range of choices available to express positions concerning civic life is seen in the increasing use of Web presence in political campaigns. Conventional wisdom has it that campaigns do not waste money on that which does not give them an advantage and political campaigns of all types, but most notably at the national level, have come to rely on Web sites for numerous purposes (Davis, 1999). There has been an explosive growth in the use of the Internet as a political tool, affecting nearly every aspect of the campaign process. Corrado (2000) notes:

> Candidates are using new technology to inform voters of their candidacies, to share their policy views, to distribute schedules of events, to raise money, to recruit volunteers, to solicit voter opinions, and make available audio and video materials, including the ads they broadcast on television and radio. (p. 5)

Thus, the Internet has emerged as a qualitatively different venue for conveying campaign information, "one that indeed represented the birth of a new medium rather than simply a different strategy for using an existing one" (Corrado, 2000, p. 101). Although few now subscribe to the idyllic pictures painted either by early proponents of the Internet as an ideal forum for democratic participation (see, for example, Corrado & Firestone, 1996; Grossman, 1995) or the optimistic scenarios envisioned by more recent political figures such as former Clinton aide Dick Morris (1999), proof of the effectiveness of the Web in politics is the unmistakable upsurge in its use (Puopolo, 2001) and the confident predictions of its use in the future (Schneider & Foot, 2002).

In this chapter I use the dual reading approach to probe utterances in two sets of political Web pages/sites. These sites could hardly be more different in terms of their sophistication, reach, voice, and purpose. The first comes from the official candidate Web sites in the controversial 2000 U.S. presidential campaign (Dershowitz, 2001); I examine three versions of the campaign site for Republican candidate George W. Bush, and two versions of the site for his opponent Al Gore. The second set of data comes from a single activist site, "Swastika on the Lawn: A Year of Anti-Semitism in Massachusetts." After examining these pages/sites, I offer some general remarks about the study of Web pages/sites for propagating political/ideological messages.

ANALYTICAL FRAMEWORK

Although much of the analytical procedure described for EDMs in earlier chapters (see especially the section "Analytical Framework" in Chapter 3) remains the same as the method I will use for Web pages/sites, the differences in the elements of EDMs and Web pages/sites necessitate some variation in the precise ways they are analyzed. In the following, I first consider some limitations in current methods for studying Web presentations and then turn to a proposed variation in the dual reading method designed especially for these pages/sites. I then provide a brief overview of the two kinds of political Web sites to be explored in this study.

Limitations of Current Methods

Although there are many ways to analyze and classify the contents of some political Web sites (see, for example, Benoit & Benoit, 2000; D'Alessio, 2000; Kamarck, 1999; Puopolo, 2001; Schneider & Foot, 2002), few methods can be used across instances of Web pages/sites.[4] Although it is possible to analyze the components of pages (such as how to present text and images) according to standards established in other media (for example, graphic design in print, film, and so on), there has yet to be formulated an overall conceptual vocabulary of Web pages and sites that will permit observers to draw conclusions based on comparing them to each other.

A couple of obstacles have prevented us from coming up with a broadly applicable approach to categorizing elements of Web pages/sites. One is the sheer volume of possible permutations for page elements. The discursive space facing the designer of the new Web page is a free-form canvas where potentials for expression are, if not limitless, at least breathtakingly vast.[5] Moreover, options for expression are seldom limited by technical resources—anyone with Internet access can create a Web page and anyone who can create a page can create a site—but by characteristics more difficult to assess, such as creativity, visual presentation, artistry with written language, and so on. While this vast range of potential configurations benefits designers, it can play havoc with attempts to classify page/site elements from one instance to another.

Another problem is that, given the monologic assumptions involved in creating categories, any attempt to classify Web elements may be of questionable value. Even were one to come up with a category system for utterances on the Web and draw conclusions based on a large number of different page/site utterances, it would not be difficult to cite an utterance that had not been taken into account. Of course, this could be said of any utterance, but as our familiarity with other kinds of discourse has developed, we have come up with categories that at least offer the illusion that we can put different messages into the "same" category. Our time with the Internet as a widely used mode of communication has been too brief to permit us to draw these kinds of conclusions about Web sites.

Dual Reading Method

Given the difficulties just described, I propose an approach similar to the dual reading method for analyzing EDM threads (Chapter 3). Although EDMs and pages/sites comprise qualitatively quite different messages, they do prove accessible from both monological and dialogical perspectives. In other words, although there is not yet a widely used and thoroughly developed system to categorize elements of sites and pages (also a problem with EDMs, though less so, because there are fewer elements involved and many category systems to describe writing, the chief mode of EDM expression),[6] it is still worthwhile to construct a standard reading of a site or page that describes and discusses functionally defined features (such as number of elements, layout, size [for example, in kilobytes], unusual features, and so on). The dependence of the page/site presentation on a computer, through the mechanism of a server, makes available to the analyst a wealth of primarily quantitative data useful for making comparisons.

Likewise, as we have seen, Internet communication is infused with multiplicity of representation, so that another reading, the utterance reading, is needed to enable us to expand the range of possible interpretations and to explore the various ways the page/site utterance might be encountered by the numerous visitors who could potentially come across it. Given the nearly limitless potential for creative design in Web pages, the dual reading method also presents vast possibilities for utterance readings. My utterance reading for EDM threads (Chapter 3) concentrated on message text, demonstrating how composers of utterances could be seen to draw aspects of the world into the message to provide a heteroglossic "spin" on functional elements identified through the standard reading. The procedure is similar for Web pages/sites, except that the range of links to the world beyond can be seen as being much greater. Instead of making connections through (primarily) words, site designers use other modes of presentation to formulate variations on standard elements of site design.

Moreover, Web sites can be revised, leaving clues about their evolution over time. These clues are to be found in both standard and utterance readings; in the standard reading, we see indications of changing parameters imposed by the mechanics of computer-mediated communication (for example, color, text format, graphic images, and other elements defined by coding) as well as conventional forms of representation, whereas in the utterance reading, we see some of the infinite number of ways that these "same" representations may manifest in the consciousnesses of visitors to the page or site. Through application of both these perspectives, we can see how designers/maintainers respond to conditions in the world, modifying elements of the page/site to adjust to the world at large. In formal campaigns, these changes (seen primarily in the standard reading) are often tied to the changing political fortunes of the candidate they represent (dynamic sociohistorical conditions often more evident in the utterance reading). Likewise, in activist sites, site elements (shown in the standard reading) are frequently dictated by political situations the site is designed to respond to (more evident in the utterance reading). When we looked at EDMs, we saw the world in a post—looking at Web pages/sites, we can see even more of that world in a page.

Although the method is very similar for both types of data, the primary difference between dual reading for EDMs and for Web pages/sites lies in the kind of material that constitutes evidence. Obviously, EDMs are primarily, even entirely, made up of text; Web pages/sites, on the other hand, include both text and a great deal more. Web pages/sites are thus not only more difficult to perform the dual reading on, but one must be more creative in interpreting the results, since there are fewer templates to guide one in understanding them. With written text, one has thousands of years of commentary to draw on; with a very new medium such as Web pages/sites, there is little in the way of shared understanding about how to classify their elements, particularly since technological innovation means that these elements are constantly in flux. A rough analogy to the differences in examining EDMs and pages/sites would be the difference between interpreting an outstanding screenplay such as *Chinatown* and interpreting the film.

The dual reading method also provides some help with the difficulties in analyzing pages/sites mentioned earlier in this section (principally vast variability of page/site elements and their intercombinations that exceeds the categories of classification systems). The relentless and bewildering variety of page/site elements, as well as the infinite permutations among them, present no difficulties in dual reading. For one thing, the standard reading does not insist on a universally applicable monologic system of categories, but rather advances a provisional method to analyze utterance functionally in the awareness that many other possible fruitful approaches exist. Likewise, the utterance reading celebrates multiplicity and the contemplation of previously unrealized forms, thus permitting the analyst to see in multiple representations the material for a more accurate understanding of Web utterance. Nor are there in dual reading any problems with troublesome future representational forms that may elude monologic categories; both the standard and utterance readings begin with the assumption that the elements of Web utterance vary far too much (and can be expected to vary even more in the future) to permit a monologic classification scheme to be used across more than a very limited range of specific instances of Web utterance.

Analysis of Political Web Sites

To show how the dual reading method helps in analyzing utterances on political Web sites, I present detailed case studies of two very different kinds of sites. It is in this difference that we find evidence of the power of dual reading in understanding site utterances, as well as how it can be used to identify resources in the one kind of site that may prove useful in improving other kinds.

The first category is Web sites of candidates who run for elected political office. This kind of site is designed to mobilize and inspire those who already support the candidate, as well as to gain new supporters. Moreover, some of these sites are highly sophisticated and becoming progressively more so with each election. As the Internet "comes of age" as a tool of communication in formal political campaigns, candidates who survive primaries to be nominated by major political parties will also be those who have the greatest resources, financial and otherwise, to use in developing their Web presence.

The second kind of site is well represented enough in the array of Web sites (Warf & Grimes, 1997) to have established a type of its own: the social activist site. These sites typically are focused on more specific issues and are thus not generally intended to reach as wide an audience as sites for candidates for elections. Such sites also tend to be constructed and maintained on a shoestring budget, often through the good graces of educational or other institutions. Also, activist sites are often developed by the very people who want to get their message out, rather than highly trained teams of analysts and developers of the kind who work on candidate sites. Although in many ways these two types of Web utterance could hardly be more different, I will show through the dual reading method how both kinds of sites interweave civic discourse while expressing their unique political ideologies.

PRESIDENTIAL CANDIDATE WEB SITES

Though still a comparatively new medium of communication, the Internet has already proved a useful, though not perfect, tool for propagating political ideas, both for conventional political candidates (Bucy, D'Angelo, & Newhagen, 1999; Davis, 1999; Hansen & Benoit, 2001; Johnson, Braima, & Sothirajah, 1999; Klotz, 1998; Margolis & Resnick, 2000; Margolis, Resnick, & Tu, 1997; Novotny, 2002; Puopolo, 2001; Schneider & Foot, 2002; Tedesco, Miller, & Spiker, 1999) and activists (Bimber, 1998; Bonchek, 1997; Brown & Duguid, 2000; Bucy & Gregson, 2001; Castells, 1997; Jacques & Ratzan, 1997; Kollock & Smith, 1999; Servon, 2002; Sparks, 2001; Warf & Grimes, 1997). Puopolo (2001) offers this optimistic picture of potential benefits of political communication on the World Wide Web:

> For those who choose to use it, the Web offers reams of information and an extraordinary capacity to communicate with others and form online communities. It offers more accessible services, changes the contours of older media technologies, expands the capacity to present diverse viewpoints, and gives people and groups an opportunity to operate in a region or nation without regard to geographic boundaries. Indeed, if one posits that democracy depends upon an informed, committed, and connected electorate, the Web has the potential to alter the face of democracy. (p. 2030)

While this vision of the future of the Web as a place where alternative ideological views can be freely propagated is not shared by everyone (see, for example, Graham, 1999; Lessig, 1999; Margolis & Resnick, 2000; Warf & Grimes, 1997), Puopolo (2001) nevertheless neatly summarizes the advantages of the Internet as a tool for political communication. Schneider and Foot (2002) take a similar view, arguing that various features of the Web work together to provide information that structures political participation, since "citizens seek information as a first step of political action, and campaigns seek to persuade information seekers to become supporters" (p. 6).

Although the Internet, as a medium widely available only since the early 1990s, has not been in existence long enough for campaigns to formulate firm guidelines about best uses, its growth in political campaigns has been extraordinarily rapid. A brief but telling indicator of the Internet's looming importance in presidential campaigning occurred in 1996 when, at the end of a debate with Bill Clinton, Bob Dole gave the television audience the URL of his Web site and asked viewers to visit (Davis, 1999, p. 85). Hansen and Benoit (2001) report figures from the Pew Research Center that, as of January 2000, 54% of the U.S. population uses the Internet, as compared with only 14% in 1995. Even more significantly, similar surveys in 2000 by the Pew Research Center show that almost 25% of Americans "indicated they used the Internet to learn about a presidential candidate in the 2000 primary" (Hansen & Benoit, 2001, p. 2087).

One reason for the increased popularity of candidate Web sites is that they not only offer advantages to those who visit, but considerable value to the campaigns. This is particularly true when it comes to extensive, substantive information helpful in defining the candidate's views, but difficult to express through other media:

> Space on Web sites is virtually unlimited, compared with that of other message forms. The cost of adding an additional 10,000 or 100,000 words to an Internet site is minuscule compared with the costs of producing and airing more television or radio spots. (Hansen & Benoit, 2001, pp. 2093–2094)

A Web site offers more than simply advantages in housing large quantities of information; it is also fast and flexible in adapting to changing circumstances. Also, a Web site can be designed to simultaneously accommodate either the surfer with neither time nor inclination to delve into issues, or the enthusiast with an insatiable appetite for political minutiae. Sites can be bare bones or incorporate a wealth of features such as video, audio, photo galleries, and resources for the visitor to configure a personalized account. Although some campaign sites are sophisticated enough to satisfy the most Net-savvy visitor, visitors need not be drawn into issues to a very deep level. For example, the final versions of the Bush and Gore 2000 presidential campaign sites seem to have focused on voters with less time to spend gathering information. On the other hand, campaign sites do not have to sacrifice their capacity to store significant amounts of information for those who wish to take a more leisurely look at the candidate. Other campaigns use the Web site's impressive storage capabilities to provide an extraordinary amount of ancillary information about candidates (Schneider & Foot, 2002). The Web appears to offer both candidates and the electorate the best of all worlds.[7]

Data analyzed in this section (five sites from Bush and Gore) is taken from a larger database comprising the major pages of Web sites from ten Republican candidates for president in 2000 (Lamar Alexander, Gary Bauer, George W. Bush, Elizabeth Dole, Steve Forbes, Orrin Hatch, John Kasich, John McCain, and Dan Quayle) and from two Democrats (Bill Bradley and Al Gore).[8] The main pages (including the home page and pages linked directly from the home page) were recorded as separate pieces of information (for example, page background and graphics) in individual folders, permitting later recovery/reconstruction of most of each page from the database. Pages were recorded at approximately the beginning and middle of each month, starting (for most candidates) around July 15, 1999, and continuing through the month after the election in November 2000.

The only complete revision of the Gore site was retrieved on August 19, 2000, two days after the end of the Democratic National Convention. The first revision of the Bush site was retrieved on October 25, 1999, and the second on the day the second revision of the site was premiered, July 21, 2000. Rather than dwell on relatively less extensive changes of each version, which in most cases varied hardly at all from one sampling period to the next, I concentrate on comparing the major versions and particularly the all-important home page. The home page is not only the portal to the rest of the site, but sets the tone for both content and appearance of other site pages.

Analysis of the Web Sites of George W. Bush

Standard Reading of the Bush Sites
The Bush site begins conventionally, renders conventional elements in a somewhat more complex fashion in version 2, and turns radically different in version 3. Version 2 involves many elements customarily associated with sites for presidential candidates. Like version 1, it comprises conventional features, albeit in a more intricate way: standard layout (for example, banner logo at the top, navigation area on the left side, and so on); traditional red, white, and blue color scheme; prominently displayed news items; at least one relatively large logo and/or photo of the candidate; the usual types of secondary pages (for example, contributions, details about the candidate's family, a version of the site in Spanish); and so on. However, version 3 departs dramatically, not only from the previous versions of the Bush site, but from all other presidential candidate sites in the database. Version 3 does not even

resemble most candidate Web sites, but looks like a commercial site, both in terms of its design and what elements are included.

The Bush site starts tentatively and even amateurishly. According to fairly widely endorsed (hence, monologic) standards for designing pages in English (Horton, 2000; Lemay, Murphy, & Smith, 1996; Siegel, 1997), the home page design is poor, unbalanced (for example, the major portion of the page, that is, the white space below the main banner and to the right of the navigation menu, often has very little text display, so that the text looks overwhelmed by the red, white, and blue colors), and very conventionally laid out. Also, there are errors in presentation: for example, the graphics that provide the background for the navigation buttons on the left side (light blue stars on a dark blue background) display as discontinuous, because the text of each navigation button has been separately constructed with its own swatch of background; hence, the stars frequently look incomplete or broken (see Figure 1). Version 1's navigation area has fifteen major links to secondary pages.

Version 1's home page is very simply laid out. It lacks the sophistication of some political Web sites, which now commonly use systems for delivery of information, such as videos, sound recordings, photographs, pop-up windows, and so on. Clearly, at this point, the Bush team has not yet decided to avail itself of these mechanisms.[9] The version 1 home page has links only to pages that are primarily text, such as "fact sheets," speeches, or continuations of stories introduced briefly on the main page.

Version 1 leaves the visitor with an impression sometimes gotten from other candidate sites: the site exists because it is expected as part of a modern campaign, and not because it is integral. Also, at this time, the Bush campaign was concentrating on fund-raising, at which it proved enormously successful (Van Natta, 2000). This is explicitly acknowledged on several samples of version 1 through a linked page with an extensive list of contributors.

FIGURE 1
"Broken Stars" Background, Bush Site Version 1

By version 2, the team has learned more about Web presentation. The home page has a more professional, engaging look; in place of the sparse text area, which in version 1 was in plain black letters in the default font for the user's browser, we find a more substantive presentation, involving different color fonts, some of which are sans serif type (generally thought to give text a less dated, more modern look [Craig & Bevington, 1999]). Increased awareness of presentational possibilities is also revealed by the fact that the coding for the main page now specifies fonts to be used for display.[10]

Other site features suggest a more extensive awareness of page design possibilities. Unlike version 1, version 2 has forms,[11] repositories for information that, on this page, permit visitors to search the site, "personalize" it to conduct their own "e-campaigns", and sign up to receive an e-mail newsletter. This last feature became very important to many 2000 presidential candidates. Schneider and Foot (2002) report that of the eight presidential candidates whose campaign sites they analyzed, only two minor candidates, Gary Bauer and Alan Keyes, did not offer a newsletter. This feature of sites is likely to be even more important in future campaigns. The possibilities for simultaneous mailing promised by e-mail, especially as compared to more conventional mail systems, are extraordinary; indeed, e-mail seems ideal for candidates seeking mass distribution of information.

Version 2's design is also improved. Designers have jettisoned the broken stars background and replaced it with a shorter list of links (11 in all) set over a much shorter navigational area. Although the background graphics are (like the broken stars in version 1) individually designed as part of each button, and although they combine to form a more complex graphic (a faint waving flag in blue fading to red), they do so continuously, revealing the designers were paying a great deal more attention to this aspect of the presentation.

Version 2 also does away with a photograph of the candidate (displayed in version 1 in the upper left-hand corner of the page [see Figure 2]). By any standard, this photograph of Bush is odd. Although his portrait is face-on and tilted slightly upward, evidently intended to suggest vision and looking forward, Bush has a boyish appearance and looks a bit confused. Perhaps to counteract common negative perceptions of Bush (young, inexperienced, uncertain), version 2's designers substitute simply a logo, "George W. BUSH for President," along with an American flag (BUSH in addition to being in all caps is set in a much larger font). Another up-to-date feature is

FIGURE 2
Photo of Bush from Banner Logo, Bush Site Version 1

a pull-down menu displaying the states,[12] under this notice, "Get Active in Your State," at the bottom of the navigation buttons. This feature, too, will probably gain greater prominence in national campaigns, as it permits the campaign team to direct visitors to the important state (and local) organizations that remain in closest immediate touch with voters.

Finally, version 2 shows a hint of the Bush team's growing awareness of the possibilities of using multimedia. Positioned between the text box for "personalizing" one's own e-campaign (new to this version) and links to continuations of leads for news stories (largely unchanged from version 1), there is another new feature: a "Message of the Day," presented both as an audio file and as a text. Although this does not as yet approach the sophistication displayed later in the campaign by both Bush and Gore, this shows, along with forms, pull-down menus, and other up-to-date features, that version 2's designers have learned that Web pages provide candidates unique ways to communicate, even though at this stage they do not fully exploit this potential.

The two versions are both readily identifiable, in a monological way, as part of what one might call the "genre" of presidential candidate Web sites. Features defining this genre include conventional symbology, not only in visual symbols (stars and stripes; red, white, and blue color schemes; flags) but words and phrases (*prosperity*; *leadership*; *volunteer*; *get active*). Despite minor variations, the 11 candidates whose sites I analyzed all conformed to the "rules" of the genre, and those who did not initially (such as Elizabeth Dole) quickly changed their initial sites to be more traditional. On one level, this could be seen as a lack of creativity; on the other hand, it may reflect the fact that, like campaign speeches that "work" by invoking what audiences already believe, such conventional Web presentations succeed precisely because they are *not* surprising, different, or creative.

These points make version 3 of the Bush site all the more remarkable. By version 3 (see Figure 3) the Bush team has learned a great deal about Web presentations.[13] A dramatic indication is that, at the first presentation of the site the "Top Story" area announces a television commercial promoting the new Web site: "Austin, TX - Governor Bush Unveils New Campaign Web site. Also Releases First Campaign Commercial Solely Devoted To A Campaign Website." The increase in awareness of the Web's potential here is startling: not only is Bush making the introduction of his new Web site the top news story, he is emphasizing its status by granting it a place in the mixture of other media presentations. This public designation of a site as a key factor in the campaign was, at the time at least, unique in political history,[14] and arguably the release of this version is one of a few key events that mark the full entrance of Web politicking into the modern political arena.

More unusually, version 3 is different from all previous candidate sites of which I am aware. The most obvious difference is the background. Most candidate sites are on a white (occasionally pastel) background, highlighted by primarily red, white, and blue graphics and/or text. Version 3 of the Bush site is on a black background. Black backgrounds are generally used on sites that provide entertainment (music, pornography, sports) according to conventional wisdom because black provides a dramatic contrast, highlighting other colors, and making them seem more intense. Nothing even approaching this strategy occurred on any other 2000 presidential candidate Web site.

Furthermore, there is no prominent use of the red-white-blue motif, except in the photograph of Bush looking older, wiser, and more experienced than he did in the version 1 photo (compare Figure 5 on page 156 with Figure 2), placed in the upper left corner. Especially in light of the link between the Web and television in the "Top Story," this photo is quite revealing. It is a profile shot of Bush, turned just very slightly outward (the version 1 photo had him almost directly facing the camera), against a background of several "real" flags (that is, not graphics representing flags), overprinted with the text portion of the logo from version 2 ("George W. BUSH For President").

However, the most remarkable feature of this photo (also not replicated in any other site) is that it is scored across with parallel, very thin horizontal lines suggesting that the picture is being seen on television. This conflation of television and Internet confirms the

FIGURE 3
Bush Site Version 3 Layout

rapidly increasing media awareness of the Bush team; along with other indicators I will explore in the utterance reading, it reveals the team may be working according to a model similar to what advertisers call "integrated marketing communication" (Caywood, 1997). They seem to realize that the Internet is not simply another channel of marketing communication, but part of an overall strategy in which the various channels work with and contribute to one another. This sophisticated understanding of the potentials of Internet communication (anticipated in somewhat more elementary form in the first version of Al Gore's site) is a turning point in the use of the Internet as a tool of political communication.

Other noteworthy features about the site, reflecting its Internet-aware qualities, include the fact that on the main page there is no extended textual message at all; the longest string of text, ironically titled "Issues In Focus," comprises fewer than 30 words! Instead, one sees headlines linking to complete stories; this is a strategy that survives both revisions, though here there is even more compression, in that, with only one exception, stories do not begin on the home page, to be continued later, but are continued on another page from headlines on the home page. This may be yet another indication that the team is increasingly aware of typical audiences for Internet political messages. Designers are warned that the attention span of the typical Web surfer is remarkably short, and that the presentation of too much text can hinder efficient navigation of the site. It is significant that, in a time when social commentators lament the decrease in knowledge about and substantive discussion of the issues in political campaigns (Patterson, 1983; Postman, 1985; Putnam, 2000, p. 36), the most thorough revision of a presidential candidate Web site, by the campaign team whose candidate won, shows a shift from using the Web to propagate substantive information toward a more superficial treatment of the issues.[15]

Finally, there are significant changes in graphical presentations. Almost entirely gone are the conventional symbols of traditional politics (stars, stripes, and so on); in their place are perky, nicely designed graphics reflecting modern appearance and professional composition that are in line with the principle that navigational graphics should provide users visual information to help them navigate a site. There is, for example, a tall question mark for the section, "why george w?" (see Figure 4 on page 150); a microphone in front of a television set for the section, "live! On-Line" (see Figure 6 on page 157) (note that this is yet another conflation of the Internet and television channels); a cartoon of a raised right hand, fingers splayed outward, for the section, "Volunteer"; and so on. Nor is it that the "usual suspects," the text links to major pages, have vanished; however, unlike versions 1 and 2, where text navigational links by size and color tended to dominate even the major text area, in version 3 these sets of links (there are two, one running horizontally just above the "Bush on Television" main logo, and the other vertically just below it) are in very small type (as is most of the text, but not the graphics, on the home page). Against the black background, they are barely noticeable, being dominated by the larger and visually livelier graphic links.[16]

It is remarkable that the Bush team chose to make this radical departure comparatively late in what many observers had consistently predicted would be the closest presidential election in American history (Norris, 2001). Moreover, the way the Bush team shifted from the conventional Web site reflected, perhaps for the first time, that they saw a different audience for Internet utterance. While other campaign teams, such as those for Al Gore and Steve Forbes, much earlier made inroads in realizing the technical potentials of Web politicking, it was the Bush team who first acted on the belief that users of the Web are not like users of other media. For better or worse, the Bush conception of those who use Web sites for political information seems to be that they are impatient and not prone to explore deep or serious presentations; they are thought to be eager to see what the site has to offer, and then get on with their other Web pursuits. We will have to wait for confirmation, but I predict that the presidential campaigns in 2004 and beyond will be characterized by sites based on Bush version 3, and not on more traditional approaches.

The Bush campaign first embraced what the public expects of presidential candidate Web sites, only later to forcefully reject them. I find it useful to look at the Bush sites according to an entrepreneurial metaphor: a young, inexperienced firm with impressive start-up capital that learns quickly and responds promptly to changes in a volatile market.

While the standard reading explains some aspects of site development, there remain some intriguing questions about why specific utterances were framed as they were. First, it is puzzling why the most senior members of Bush's team (such as Dick and Lynne Cheney) are nearly absent from version 3, at least in its early presentations.[17] Management principles would suggest that people as experienced as the Cheneys should be given more prominence to bolster the stability of the campaign (as the Gore campaign does with Joseph Lieberman). Another puzzle is the dramatic increase in emphasis on the Spanish-language version of the site. While the standard reading might suggest spending more time and resources on voters whose support can be counted on (analogical to making safe investments), the Bush team prioritizes a comparatively minor portion of the electorate, one moreover that has traditionally overwhelmingly supported the Democratic Party (Weigel, 2002). Finally, the standard reading might suggest site revisers take a safer course, arguing against the risk of going far beyond what voters expect, especially as the campaign draws to a close, according to the well-known principle that it is foolish to risk one's resources with little expectation of reward. Yet the Bush team takes just such a risk with its groundbreaking redesign of the site in version 3.[18]

To account for these and other anomalies, we must go beyond the standard reading to dialogically open the problem space in analyzing the Bush sites. To do this, I adopt the same strategy used in analyzing EDMs in Chapter 3: I examine four specific features of utterance that work in various ways to import facets of the unpredictable and unclassified sociohistorical world into composition and perception of the Web site/page utterance. Through this process, I will show how the "real" Bush sites "spin off" centrifugally from the abstracted features on which we primarily concentrate when we view them according to the standard reading.

Utterance Reading of the Bush Sites

As I apply the tools of utterance reading to the Bush sites, it is clear their evolution is governed by a change in the way the Bush team sees the audience for political Web sites and indeed Web sites in general. In fact, of all the sites in my database, only the Bush sites reflect a consistently evolving awareness that the Internet is a form of communication qualitatively different from all others.[19] Performing the utterance reading on the Bush sites results in two chief indicators—conceptually interlinked—that offer clues to the thinking of the Bush team about the emergent Internet audience. First, the team sees the audience as progressively less cognitively complex; second, the team views the audience as progressively more familiar with the Internet as a unique form of communication.

It is perhaps unfortunate that as the Internet has grown in popularity the quality of discourse on it has decreased, at least according to monological standards of composition. Therefore, that the Bush team finds an approach that resonates with this decrement in quality would be, for many, a disappointment. But this is yet another manifestation of the struggle between monological and dialogical qualities in discourse. The Bush team defies the dictates of monologic views, devising a more appropriate way of addressing an audience that is impatient, reads and thinks less, and is more attuned to visual rather than verbal presentations. Lament as we might the decline in the quality of political discourse, the fact is that the Bush team felt the pulse of the Internet generation and responded to it, and I predict future campaigns will follow their lead.

To see the first indication of this decreasing concern for substance, we need only look at an instantiation of OTHER MEANING, invariably found on Web sites of presidential and other candidates: the link to the candidate's position on "the issues." As we have seen, OTHER MEAN-ING occurs when the composer of utterance brings in evidence and other support that invoke various meaning systems. Issue statements are a good example—a collection of issue statements invokes a whole universe of meaning systems that modify how the site visitor will view the candidate. Even though conventional wisdom has it that there is decreasing emphasis on depth exploration of issues, reference to "candidate positions" in all political communication, including Web pages/sites, is obligatory. One suspects this is not because visitors will read such utterances, but because a campaign, to be considered legitimate, must put into public discourse resources to help voters make an informed decision (a key element in "classic" democracy [see Chapter 1]).

Various instances of OTHER MEANING invoked in the three versions of the Bush site reveal an increasingly sophisticated understanding of an audience of Web surfers more oriented toward vision and sound, than to reading. In version 1, the "issues" link is expressed in conventional, even stuffy, terms: "The Message: Proposals and Policies." This link is in the fourth position in the left-hand navigational area, just below "The Committee," but far above "Tours and Events" and "W.tv," showing that these latter visual presentations, much more prominent by version 3, are here relegated to the lowest point in the navigational area.

Version 2 finds the language of this link truncated, to simply "Issues." It is positioned in the vertical middle of the left navigational area, just under "Speeches." The abbreviation of the link title, between versions 1 and 2, together with the overall streamlining of the navigational area, seems to indicate that the Bush team realizes they are dealing with an audience that may not respond favorably to standard, conventional representations.

By version 2, the team seems to have caught on to the fact that to hold the interest of many Internet visitors one must be brief and colorful and use navigational links to direct visitors to parts of the site they might wish to explore more thoroughly. In other words, the purpose of the "issues" link is to get issue-oriented visitors (a group probably far fewer in number than casual visitors) to a more information-rich, substantively researched area of the site. The team also seems aware that any attempt to persuade with the link itself (by using stuffy phrasing, serif type, and noticeable capital letters, as in version 1's "The Message") is fruitless and probably counterproductive. Thus, by modifying how the link to the systems of OTHER MEANING invoked by the candidate's stances on issues, the site designers in effect alter the way this OTHER MEANING will be incorporated into a perception of the site.

However, the most overt indication of the change in the Bush team's orientation toward OTHER MEANING, as it relates to issues, occurs in version 3. Like other navigation area links more prominently displayed in version 2, the "issues" link is part of a much smaller, less prominent left-side navigational area, in very small letters, and nearly invisible (at least with the color setting for followed links in my browser) against the black background. However, version 3 features in the more prominent middle area a new region, made even more noticeable by its display immediately beneath the colorful "Top Story" area. This new area is marked by a tall, stylishly designed, three-dimensional picture of a question mark, with the words, in maroon, noncapitalized, "why george w?" (see Figure 4). Beneath this eye-catching visual are three conventional text links: (1) "Reforming Social Security"; (2) "Lowering Personal Income Tax"; and (3) "Putting Education First."

This change in instantiation of OTHER MEANING is rich in implications. The first point is the severance between the traditional link to issues (present in some form on all three versions), and this new, simplified approach. The Bush team, even while clinging to one type of instantiation of OTHER MEANING (traditional presentation of candidate positions), hews to the new view that the best "platform," both for Internet audiences and the public generally, is to keep one's message brief, basic, focused on what is most important, and hopeful.

In all these examples of OTHER MEANING, I have referred to systems of meaning, with their associated concepts, vocabulary, and all the rest, upon which the composers of site utterances apparently have had to rely in constructing pages/sites in order to make their meaning clear. Due to the cultural understandings that are (to some extent) shared, the ways in which these designers invoke other systems of meaning will likely involve them in the coconstruction, along with site visitors, of the meaning of the page/site utterance. The importance of OTHER MEANING lies, first, in the idea that the way site composers and visitors invoke OTHER MEANING will always be different for each individual, and second, that the combining of these "individual" meanings for the utterance will result in unique shared meanings, in a way similar to the process of collaborative learning described by Vygotsky (1978; see also Chapter 2 in this volume). Thus, OTHER MEANING is never unitary but will vary according to the specific perceptual horizon of the person who refers to it, either in composing or

FIGURE 4
"why george w?" Graphic, Bush Site Version 3

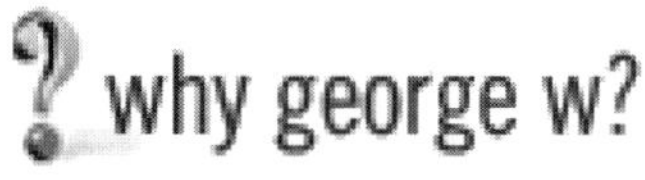

? why george w?

perceiving the Web utterance. As we have seen through the ways site designers change in their use of OTHER MEANING on the Bush sites, OTHER MEANING is the essence of dialogism: we learn alternative ways to view the site by contemplating this infinity of "other meanings" available to those who make and view the site, even as we realize it is impossible to achieve any closure in understanding them.

Additionally, in the prominent display of three basic issues, in just this way, there is an emphasis on activity. Notice the stress on action in the chosen verbs *reforming*, *lowering*, and "*putting* [first]." Although these are technically (and monologically) the transformation of verbs into nouns, they suggest that Bush, if elected, can be expected to do these things. I suspect this is as much "action" as they felt comfortable with; more active phrasing—*reform*, *lower*, *put*—might be considered too imperative. Again, the variation in the kind of OTHER MEANING referred to is striking; depending on the site, there is a marked difference in which systems are invoked. In version 1, OTHER MEANING is noticeably of the most conventional variety: links (usually only text) to documents, such as speeches or press releases. In version 3, however, this is changed to a link (through the active verbs) to meaning systems that suggest Bush is a "take-charge" leader and probably is so regardless of whether traditional supporting evidence reinforces his decisions or not.[20]

Finally, version 3 is noteworthy because of OTHER MEANING about issues it avoids instantiating. In politics, invoking the familiar through OTHER MEANING is much the preferred strategy, since conventional wisdom cautions against startling voters with too much difference; hence, one often finds, in political discourse, the absence of invocations of OTHER MEANING that one might expect. So prevalent is conventional thought and expression in politics that the omission of such references usually reflects a conscious choice on the part of the candidate's team. If candidates do not mention family, for example, this might mean, for one reason or another, they wish to have that aspect of their lives played down. Significantly, Bush site version 3 has no references to important but more controversial issues likely to alienate some visitors, such as abortion rights, immigration policy, gun ownership, and so on. Although, if one looks deeper into the site, one is able to discover the positions Bush takes on such issues, apart from an inconspicuous pull-down "issues" menu at the top right, there is no reference to these divisive matters on the main page. The three positions referred to in the "why george w?" section (the tone is affable, with no last name and exclusively small letters that suggest egalitarianism) are hardly controversial. Most people would want to "reform Social Security," "lower taxes," and "put education first." By offering visitors positive, upbeat "positions," the Bush team makes the candidate's positions more palatable to the less patient, visually oriented Web surfer. One instantly gets the gist of the candidate's views, in the space of a few seconds, by reading ten words: "Reform Social Security," "Lowering Personal Income Tax," and "Putting Education First."

Another way we know the Bush team is moving away from conventional verbal expression as a way of communicating to visitors is that as emphasis on written text decreases the emphasis on visual presentations increases. In the utterance reading, this tendency can be revealed by seeing references to visual presentations as forms of OTHER CONCEPTION. OTHER CONCEPTION, as previously, refers to how composers and perceivers of utterance view people, as opposed to OTHER MEANING, where one invokes ideas and meaning about subjects that are not explicitly person related.

A shift in emphasis, from text to visual, can also be seen in how prominently placed are links to video presentations on the various main pages. Development of technology for displaying video on Web sites offers a greater range of opportunities to present the candidate and his or her views. Television is vital to the modern presidential candidate and it becomes more so with each campaign (Pfau, Cho, & Chong, 2001).

The added opportunity to bring together video and other channels (that is, the Internet) offers unique advantages for the candidate's team to demonstrate OTHER CONCEPTION. First, it gives the site a modern appearance, permitting the candidate to promote an image of the visitor as interested in and willing to use the latest technology. Even if a visitor cannot view the presentation, due to limitations such as slow transfer speed through a dial-up connection, computer hardware (such as memory), or software, the fact that some can do so is a powerful way to persuade all visitors that the candidate is at the "cutting edge" of campaigning. This is a multiplex example of OTHER CONCEPTION in that numerous ideas about potential visitors are intertwined by the composers in the apparent expectation that the site will interest a range of people who vary widely in technological sophistication, as well other characteristics already mentioned.

Second, the candidate can present political advertisements not available in the visitor's television coverage area. Political advertisements, though formulated for a national campaign, are often precisely targeted toward specific geographical areas. Hence, a given advertisement might be seen by only a comparatively small portion of the electorate. With video on a Web page, anyone with access to the site and requisite computer capability can view any advertisement the campaign team wishes to present. Here too OTHER CONCEPTION is involved in various ways. Visitors are apparently seen by site designers across a spectrum of technological sophistication, varying from primitive to advanced, as well as unlikely to be surprised to see a television commercial on a Web site.

It is not until version 3 that video presentations become prominent on the Bush site. In version 1, the link to video presentations—labeled "W.tv"—is 9th in a list of 15 in the left-side navigational area. Considering version 1's staid tone, this designation is rather creative. In a remarkably brief use of symbols, "W.tv" suggests several points about the team's OTHER CONCEPTION of the visitor. First, it doubtless refers to MTV, once and perhaps still a widely known symbol of youth market appeal. Second, "W" suggests that the video presentations have a particular consonance with the Web. Finally, of course, "W" is widely known as George Bush's middle initial (one suspects far better known than the middle name [Walker] for which it stands). OTHER CONCEPTION here manifests itself through invocation of what is assumed to be a widely shared popular cultural meaning: the people who view the site seem to be assumed familiar with the initial "W" and what it means with respect to the candidate. The "W" device thus represents a concise summary of cultural assumptions apparently ascribed to a significant number of individuals (a multiplex instance of OTHER CONCEPTION) who might visit the site. Despite the novelty of the formulation, however, nothing on version 1's main page denotes "W.tv" as a link to anything remarkable.

Version 2's home page has no references to video presentations, either in the navigation menu or in the main page area (to the right of the navigation area) where most of the page's information is displayed. It is not that version 2 is devoid of video presentations; for example, there is one per page, on pages linked by "George & Laura Bush," "En Español," "On the Road," and "Speeches." However, these scattered references seem more an afterthought to elaborate themes on specific pages than part of an overall strategy to incorporate visual presentations into the design of the site.

Even as the team develops the view that Internet audiences respond less to written messages, it sees the same public as more likely to know the rudiments of communicating via the Internet. One way to see this OTHER CONCEPTION is in the increasing number of enhancements, distinctive to Web sites, appearing on each successive version.

Version 1 has very few such enhancements. On the main page, with the exception of the "W.tv" link (to a page that in fact has links to six video and two audio files), little on the main page shows that the site has advanced beyond what Siegel (1997) calls a "second-generation" site, that is, basically a text site with some illustrations and graphic buttons. On the edition of version 1 used for this analysis (retrieved September 15, 1999), there are also two text-only links to documents representing Bush's stance on education—these can be delivered in a PDF (portable document format).[21] Apart from these minor exceptions, nothing on the main page suggests the Bush team is aware of the potential for Web pages/sites to present political communication in ways specific to the medium, even though at the time the site was composed, these features had been in wide use for many years.

By version 2 things have changed considerably. In addition to text links, one finds a pull-down menu, listing all the states, under the heading, "Get Active in Your State." Choosing one of the menu items directs an inquiry to that state's (or another local) Republican Party organization. As the dialogical perspective tells us, imagining the exact qualities of the individual who will be perceiving one's utterance is impossible, since they could conceivably be anyone; hence, site composition involves imagining who might be looking at one's site, and it is to the elements of the page or site involved in its construction that we must look for clues as to what sort of OTHER CONCEPTION is involved. Considering such factors reveals the Bush team seems to have changed its ideas about visitor familiarity with Web technology between version 1, where they seemed to avoid technological enhancements, and version 2, where there is almost a surfeit of them.

Version 2 also uses CGI (common gateway interface) scripts, that is, code on the server to gather information and assemble it for delivery to some other location.[22] Version 2 uses such scripts to obtain subscriptions to an e-mail newsletter. This also represents a change in OTHER CONCEPTION, showing the campaign has altered its view of the audience and what it knows and is likely to expect. Subscribing to the e-mail newsletter involves having the visitor fill in her or his name and contact information. Thus, designers (perhaps unconsciously) assume certain things about their audience, including that they know what it means to receive e-mail on a regular basis; that subscription involves entering information about oneself; that unrestrained provision of personal information over the Internet is not a good idea (Garfinkel, 2001), so the site needs to have a "privacy policy"; and so on. There is none of this in version 1, whereas by version 2, these elements of common Internet transactions are part of an array of other enhancements, all of which the team assumes visitors will be able to deal with.

These trends reach their peak in version 3, where the home page has all the enhancements of version 2, as well as a popup window, "This Week's Action Items," with four buttons: "Nationwide Literature Drop-off," "Send a Letter to Your Editor," "Today's Trivia Contest," and of course the inevitable "Donate." Not only does this represent the team's greater awareness of Web capabilities, it is a risky move: many Web users find pop-up windows annoying and indeed use software to suppress them. The fact that the Bush team uses this technique reveals that they are becoming more certain of their OTHER CONCEPTION. That they would combine this action with so many other departures from the norm for political Web sites indicates that they think they can, in a very close election race, accurately predict what visitors are likely to do.

Finally, on a more subtle level, a remarkable conflation of symbols in version 3 suggests the team's deeper view of the Internet audience. This insight is most accessible when one thinks of the symbols as EFFORT AT SHARING. This EFFORT AT SHARING is complex, involving the tying together of references to what, monologically conceived, are discrete channels of communication. The team reaches the conclusion that Internet communication is best conceived, not as a separate channel, but as part of an array of channels that includes print, radio, but, most importantly, television. The Bush team merges references to channels of communication, in overt and covert ways, and then presents these conflations to the visitor to suggest that Internet communication is one aspect of a new media megachannel that may come to characterize future political communication. Both the idea itself and the ways in which it is executed are revolutionary and, I argue, destined to have far wider impact on presidential campaign Web sites.

An important indicator of this process is the way multimedia is treated in the three versions. In version 1, we have already looked at the "W.tv" designation; however, apart from its creative combination of symbols, the link to "W.tv" is not prominent, near the bottom of the navigation area. Although "W.tv" does link to a page that, by version 1's modest standards, is not uninteresting (two audio and six video presentations), the idea of site visitors as amenable to EFFORT AT SHARING through conflation of channels remains nascent. Like much else about version 1, information about newer channels is presented conventionally, and while the notion of merging Internet and other channels is vaguely suggested, it is not actualized.

In version 2, indications of the conflation are even more eclipsed, since there is no reference to video presentations on the home page, only scattered theme-specific videos on certain pages. Indeed, the team seems largely to have positioned video presentations as an afterthought to their main purpose—even the provocative "W.tv" has vanished.

However, in version 3, we find a full-fledged conflation of video and Web communication. This is indicated in many ways; I will mention two. First, the most prominent graphic in version 3 is the large profile photograph of the candidate in the upper left-hand corner (see Figure 5). A highly interesting feature of this rendering is that, as noted previously, it is scored through with faint horizontal lines, suggesting the image has been taken from television. This appearance, obviously carefully planned, suggests the immediacy that many associate with television campaigning.

A second clue indicating intention to bring together images of television and Web presentations is in the main area (white background) with a graphic of a microphone, together with a television screen (of the more modern, large-screen type), with the words, "live! OnLine" (see Figure 6). Beneath these graphic indicators is a text message: "George P. Bush July 20 @ 12:30 pm" and the text link "LISTEN." George P. Bush is the son of Florida governor Jeb Bush and his Mexican wife, Columba, widely acknowledged as a very attractive young man, and chosen by *People En Español* magazine as number 4 of America's 100 most eligible bachelors (Ballestero, 2000). Note also that instead of the word *at*, there is the symbol "@," a common feature in Internet addresses.

These indicators combine for a highly interesting array reflecting EFFORT AT SHARING. Not only are the channels combined to form a new, unique view of communication (unique, that is, to presidential campaign Web sites), the effort seems directed toward modifying the

FIGURE 5
Main Logo, Bush Site Version 3

visitor's worldview. Version 3 presents the conflation as part of an overall strategy seemingly designed to involve the visitor in a new experience with presidential candidate Web sites. This is perhaps the epitome of EFFORT AT SHARING, which aims not only at introducing what seem to be disparate worldviews to each other, but at modifying each "separate" worldview, based on what is discovered through contact with these other systems of thought.

In addition to unique features in version 3, we also see certain features shared by nearly all other presidential candidate sites nevertheless receive idiosyncratic treatment, revealed through the utterance reading. From the many examples of this process, in the following I discuss three: (1) providing a Spanish-language version of the site; (2) competing for contributions; and (3) providing ways for visitors to personalize the site.

One specific system of OTHER MEANING that has become nearly de rigeur for candidate Web sites is the version of the site in Spanish. To invoke Spanish language and associated cultural meanings is to import a vast alternative worldview, presumably (according to the monologic perspective) a consistent, complete system of OTHER MEANING. In gubernatorial contests in Texas ("Bush Ads," 1998), and to a lesser extent in the race for president, Bush depended heavily on the Latino vote, achieving a 35% share, far higher than any other Republican candidate (Weigel, 2002). Despite this connection between Bush and Spanish-speaking voters, however, and despite the

FIGURE 6
"Microphone and Television" Graphic, Bush Site Version 3

live! OnLine

fact that a Spanish-language version is part of many sites, there is a difference among the three versions of the Bush site with respect to how prominent the link to the Spanish-language version is.

In version 1, the link is next to the bottom of 15 links in the poorly designed left-hand navigation area. In fact, since the bottom link is "Home," its usual position on Web sites, the placement of the link "En Español" seems almost an afterthought, and like much of the rest of version 1, carelessly executed.

In version 2, the link's placement is dramatically altered, moving to the next-to-top position, just under the "George & Laura Bush" link. The change could hardly be more overt. The move in vertical placement (which is important in attracting visual attention within a specific spatial area) is, literally, from bottom to top.

In version 3, "En Español" (in Spanish) is removed entirely from the navigation links (again, this area's links are much tinier and less noticeable). Instead, the graphic link is now in the highly visible white area, more noticeable because of its contrast with the overall black background. The text description of the link has also changed to "¿HABLA ESPAÑOL?" (Do you speak Spanish?). The link is also more prominent visually, with a nicely designed button (see Figure 7) and grouped at the center of the white area following only two other links ("Volunteer" and "Contribute").

A standard reading of this home page might conclude that the change in emphasis on these links simply reflects an awareness that Spanish-speaking voters are increasingly important in national elections, which by any measure they certainly are (Len-Rios, 2002). Moreover, among increasingly influential ethnic voting blocs in America, Latino voters are probably the one with the most readily identifiable and widely spoken language.

However, according to the monological standard reading, it would also be assumed that the Spanish-language page link serves one or a few functions regardless of the Web site it is on. According

FIGURE 7
"¿Habla Español?" Button, Bush Site Version 3

to the utterance reading, though, we can examine various versions of the site, and consider alternative functions that the "same" link serves. On the Bush site, then, it is not simply that the "En Español" link presents different appearances in the three versions; the link changes with respect to how it is illustrated (that is, text versus graphic) and how prominently it is placed. Such variations in utterance invoke different systems of OTHER MEANING, doubtless reflecting the importance to candidates in general, as well as to this candidate in particular, of the Latino voter, whose changing role in elections in turn reflects alterations in the makeup of civic society. Because site design is such a deliberate act of utterance construction, considerable thought and planning must have gone into the redesign and resituating of the link.

One final element indicating an OTHER MEANING shift has to do with the change in phrasing, from "En Español" to "¿Habla Español?" Here the alteration concerns a change in the activity suggested by the phrase. "En Español" is what we might call conventional "link language," that is, it identifies a different location with the intent that the visitor go to that location ("follow the link")—it is more like a street sign. "¿Habla Español?" is a question, suggesting a more personal interaction with the visitor—it is more like directions you get from asking how to get to a location from a living person. Thus, this reformulation is very much in line with the tone of the radical revision of the site genre seen repeatedly in version 3. Gone are traditional conceptions of the link, in favor of a more engaged, active, and prominent version of what was once considered a "standard" link on most candidate Web sites. This subtle yet powerfully significant alteration may signal a change in the Bush team's desire to engage the Latino voter directly—"speaking" the language, as opposed to simply using it ("En Español")—and thereby indicating a shift in the meaning system invoked, deepening the level of cultural meanings accessed, from the convention "En Español" (which appears on many political sites) to the more personal "¿Habla Español?" (the change in the design of the button, the more prominent placement of it, and the addition of genuine punctuation, may all be additional indications of this).

Another standard feature of candidate sites given idiosyncratic treatment is the appeal for contributions. As everyone knows, political campaigns run on money, and generally speaking the more well-funded a candidate is, the greater that candidate's chances of success.[23] In some ways, the Internet has proved to be an enormous boon in political fund-raising, tapping a source of individual, as compared to group, contributions. Since there is competition for the financial resources of the Web visitor, the way appeals are phrased and displayed reveals a great deal about the campaign's conception of its audience, despite the fact that nearly all Web sites provide for the visitor to make contributions to the campaign.

In the utterance reading, this characteristic of Web sites came into focus for me through applying the idea of CONTESTING OWNERSHIP. The targets for contesting contributions are, at least on the Internet, not primarily large monied interests, such as corporations or political action committees, but individual contributors. The competition for money from individuals is intense, and has worked (and will continue to work) to drive important technological enhancements to political Web sites. An example is the pop-up contribution window that comes into view when the visitor accesses the main page.

This evolution of solicitation techniques on the Bush site appears to be affected primarily by two forces. First, the Bush team follows a steep learning curve, accelerating through the three versions through understanding and using more advanced possibilities of Web pages/sites. Second, there is an accelerating demand for funds, in general, by all candidates, as the campaign advances inexorably toward Election Day.

On version 1, the appeal for contributions is like other references on the home page. The link is located in the unremarkable left-side navigational area, 11th of a list of 15. On the home page is a lead story stating that the Bush campaign has been the first to disclose its contributions. However, this is portrayed as a news item and, unless one assumes some tortuous logic by which the lead story could be considered an enticement to contribute, has nothing to do with a direct appeal for money.

In version 2, the link in the left navigation area to the "Contribute" page occupies roughly the same relative position as in version 1, 8th of a list of 11 links. Although this does not indicate a higher relative priority for the item, because the navigational area has been re-designed, simplified, and streamlined, the "contribute" link, along with all other links in that area, stands out more. This effect is heightened because the background graphic for the navigation area, a stylized waving flag, changes from deep blue through a brief combination of red and blue, to a deep red—the "Contribute" link is positioned at the end of the blue area, just before it changes to red, and thus the eye is naturally drawn to it. Still, even following the link leads one to an extraordinarily subdued "Contribute" page; there is a picture of a younger George Bush (with almost no gray hair) and his wife, Laura, and the message at the top reads "Will you contribute to help me win the White House?" followed by a fairly brief text message explaining the status and history of the campaign, and beneath that, two more text links, "Credit Card Contributions" and "Check Contributions." All in all, the approach taken by the Bush team in version 2 can hardly be characterized as a hard sell of the need for financial support.

The more direct approach is reserved for version 3, where the home page has no fewer than three separate appeals for contributions. Indeed, the first appeal is the first thing one reads on the page: a horizontally arranged menu bar tops the "television" picture of Bush (see Figure 5) and the leftmost item on this menu bar is "CONTRIBUTE TO GwB." (It is interesting how the designers, when they must use capital letters to designate a link, emphasize the middle initial by making it lowercase.) Then, in the middle, white-background text area, a "DONATE" button is placed between two other buttons ("VOLUNTEER" and "REGISTER TO VOTE") vying for visual attention in nearly the exact center of the area. Finally, a replica of this same button is placed on the pop-up window, "Action Items," where it is emphasized by its placement *separate from* three other buttons arranged horizontally ("Nationwide Literature Drop-off," "Send a Letter to Your Editor," and "Today's Trivia Contest").

Although one obvious factor driving this increase in intensity in appeal for money is that the campaign is entering its final stages, and the candidate needs increasingly more funds, I believe this specific form of multiple appeals is yet another indication of the Bush team's understanding of Web page design and how it can be used in campaigns. The team seems more aware that such qualities as brevity, color, and repetition are key elements in how visitors attend to and understand utterances on the site. Furthermore, with multiple appeals, there are more possibilities for success. That which is contested here is the almost inevitable claim to the limited resources of the visitors to the site, a complex notion that involves not simply money, but commitment to the candidate's positions on issues and ideology. In essence, the increasing competition for political contributions via the Web is a battle, a CONTESTING OWNERSHIP, for voters' hearts and minds, with the manifestation of voter allegiance in quantifiable terms the amount of money candidates can raise.

EFFORT AT SHARING grants entry to a third example of the Bush team's elaboration of a common candidate site feature: the "personalizing" of the Web site to reflect the specific preferences of the individual visitor. In version 1 there was little capability on the main page or elsewhere to configure the site's resources to individual needs. The only products accessible from the main page are two PDF documents, which cannot usually be modified by the user.[24] Version 2 has a number of user-configurable features. I have already noted the pull-down menu under "Get Active in Your State" and spaces to enter information to subscribe to the newsletter. Version 2 also features a search engine (something version 1 did not have, making it nearly unique among nationally positioned sites), as well as a relatively small text link in the main area, "Personalize!", under the heading "Create Your Personal E-Campaign."

By version 3, there is a thoroughgoing effort to enlist the visitor in the campaign. The "Personalize" area has been renamed "myGEORGEW" (note the implication that the voter "shares" by "possessing" the candidate). This area is greatly simplified, the visitor being directed merely to enter his or her e-mail address "to get started." Likewise, space to sign up for the newsletter is more prominently placed in white letters (and here designers reap the benefits of the black background) and requiring, again, only that the visitor enter an e-mail address. Finally, version 3 has at least two direct attempts to immediately enlist the participation of the visitor. First, the pop-up window lists, not unlike a personal digital assistant, the visitor's "action items." Second, there is also a section at the bottom, "Opinion Matters," asking visitors to vote on what they think is the most important issue in the election (education, Social Security, moral values, or health care), as well as permitting visitors to look at past poll results. These moves toward personalization epitomize EFFORT AT SHARING because they, individually and together, aim at creating a more "one-to-one" relationship with the candidate, perhaps to counteract the feeling of depersonalization the Web sometimes creates in site visitors.

At the same time, much of the above can be seen as CONTESTING OWNERSHIP because site designers, along with all other political professionals, need to counteract the increasing lethargy of the American voting public. Due to a variety of factors (Putnam, 2000), increasingly American voters seem not to care much about politics. The job of the campaign team, particularly as Election Day approaches, is to break through apathy and motivate people to go out and vote for their candidate. This presents a unique and highly difficult challenge. The team must find some way to ascertain the source of voter apathy, contest that, then find the key to motivation, thus contesting the natural inertia of voters, and finally, confront the view of the voter that "my vote doesn't count." At each stage, differing worldviews about participation in the political process must be assessed, breached, and reformulated by means of multiple acts of CONTESTING OWNERSHIP.

Analysis of the Web Sites of Albert Gore

Standard Reading of the Gore Sites
In contrast to the Bush presentations, the Gore sites show a less consistent pattern of alteration. The Gore team performed a complete revision of its site once, a version I picked up in the sample for August 19, 2000. Although the Bush team's final revision (version 3) showed a radical departure from the category of presidential candidate sites, the Gore team's final version (version 2) in some ways went in the opposite direction. From a somewhat creative and distinctive site in version 1,[25] perhaps reflecting Gore's often-stated (and lampooned) interest in the Internet, the team moved to a more conventional site. One is tempted to attribute the shift in the approaches of the two teams to the conventional wisdom that as the election draws near the candidate, who can count on the support of her or his base, should reach out to those not in that base (for Bush, the more adventurous voter; for Gore, the more conservative).

I label version 1 "somewhat creative" because, although the design is unusual, it has many conventional features associated with presidential candidate Web sites. For this analysis, I looked at the site retrieved September 16, 1999, to match as closely as possible the period for the retrieved version 1 Bush site (September 15). Portions of the site have a rather dark bluish purple background and unlike most candidate sites in which content fills the entire browser screen (as with Bush versions 1 and 3), Gore version 1 has its content centered in an area comprising a little over 500 pixels of horizontal space in the visual field.[26] The colors in this centered area are primarily the traditional red, white, and blue, though with some variations. For example, the color of the background depends on the user's browser preferences. At the top (in a large version) and bottom (in a much smaller version) is the well-known Gore "shooting star" logo: this is an animated GIF (graphic interchange format) showing, against a dark blue rectangular background, the white letters "Gore 2000," together with a red upward curling ellipsis terminating in a white star.[27] The effect of the animation is that the star appears to follow the curve of the ellipse upward, terminating at a point just over the last letter of Gore's name. The lettering of the main text area is black with large headings in red, against a white background. To this extent, the site follows the more traditional color scheme favored by many candidate sites.

However, version 1 offers some variations in color. Predominating is a region of the main text area, extending from the right over about one-third of the horizontal space (this is positioned, rather dramatically, next to the other text area, in white, extending over the remaining two-thirds of the visual field). The color is in "color-safe" HTML terms "#66 66 CC," denoted verbally in Netscape Composer as "violet duskish," a bit darker than lavender.[28] This is an interesting color that departs somewhat from the standard candidate site color scheme, though not entirely, since violet is after all a combination of red and blue, and it is positioned side by side with white.

The top navigation menu (of purplish background as well) also departs from the norm, being positioned above the shooting star logo, and displayed in two rows of five graphic buttons each. The conventional placement, seen to a greater or lesser extent in all three Bush sites, is to show at least one version of the menu with the links running vertically down the left side of the page. The designers of Gore site version 1 seemingly wished to avoid this common practice, and indeed to generally play down emphasis on links in the main area of the page: in addition to the top menu, there is also an all-text link menu at the bottom of the page (a standard practice in Web design, and present on all Bush and Gore sites).

Unlike the Bush team, Gore's staff hits the ground running when it comes to exploiting the Web medium, with several Web-specific enhancements on version 1. The first is the animated shooting star GIF. Version 1 also has links to video archives (although Bush version 1 has the link to "W.tv," there is no mention, on the main page, of which specific clips are available, whereas the Gore main page mentions four video clips by name; a link to RealAudio's page so the visitor can get a copy of RealPlayer;[29] and a gallery of photographs). One other feature of the Gore site has since become part of political legend: a campaign message in the HTML code for the main page. This message reads, in part: "Thanks for checking out our source code! . . . The fact that you are peeking behind the scenes at our site means you can make an important difference to this Internet effort."

Compared to the Bush sites, version 1 of the Gore site is densely packed with information. The lettering is small and the HTML code specifies it be rendered in sans serif type (for example, Verdana, Arial), so it seems even smaller. This is odd, given that the width of the page on many screens would be wider than the 500 or so pixels allotted for display of the information.[30] In other words, much of the space is wasted and the information in the main text area is sometimes difficult to read. Nevertheless, this way of displaying elements of the page is very different from conventional layout practices.

With respect to areas of interest, version 1 of the Gore site is similar to the Bush sites versions 1 and 2. The top menu's items are, in order, (top row) "The Agenda," "The Gore Family," "Tipper Gore," "Briefing Room," "Town Hall"; (bottom row) "En Español," "Get Involved," "Register to Vote," "Contribute," and "Speeches." Although the same basic subjects as Bush site version 1 are covered, on the Gore site they are phrased in more interesting and creative ways (not "The Message," but "The Agenda"; not "News Room," but "Briefing Room" and "Town Hall"). Moreover, the home page links to locations describing two separate aspects of Gore's family; in addition to the link to "The Gore Family," there is a separate link to "Tipper Gore." In contrast, on Bush site version 1, there is a single link, "Meet Governor George W. Bush," and another, "Meet First Lady Laura Bush"; the notorious Bush daughters (Thomas et al., 2001) are never pictured on any version of the Bush site, though they are mentioned perfunctorily as part of Bush's résumé on the "Meet Governor George W. Bush" page. On Gore site version 1, all members of the family (Al, Tipper, and their five children) are pictured on the page "The Gore Family."

Version 2 of the Gore site is, in its own way, nearly as radical a departure from its earlier version as Bush site version 3 is from its predecessors. Despite this fact, Gore site version 2 is actually more a reversion to conventional modes of expression, certainly more so than the last revision of the Bush site. Gore version 2 is extremely densely packed with information, so much so that here it will be possible to describe only a few of its more prominent features.

The focus of the Gore team's revision is immediately apparent: the event said by some to have rejuvenated Gore's campaign, the naming of Senator Joseph Lieberman as his vice presidential running mate. Version 2's main page (see Figure 8) is laid out in three basic sections, on a white background.[31] At the top of the area is a large photo of Gore and Lieberman, each with one arm around the other, and each man's remaining arm raised high. In large blue letters, over the two men, are the words, "YOU AIN'T SEEN NOTHING YET" (see Figure 9).

Even more noticeable, just under the Gore/Lieberman logo (a variation on the shooting star logo, except this is not animated and the star is red, not white), are four small equal-sized photographs under the legend "GET TO KNOW US": the photos are of Gore; Gore's wife, Tipper; Lieberman; and Lieberman's wife, Hadassah. Under the photos are the words (in red), "Meet the Gores and the Liebermans" and under that (in blue), "Al and Tipper, Joe and Hadassah." This display, nearly at the visually dominant top left corner of the page, is extraordinary in its contrast with Bush site version 3 (put online after the selection of the vice presidential candidate), where images of Bush predominate and there are hardly any pictures of his running mate Dick Cheney, certainly not on the main page.

The total width of version 2's main page is about 1,280 pixels (more than twice the width of version 1); the left area measures about 182 pixels in width, the right area about the same (196 pixels). This means that the middle area dominates the horizontal visual field, occupying about 902 pixels or about 70% of the area. Nevertheless, because of the density of graphics (according to the "Page Info" feature of Netscape, this main page contains an astonishing 88 graphic images[32]) and written information, this center area does not seem very large; indeed, it appears dwarfed by the navigational links on both sides, as well as the large photograph of Gore and Lieberman that dominates the horizontal visual field at the top of the middle section.

Earlier I noted the increased number and variety of Web-specific technical enhancements on Bush site version 3. However, compared to Gore site version 2, the Bush team's effort is paltry. A partial list of the more advanced features of the revised Gore site includes (1) two pull-down menus to direct visitors to more specialized Internet locations (the first, as on two versions of the Bush sites, routes visitors to the appropriate state, while the second directs them to locations for

FIGURE 8
Gore Site Version 2 Layout

FIGURE 9
Gore/Lieberman Photograph, Gore Site Version 2

specific groups, such as ethnic groups [for example, Latinos], groups based on gender roles [for example, women and gays/lesbians], veterans, and so on); (2) a "Send This Page" link; (3) a link to optimize instant message services to receive updates; (4) a "debate duck" clock, a constantly updating digital clock recording how long the Gore campaign says George Bush has been avoiding ("ducking") a debate with Gore; (5) numerous links, not only to video clips, but to versions of these, based on various user platforms and connection speeds; (6) a live feed from Gore's headquarters ("NashvilleCam"); and (7) "Campaign to Go," a link that provides campaign updates for PDAs (Personal Digital Assistants).

This range of use of Web page capabilities is not merely breathtaking, but, because of the small space in which these links (with numerous others) are confined, overwhelming. Were many of these links rendered simply as text links, it might be easier to manage the information visually; as it is, however, nearly every text link is accompanied by its own small graphic button, and though these are quite attractive and creatively designed, their sheer number does not allow the visitor leisure to appreciate their appearance.

These are the basic elements of the two versions of the Gore site main pages. Given the large amount of information, particularly on version 2, I have only been able to mention a few features in the Gore site revision. I will refer to more of these, as well as selected features on subsidiary pages, as I discuss particular aspects of the sites in the utterance reading.

The conventional, monologically inclined, reading of the Gore sites indicates the Gore team seems content with its acknowledged superiority in information technology. While a conventional indicator of this is that the Gore site changed only once, the reason the Bush site changed more than once was because it had to, the first version having been less than a success. On the other hand, the reversion of Gore site version 2 to the kind of design users have come to associate with presidential candidate Web sites shows that their advantage in knowledge of technology may have overridden their sense of design.

One must also take note of the relation between the site utterances and the discontinuity in sociohistorical climate experienced by the Gore campaign. Whereas the Bush team followed a clear path in developing their site, the revision of Gore site version 2 seems motivated by a change in the Gore campaign's direction. With the selection of Joe Lieberman as his running mate (a choice that surprised some), Gore may have found it necessary once again—using a word that has become identified with him—to "reinvent" his candidacy (Turque, 1999). However, unlike the thorough revision of the Bush site, which seemed driven by the campaign team's newly acquired awareness of the idiosyncratic nature of the Internet audience, the Gore team's revision seems more an accumulation of what it saw as its advantages (more Web-specific bells and whistles, more inclusion and egalitarianism, and so on), complicated by a perhaps overly abrupt change in the campaign's trajectory, leading to a situation in which the Gore team never quite reconciles the former with the new approach.

At the same time, designers of the Gore site (both versions) maintain high standards for keeping focused on substantive issues. Although the Bush team increasingly phases out discussion of, and material on, substantive issues, in truth they were never truly focused on these from the outset and become less so with each revision. Gore version 2 concentrates a little less on substantive discussion, certainly less than the considerable attention it received in version 1.

As with the Bush sites, however, standard reading of the Gore sites takes us only to a certain point. For example, the standard account of the Gore sites' development does not immediately and obviously present a rationale for the extraordinarily dense presentation in version 2. Even a neophyte Web designer is constantly reminded not to overload a page with information and the Gore team, based on the quality of its presentation of version 1, certainly were not neophytes. Another issue left largely unanswered by the standard reading is why the Gore team would so strongly emphasize the presence of Joe Lieberman on the ticket, even to the extent of using symbology to suggest equality among the candidate, his running mate, and their wives. Certainly, as a government official who worked in the shadow of President Clinton for eight years, Gore must have been sensitive to the need of defining himself as a leader. Finally, the standard reading does not on first inspection reveal why the Gore team undertook a reinvention of its Web campaign image in the closing phases of the election, and indeed even forecast further changes by calling attention to the slogan YOU AIN'T SEEN NOTHING YET (note the word *YET*). Given the closeness of the race, conventional political wisdom would argue against a thoroughgoing reformulation; yet the Gore team's exuberance at its boost in the polls after Lieberman's selection seemed to provide entrée for a complete shift in the Web presentation's trajectory.

As with the Bush sites, the way in which the Gore team brings the broader world of sociohistorically specific information into site utterances reveals information that will begin to answer these questions. Final answers are not possible, these being based chiefly on monological presuppositions. However, dialogistic inquiry serves the analyst best by opening alternatives to standard readings. With the Gore site, this expansion of the problem space proves to be very revealing.

Utterance Reading of the Gore Sites

In this utterance reading, I will refer not just to what is evident on the Gore sites themselves, but, since we have a similar analysis for the Bush sites, comparisons between the two standard and utterance readings. Evolution of the Bush sites appears to be governed by a pragmatic response to stimuli connected to an alteration in their view of the site visitor; evolution of the Gore sites seems governed by a much more abrupt change in the conception of the candidate, particularly as defined by his relation to others in the campaign (chiefly, the vice president), and of course at the same time changing conception of the candidate means the team also changes its conception of the audience, to the extent that they think those who do, or who might, support Gore would be comfortable with his "reinvention." The essence of the divergence between these two candidates lies in large part in the relation between how conceptions of audience and technology are interrelated. Although the Gore campaign team clearly realizes the potentials of the technical aspects of communication via Web sites much earlier and more thoroughly than the Bush team, the way their technical expertise is used seems to work against them, given the idiosyncratic nature of their audience. The Bush team devised a site for the masses to use, but without the masses in mind; the Gore team devised one with the masses in mind, but not for the masses to use.

Since the technological divide between the two teams is an issue, we can begin by discussing how the Gore team introduces technology through OTHER MEANING (the importation of meaning systems through use of evidence and support). One way is through providing technical "support" for various specific forms of technological enhancements. Although there is some evidence of this on both versions, it greatly predominates on version 2. For example, there are references to the numerous modes in which video presentations can be viewed: for the two primary brands (RealPlayer and Windows Media), there are three links each provided in the main area (for three different connection speeds), making six links in all, and this in the area of the page where one expects key information. Here the Gore team uses its knowledge of the alternative meaning systems involved in defining various parameters of video presentations to make it easier for visitors to access different modes.

The team's awareness of the potential for employing its technological expertise is also shown in a revealing EFFORT AT SHARING, also especially prominent in version 2: providing many possible channels for feedback. In the utterance reading, this insight emerged through applying EFFORT AT SHARING because it is an act of opening channels of communication, again, not necessarily because information is exchanged, but because the candidate wishes to appear to be in touch with the electorate. This is more than merely sharing information, per se, but involves sharing expertise in the means of communicating, in the apparent hope that both the information itself and the way it is conveyed will serve to enhance the credibility of the candidate—that is, it will establish that Gore is knowledgeable both about politics (because of information he is willing share) and about how to convey it most efficiently (because of his facility with technology). It is worth noting that both of these are qualities that Gore's team sought assiduously to connect with the candidate during the campaign.

Although version 1 does noticeably try to provide a means to contact the campaign via specific channels (segmentation of visitors to state organizations occurs, for example, much earlier in Gore's version 1 than it does on the Bush site), the number of channels offered on version 2 is astounding. The left-hand navigation area, already dense with the pictures of the candidates and their wives, as well as the two pull-down menus for state and issue segmentation, has just below these areas a set of eight links, each with its own accompanying small graphic and specifying some distinct communication channel or process: (1) "GoreNet" (a "network of young Americans"); (2) "Send this Page"; (3) "Join the Gore I-Team"; (4) "Instant MessageNet"; (5) "Get Involved"; (6) "Register to Vote"; (7) "Join the Fight!" (soliciting contributions); and (8) "MyElection" (a way of updating online preferences). Notice, in the latter stages of the campaign, the similarity in the shift to imperative voice, as on the Bush version 3 site. This could almost be viewed as an example of sharing run to excess; it is as if the team is intent on establishing that no matter how you communicate with the campaign, they "have you covered." In terms of the utterance reading, it is the first presentation of a theme that will be repeated many times on both versions of the Gore site: the campaign is set on portraying itself as inclusive, and reinforces this dialogical variation of a conventional element of most political campaign sites.

However, even this is not nearly the entire roster of proffered channels on version 2. In the middle of the page, more toward the bottom, the Gore team offers what it calls "e-mersion" coverage of the Democratic National Convention, held on August 14–17, just prior to retrieval of the site on August 19. This link, which is in fact a rather sizable banner advertisement that promises streaming video, digital logs, podium chats, and so on, is an attempt to convey, via EFFORT AT SHARING, what visitors might have missed from mass media coverage of the event, which was somewhat less than in previous years (Kern, 2001). Thus, here the EFFORT AT SHARING extends even to presentations that have already occurred in other mass media (serving some of the same purposes as the presentation of television and radio advertisements on the sites of both candidates).

Then, on the right side of the page are still other links to channels of communication. From the top, there is, first, a search engine for the site; second, a sign-up mechanism for receiving campaign updates by e-mail; and third, a section headed "WATCH & LISTEN." This last section has another four links specifying communication to and/or with visitors: "Video," "Audio," "Photos," and "NashvilleCam" (with live shots of the Gore headquarters in Nashville, Tennessee). Finally, at the bottom of this right navigational area is a link to a location where one can sign up to get campaign messages delivered to one's PDA ("Campaign to Go"). Not even taking into account subsidiary pages (such as "Town Hall," which solicits questions), that makes a total of about a dozen separate requests for participation on the home page alone.

While it is a truism that one of the most important things a candidate can do is listen to the electorate, this goal becomes, by version 2, almost frantic, as well as unwieldy. Although these graphics are interesting and well designed (and in line with good design practice in that they do not take too long to load), their presence simply adds to the sense of visual crowding as well as making it difficult for the visitor to perceive and respond to the more relevant links. To take just one example, it does not seem reasonable to expect that many people will want to get campaign updates downloaded to their PDAs.

Although the Gore approach (which contrasts sharply with the leaner and simpler Bush version 3 site) may be optimal for more traditional modes of communication, it is less so for the Internet. Moreover, the profusion of channels seems to be pressing a point that hardly needs to be made: that Gore is an enthusiastic supporter of technology. That point was made far more subtly in the campaign message in the HTML coding (which is also in version 2, though in abbreviated form), whereas in this perhaps overzealous example of EFFORT AT SHARING, it is too obvious and unwieldy to be effective.

As was the case with the Bush sites, several features of the Gore sites reveal how the Gore team places a distinctive stamp on conventional features of the presidential candidate site. These are, as it were, heteroglossic "spins" on features we have come to expect in campaigns. As before, much of what I have to say will involve not just data from the Gore sites, but comparisons between the sites for the two candidates.

The first of these elaborations has to do with declaring the candidate's position on the issues. A distinctive feature of OTHER MEANING in the Gore sites—contrasting sharply with the Bush sites—is the extensiveness of references to Gore's positions on a wide range of issues. Beginning with version 1, there are links to a page titled "Briefing Room" where Gore lays out a wide range of detailed positions, as well as discussing initiatives he has taken over the years on issues such as AIDS care and prevention. There is also a link to the "Town Hall," an "interactive" forum through which visitors can pose questions for Gore to answer (an archive of answers to questions on numerous specific issue areas can be accessed through a pull-down menu). This strategy gives Gore numerous opportunities to call on his experience in politics to import OTHER MEANING to answer specific, targeted questions. Moreover, this use of OTHER MEANING epitomizes a principle referred to several times in this analysis: the importing of knowledge from other realms serves to clarify and define positions. Through extensive linkages to OTHER MEANING, Gore defines himself through defining his connections to broader realms of knowledge.

Strangely, though, on version 2's home page there is a less noticeable emphasis on issue stances. For one thing, the link to the "Briefing Room" has been removed. Also, even though the "Town Hall" link remains in roughly the same position at the top center of the page (the linked "Town Hall" page is also streamlined and more efficiently designed and presented), it becomes even less noticeable because of the profusion of graphic buttons linking to other facets of the site, not to mention the visual domination of the photograph of Gore and Lieberman. In other words, one of the most noticeable features of version 1 is less visible in version 2.

One could almost see this situation as a competition among different kinds of OTHER MEANING, with links to biographical details and technical enhancements in version 2 forcing out more overt references to the discussion of issues in version 1. Clearly, this confirms the principle that the way to make meaningful utterances on the Web (or elsewhere) is to choose which systems of knowledge one wishes to emphasize via instantiations of OTHER MEANING. The specific kind of OTHER MEANING one wishes to connect to will determine how one's message is perceived. The shift in emphasis between types of OTHER MEANING on versions 1 and 2 of Gore's site confirms the importance of this principle in site design.

One fascinating example of how OTHER CONCEPTION serves to advance a specific elaboration of a conventional campaign element, seemingly important to most presidential campaigns (though, oddly, not so much to Bush's), is the portrait of the candidate as a family person. The near-universal need for candidates to establish their connection to institutions such as "the family" is an ideal example of OTHER CONCEPTION. It indicates a perception (whether accurate or not) on the part of site designers that visitors will be interested in candidates who come from, or who are able to sustain, "good families." The Gore team's need to portray their candidate as part of a family, concerned with families in general, is extremely strong on both versions of the site. We have already seen on version 1's home page two links about Gore's family, one to a page devoted to his wife and one to a page for the family as a whole. On version 2, we also noted the presence, at the top of the page, of a series of small equal-sized photographs of the Gores and the Liebermans; these photos are linked to separate pages describing these individuals.[33]

This is a distinctive use of OTHER CONCEPTION, in that it must simultaneously portray conceptions of other people, together with the target (the candidate), to create a kind of reality in which the role of Gore as a family man will appeal to the visitor. That this is a concerted effort shows that the designers are aware it is an important issue.

It is interesting that this rather traditional conception of the family (in version 1, all seven members of the Gore family are shown in a photo on a back porch) is normally more associated with Republicans. Given the negative associations of the sexual scandals of the Clinton adminis- tration of which Gore was part, this array of utterances may be used to establish that Gore has a very traditional American family (although it is also interesting that an alternate conception is established by showing Tipper Gore as not simply a political wife, but, on a page of her own, an activist with a personal agenda and accomplishments, perhaps to satisfy another American ideal, that of the independent woman). It is also in- teresting to see how the utterance reading brings out indications of how the meanings for these powerful symbols are constructed out of the so- cial realities experienced by the different parties involved. For example, although it is important to many American voters that Tipper Gore is both wife and mother, it is equally important to many American women (and this is probably particularly true of Democrats) that she be seen as an independent woman. This can be seen in the contrasting images that Gore's team is obliged to include in the site; and of course it is also the case that visitors to the site will encounter the symbols according to their own ways of viewing the world. One visitor might come to the site ap- preciating the attempt to portray Tipper as devoted to both family and career, another might find one or the other portrayal inappropriate for a political site, yet another might think that Gore is not being portrayed as his own man, and so on. The point is that each visitor will engage the symbols in the variegated ways in which the designers of the site used elements of Web page/site composition to fashion them.

This also seems to be the strategy behind both the selection of Joseph Lieberman (well-known for his moral stances, based in part on the fact that he practices Orthodox Judaism) and, following that, the prominent display of Senator Lieberman and his wife, along with Gore and his wife, on the main page of version 2. Version 2's display of Joe and Hadassah Lieberman complements the large background photo of Gore and Lieberman that dominates the center of the page. Taken to- gether, these utterances reveal the Gore team's effort to provide a distinctive flavor to the site to appeal to a sector of the electorate that is not, perhaps, traditionally associated with liberalism and the Demo- cratic Party. The dialogic method is useful in that it shows both the monologic standard (that is, the conventional presentation of the candidate as a family person), as well as the possible dialogic alternatives raised by the pronounced emphasis on this factor on Gore's site.

Most interesting of all, though, is that version 3 of the Bush site evolves in almost *exactly the opposite direction*. Even though the Bush campaign never really does foreground the Bush family to the same extent as the Gore campaign, in version 3 the Bush team focuses almost entirely on Bush himself. There is no mention of vice presidential candidate Dick Cheney on the main page; no prominent reference to Bush's wife, Laura; and no reference at all to Cheney's wife, even though Lynne Cheney (*Biography of Lynne V. Cheney*, n.d.) has considerable management experience in government, education, and charitable work. The Gore team uses OTHER CONCEPTION to conceive of an audience who will favorably respond to an administration in which there will be participation by a number of people; the Bush team's OTHER CONCEPTION forecasts an audience who will respond to a take-charge executive who will be the central figure in his administration. With this element, as with others on the Gore (and Bush) sites, OTHER CONCEPTION actually functions in at least two ways. It reveals clues about how the designers see the audience, and at the same time, because one can presume that designers' methods of appeal reflect what political experience tells them the audience is likely to think, it hints at what visitors will bring to the table in interpreting the site: in this case, their ideas about what an effective leader is. As we have seen, the Bush team (promoting a take-charge image) is very different from the Gore team (promoting a team-player image).

Along with these idiosyncratic elaborations of conventional themes, the Gore site also provides some distinctive features not readily noticeable on most other sites. One manifest instance of this, again contrasting sharply with the Bush sites, is the amount of verbal information. In looking at the evolution of the Bush site, I noted that the Bush team appeared to adjust its mode of communication with its conception of the Internet audience in mind, using fewer words and more pictures, and making messages "punchier." This is not of course to say the Bush team is correct in their assessment of Internet visitors, though it does resonate with the often-heard gloomier predictions of those who lament what they see as an Internet-stimulated decline in skill with conventional rhetoric.

On both Gore sites, however, there is a considerable amount of verbal information, even in version 1, where a comparatively lesser amount of the available page space is used. One easy way to get a rough idea about this difference is to count the number of words in the principle text area for the main page for version 1 of both sites. On the Gore site is a total of about 320 words, whereas the Bush site has only about 200. However, whereas the main text area of the Bush site is the only area for text display on the page, on the Gore site this area is placed side by side with another area, which also contains a significant amount of text.

An implication of this difference is that with more text it is easier to import significantly greater amounts of OTHER MEANING. However, taking advantage of this increased opportunity is not without risk. Too much "verbal" information, designers generally agree (Krug, 2000; Lynch & Horton, 2002), can inundate the visitor with too much to process, since those who visit Web sites are unwilling to do much reading (largely because it is uncomfortable), preferring instead to have their navigation through the site (not to mention their assimilation of disparate ideas) handled for them by clever and unique design. Making the Web site visitor read too much is considered fatal to "good" design.[34]

Clearly, the Gore team's choice is more in line with an ideal of civic discourse: given enough information, and provided it can be discussed freely and openly by citizens, better government policy will result (Dahl, 1989, 1998). Whether this ideal applies to the Internet, and particularly Web pages, is open to question. Here we see the paradox: what is held to be ideal discourse in a participative form of government may not be appropriate in the medium that holds perhaps the greatest promise to improve that very participation.

Although dialogistic insight is often beneficial, even inspirational, using it can be frustrating because it does tend to highlight troublesome contradictions, such as the one I have just described. However, at another level, this may be yet another manifestation of the fact that monological perspectives tend to obscure the often chaotic and "messy" reality of living language. According to the monological view, it would be easy to see the Bush and Gore sites according to simplistic dichotomies about the candidates they represent: Bush is portrayed as shallow, Gore as deep; Bush is engaging, Gore is boring; Bush is egocentric, Gore is a team player; and so on. Yet dialogistic inquiry shows us that such simplistic dualisms are inadequate to the task of understanding Web utterances, and therefore ultimately of ushering such utterances into full usage in modern politics. Rather, against the backdrop of the conventions of monologism, we see numerous alternative interpretations that begin—and *only* begin—to indicate the underlying richness of potential interpretations. Perhaps what dual reading of Web utterance reveals is that democracy, like other ideals, has been too long associated with monologic expression. Indeed, it may be that the ideals of democracy will be satisfied, on the Internet and elsewhere, not by appeals to what civic discourse "should be," but by solving the considerably more difficult problem of forging new modes of expression that take account of its many interesting contradictions.

Another, less confrontational, type of CONTESTING OWNERSHIP unique to the Gore site is to be found in the slogan that accompanies the large photograph of Gore and Lieberman that dominates the center section of the main page in version 2: "YOU AIN'T SEEN NOTHING YET." This phrase is placed in a position of startling prominence, in blue letters against a white background, and a font size that makes it nearly as large as the photograph of the candidates themselves (see Figure 9). The phrase implies that the Gore campaign has recently embarked on a new direction and that there will be further, more extensive changes in the future. It is not difficult to guess that the "new direction" relates to Joe Lieberman, a move that, according to many observers, gave Gore a boost in the polls (Norris, 2001). The phrase seems intended to capitalize on the momentum gained through nominating Lieberman. It is an example of CONTESTING OWNERSHIP because it appears to provide a number of preemptive answers to challenges not yet explicitly made. In these utterances about Lieberman, the Gore team seems to position itself with respect to the question, Why Lieberman? (who was not the choice expected by many political analysts) by providing an answer in advance: "Gore's decision about his running mate is not an anomalous occurrence, but is part of our overall strategy." This preemptive CONTESTING OWNERSHIP is a very common feature of political discourse, whether on the Web or elsewhere.

Yet, just as with the abundance of links to communication channels, this new slogan may be overly zealous. As noted, Gore has always been fond of the idea of reinvention (he has, for example, closely associated himself with the popular slogan "Reinventing Government"), even though too many attempts at "reinvention" may have worked against him in the campaign (Turque, 1999). If one already has a reputation for ongoing reinvention, perhaps one should aim for consistency (again, there was an opposite direction in development of the Bush sites, the Bush team settling on a very few, albeit oversimplified, messages, presented redundantly). One good way to see the difference is to conceive of the two approaches as tending toward centripetality (holding together) or centrifugality (splitting apart) (see Chapter 1). The Bush site's strategy of simplification means that symbols, written and otherwise, cluster around fewer basic themes, and this clustering makes the site hold together. On the other hand, the Gore site's relentless inclusion of numerous concepts about voter interest groups and the subtleties of issues means that the range of themes is expanded, and thus the site suffers from too much expansion of its focus. It is ironic, though, that the basic centrifugal tenor of the Gore sites results from an overabundance of primarily monologic discourse.

Another use of OTHER CONCEPTION, more idiosyncratic to the Gore site than any site in the database, is the segmenting of visitors into specific interest groups. To use characteristics by which people can be classified involves numerous acts of OTHER CONCEPTION. This strategy begins on version 1's main page, which features a series of rotating photographs showing Gore with various interest groups (students, firefighters, and so on), and three stories about Gore and targeted interest groups (labor, Latinos, and students). We have noted on the home page's top menu a link to a page called the "Town Hall," where answers are posted to specific questions, with a pull-down menu linking to an extensive list of topic areas, each with its own questions and answers.

That the Gore team considers this OTHER CONCEPTION important is confirmed by the even greater prominence it receives in version 2. This revision of the Gore site is, as we have seen, overloaded with information. Nevertheless, in the midst of the profusion of buttons and menus, in a section on the left-hand page headed "TAKE ACTION," are two easily noticeable pull-down menus, "Your State" and "Voter Outreach." Although some segmentation is implied by use of the former menu, the idea of the latter involves getting the visitor first to identify and second to enlist the help of groups of people considered more aligned with the Democratic Party (such as African Americans, students, the elderly, and those with disabilities) than with Republicans, as well as others conventionally considered more aligned with Republicans (such as business leaders).

It interesting that the "TAKE ACTION" section is found beneath the "GET TO KNOW US" section, with its four equal-sized pictures of the candidates and their wives, visually continuing the theme of inclusion of disparate elements. The traditional knitting together of various, frequently disaffected, interest groups has long been a Democratic Party tradition. Although the presentation of a unified portrait of such disparate interests is very difficult—leading to priceless witticisms such as Will Rogers's famous quip "I'm not a member of any organized political party, I'm a Democrat"—the Web page presents unique opportunities to actualize this goal. In what other channel of communication could one simultaneously depict what seems unified ("Pick Your Group") with such a diversity of options? The dialogic mode of expression is characterized, among other things, by multivocality, that is, the presence of many voices, rather than a single dominating voice, in determining the tenor of discourse. Both the history of the Democratic Party, as well as the evidence from the dialogical reading of the Gore sites, confirm the importance of multivocality to the party's philosophy. Through its numerous indications of egalitarianism and inclusion, the Gore site forges utterances that bring together these disparate forces in uneasy tension. It is unfortunate that Will Rogers did not live to see the realization of the Internet—I have the feeling he would have understood its use by the Democratic candidate.

Another quality of the dialogic approach is that it brings to one's attention the possible reasons why an utterer might want to link to one or another aspect of the broader world in which discourse occurs. With respect to including disparate groups, it is easier to see this in Web discourse than it perhaps is in other forms. A great advantage of Web discourse is the precision with which links from Web pages can target specific audiences. While this feature is used in nearly every presidential candidate site, it is the Gore site that places segmentation of voters in perhaps its most prominent position (in contrast, although there is a pull-down menu directing visitors to state sites on versions 2 and 3 of the Bush site, there is nothing even resembling a "Pick Your Group" menu). Clearly, the dialogic reading of both the Bush and Gore sites shows a marked distinction in OTHER CONCEPTION and EFFORT AT SHARING. Taking a monologic perspective, on the other hand, it would be easy to view both sites as making some effort at inclusion, just as would be expected of any presidential candidate site.

Finally, a highly idiosyncratic use of CONTESTING OWNERSHIP on Gore version 2 depicts Bush in a negative light. Beneath the "TAKE ACTION" section of navigation buttons on the left side of the main page is another section, headed "BUSH 'DEBATE DUCK.'" In yet another indication they know about Web page design, the Gore team has placed in this section, under the question, "How Long has George W. Bush avoided debating Al Gore?", a continually updating digital clock, recording the amount of time elapsed since the Gore team says Gore extended his challenge to debate Bush. As the 2000 presidential campaign drew to a close, Gore and Bush increasingly clashed over the issue of candidate debates, with Gore pressing Bush to have debates other than those proposed by the Commission on Presidential Debates (Marks, 2000); this disagreement evolved into a contentious and complicated dispute over which invitations had been extended and accepted (Bruni, 2000; Marks, 2000).

The "debate duck clock" is one of the few instances in which either candidate negatively portrays his opponent, and considered as utterance, is a fascinating way to portray this issue, highly specific to the medium of the Web. The clock is not the only reference to Bush and debates on this home page; near the bottom of the center section, in the same horizontal position as the clock, is a statement by Gore campaign director Bill Daley: "We welcome Governor Bush's new found [sic] interest in debates. As he knows, Al Gore has been ready to debate for months, and has accepted dozens of debate proposals already." The clock, on the other hand, shows a sense of urgency, though it is unclear which campaign finds the matter more urgent. Clearly, one of the purposes of the clock is to embarrass Bush by suggesting he is afraid to debate. Nevertheless, compared to the confidence and forward-looking optimism of the Bush site, the inclusion of the clock lends a sense of desperation to the Gore campaign. Whatever the reason, it is clearly a way of directly CONTESTING OWNERSHIP of the Bush team over the validity of its position on having additional debates.

Summary

By revising their Web sites according to what they perceive their audiences to be, the Bush and Gore campaign teams, together with visitors to their sites, collaboratively construct a rich and diverse political dialogue that, in addition to serving the functional purpose of attempting to garner support for the candidate, also reveals important indications of political and other beliefs of the respective campaigns. Perhaps ironically—perhaps not—the two campaigns use Web utterance to reach out to different elements of the electorate than those conventionally (monologically) associated with their political parties. Though it is possible to see this as a purely pragmatic strategy, the utterance reading also reveals how campaigns can use the resources of the World Wide Web to fluidly and dynamically recast images of the candidates. It will be interesting to observe in future campaigns, as well as future analyses of the 2000 campaign, how the recasting of images of candidates on the Web compares and contrasts with other kinds of reformulation of image through other media channels.

"SWASTIKA ON THE LAWN": A SOCIAL ACTIVISM SITE

An intriguing feature relating to dialogical qualities of the Internet is the promise this medium holds for people to be heard on issues that concern them and others in society. This can occur whether or not such concerns are important to other kinds of media, such as television, radio, or newspapers. Indeed, with the increasing homogenization of news and the accompanying decrease in substantive reporting, the Internet has become a preferred means of expressing alternative points of view. Sites devoted to various causes are innumerable; if one discounts inevitable restrictions imposed by some server administrators on material that can be presented, just about anything about social issues that one wishes to say can be said on the World Wide Web.

Despite this widespread availability, or perhaps because of it, much of this communication is less than successful. Indeed, it can be offensive and crude, not only in terms of language but other presentation modes (such as graphics). One could argue this is inevitable, given the Web's dialogistic tendencies, arising from its unruly ancestry. However, the Web also has the potential to present a better quality product to appeal not only to its wide open tendencies (Weinberger, 2002) but also to audiences seeking a less evanescent, more permanent product that yet utilizes the Web as its mode of distribution.

A site that illustrated this potential was "Swastika on the Lawn: A Year of Anti-Semitism in Massachusetts."[35] By propounding a message framed in principally monologic fashion, in a predominantly dialogical medium, this site not only managed to respond to a number of anti-Semitic incidents during the mid-1990s in Massachusetts, but also provided an account relevant long after the events happened. Moreover, through acting as "concerned citizens," taking advantage of the range of expression available on the Web, the creators of "Swastika" called attention to anti-Semitism and perhaps even abated it. "Swastika on the Lawn" is an example of the potential for Web utterances to transcend what are normally thought of as limitations in Internet communication as a tool for social activist communication. "Swastika" seemed to me to "work" despite being constructed and maintained on a limited budget, having to deal with a difficult and delicate issue, and having to overcome what is perhaps a predisposition for visitors to see its designers as biased. In these respects, understanding a Web site such as "Swastika" may point to ways to realize the potential of the Web to bring into civic discourse the discussion of issues that might otherwise prove difficult for interest groups to get into public consciousness.

I use the dual reading method to point out both the substantial number of things I think "Swastika" seemed to perform more effectively with respect to getting its message out, and also how the site might have been improved by exploiting the more dialogistic tendencies of design. The basic idea behind "Swastika on the Lawn" can be considered as one of a number of templates for the propounding of social activist agendas, providing a way for those with a message to disseminate their views on the Internet.

Standard Reading of "Swastika on the Lawn"

"Swastika on the Lawn" was an unusual activist Web site. Although it made use of some text and graphic presentation possibilities of Internet sites, its structure tended more to the monologic. The Web pages comprising the site were arranged as in a book, with an introduction, "chapters," (for some pages) references and footnotes, and in general a more staid, sober style of presentation than customarily found on other sites. Clearly, the creators wished to infuse their utterances with legitimacy (an idea more associated with monological than dialogical approaches).

According to information on the site itself, "Swastika" was principally the product of two (as they refer to themselves) "concerned Jewish mothers," Billie Freeman, an author and former newspaper columnist; and Cindy Grossberg, photoessayist and assistant curator of the photographic archives at a well-known Massachusetts university library.[36] "Swastika" was published on the Web site for an institution of higher learning in Massachusetts specializing in Judaic studies.

The site's name was derived from an incident in a suburban town in Massachusetts, involving Daniel and Karen Green and their three children: a 20-foot swastika was burned into the family's lawn on May 23, 1994, following their receipt of an anonymous hate letter on May 10. After a candlelight vigil in their hometown on June 15, the Greens received a second hate letter on June 27. This focus is interesting because the description of the incident with the Greens is a relatively small portion of the site. Other pages deal with such incidents in Massachusetts as the defacing of synagogues, thoughts about hate and anti-Semitism from local rabbis, and broader issues such as bias in school curricula and debates about academic freedom in higher education. Thus, it is interesting that the site should have been titled in a way that does not immediately reveal what it is actually about, although the full title does provide further particulars: "Swastika on the Lawn: A Year of Anti-Semitism in Massachusetts." However, it is the dramatic initial phrase, in bolder, larger letters, that users first encountered when visiting the site and certainly the phrase likely to have made the greatest impact.

The structure of "Swastika" was, particularly compared to the presidential candidate sites, quite simple. "Swastika" was what Siegel (1997) refers to as a "first-generation" Web site, that is, comprising only text and a few graphics. In fact, apart from the color photographs (apparently primarily the work of Ms. Grossberg), "Swastika" had no graphics. The site had a total of 13 pages, mostly text, but also photographs of people, a few locations, and some objects (for example, one of the letters to the Greens). Additionally, the background of all pages was plain white with black lettering and link colors as specified by the user's browser. In other words, the design was noticeably plain and seemed focused more on the written material than on decorations for the pages.

The writing (primarily the work of Ms. Freeman) was in straightforward journalistic style. In addition to accounts of historical incidents were reports of extensive interviews with several individuals, including the Green family; Rabbis Samuel Rensick, Lev Obermann, and M. Jonathon Weiss; Professors Maureen Leopold and Randall Castell; Phyllis Feingold; Cindy Grossberg; and an official of the Anti-Defamation League of B'Nai B'rith, Lawrence Zeigler. Interviews with the rabbis focused on acts of apparently hate-motivated defacement of local religious locations and objects, while interviews with the professors had to do with freedom to challenge endorsement of anti-Semitic statements in the context of academic presentations at their respective universities. Ms. Feingold's interview concerned a program sponsored by the Jewish women's organization Hadassah: Curriculum Watch examines K–12 curricular materials to ensure that the portrayal of Jews and Israel is accurate.

Of the various symbolic approaches that could have been chosen to represent this set of Web pages, the designers selected the incidents with the Greens (and, in reality, only one of several incidents involving that family). In contrast to this sensational event, most of the pages were about more abstract, though potentially weightier and more serious issues (not of course to minimize the seriousness of hooligan- istic hate crimes). However, that the composers chose to call the site "Swastika on the Lawn: A Year of Anti-Semitism in Massachusetts" is significant. The authors seemed convinced that the seemingly dis- parate events of thuggish hate crimes and the Byzantine complexities of academic politics are connected, and this title was the first of sev- eral ways in which they tie these two realms of activity together.

As did the EDM threads (Chapter 3), the site had a core utterance, one that defined and set the tone for subsequent utterances. This was the description of the incidents with the Greens. The receipt of the two hate letters, together with burning the symbol of Nazism on the lawn of a typical American family, and this is in a suburb that (according to the Web site) is predominantly Jewish, are the sorts of incidents that in- spire terror. On the page describing the plight of the Green family were the words of Daniel and Karen Green, from interviews conducted with them after the family received each of the two threatening letters. These interviews showed not only the family's anguish, but also their deter- mination not to be victimized. Daniel Green told how he contacted local Jewish leaders to seek guidance, and how the letters and defacement of the Green property led to a Unity Rally and a candlelight vigil in Nor- ton. Despite the horror of the situation, the dominant tone of these accounts was positive and hopeful, and the focus not on how the past has poisoned some, but how the future inspires many others.

Nevertheless, although the impact of the Green incident is powerful and persuasive, "Swastika" had more complex and difficult rhetorical goals to accomplish. Freeman and Grossberg used the Green family in- cidents as points from which to initiate a discussion of the broader issue of anti-Semitism. The next three chapters, in fact, formed a bridge be- tween the personal nature of the Green case, and anti-Semitism in academia and society at large. Chapters 2 through 4 feature interviews with three rabbis concerning local acts of defacement and their connec- tion to social and religious issues. Chapters 5 and 6 introduced site visitors to, respectively, Maureen Leopold, professor of humanities at a well-known private women's liberal arts college, and Randall Castell, professor of economics at the University of Massachusetts–Edgarton.

Both professors were involved in disputes at their respective institutions over courses in Black Studies that used texts and lecture material (including guest speakers) promoting what they identified as anti-Semitic and inaccurate content.

Chapter 7 focused on Phyllis Feingold, head of Curriculum Watch, an organization sponsored by Hadassah that monitors "materials, mainly textbooks, used in grades K–12 (public and private schools) to assess whether information about the Jewish people, Israel, the Holocaust, and Judaism is presented accurately and fairly" (Introduction, para. 1).

Chapter 8 recounts how one of the site composers, Cindy Grossberg, who is also a counselor for the Anti-Defamation League of B'Nai B'rith, handled complaints of anti-Semitism. Chapter 9, the last chapter, presented the views of Lawrence Zeigler, executive director of the Anti-Defamation League, New England Region. This interview, conducted more than a year after the incidents with the Greens, was a reflection by Zeigler on his life and how the community's response to anti-Semitism had changed during the time he held his position. Zeigler also reflected on his experiences as a child growing up with anti-Semitism. It is interesting that, in this final "chapter" of the site, there was only one very brief mention of the Green family incidents; the Zeigler interview provided the broadest sweep of material in "Swastika," yet the page closed with a return to the core utterance by exhibiting a photograph of Zeigler speaking to the Unity Rally. Other pages in the site included biographies of, and information about how to contact, Ms. Freeman and Ms. Grossberg; a list of suggested readings; and an introduction to the site.

The tone of "Swastika" was authoritative, controlled, well planned, and serious—these are qualities associated more with primarily monological than dialogical accounts (dialogically inclined accounts seem antiauthority, uncontrolled, spontaneous, and unpredictable). For "Swastika," there was, at least on the surface, more a concern for alerting the Internet audience to a problem and describing its dimensions (a discursive strategy more associated with conventional monologism, especially in civic discourse), than with inviting comment and discussion to come up with an evolving, dynamic position on the issue. However, as I will show in the utterance reading, the dynamic evolution of the issue of anti-Semitism reported in "Swastika" took place, as computer people say, IRL (in real life), that is, not on the site and not principally via the interactions of Web visitors who encountered it. This unusual feature of "Swastika" presented both advantages and disadvantages to the site designer considering emulating the approach taken by Freeman and Grossberg. To explore how this works, let us turn to the utterance reading.

Utterance Reading of "Swastika on the Lawn"

Contrary to the standard reading of "Swastika" as a straightforward, monologically inclined site simply reporting on incidents of anti-Semitism, the utterance reading reveals considerable complexity. As we will see, the apparent monologism of the site was illusory, in that the incidents that informed site utterances took place prior to utterance formulation and hence were not necessarily developed on-site, but in "real life," to serve as the material for on-site presentation. This key distinction is significant in discussion of sites to be used for social activism. Indeed, one of the weaknesses of the many activist sites is their inability to situate themselves in a historical perspective, with issues emerging quickly, being discussed heatedly, and then just as quickly vanishing into the fog of ever-shifting cyberutterances. "Swastika," though perhaps going a bit too far in the opposite direction, was obviously aimed at producing something more permanent and this is the reason for its apparent monological inclinations.

As noted in the standard reading, on the surface "Swastika" seemed like the most conventional of Web sites. Yet, from the first time I encountered it, and despite its lack of sophistication, I had the very strong intuitive reaction that, among the dozens, perhaps hundreds, of activist sites I had looked at, this one "worked" better than others. This was due only partly to its relatively high degree of coherence—individual elements of many activist sites tend to be extraordinarily disjunct—and its overall "academic" tone, a quality of discourse I am comfortable with. Rather, I sensed that there was something about the arrangement of the site and its multilayered approach to a social problem that one might easily have expected to be rendered more unidimensionally and hence less credibly. When I applied the utterance reading, I was surprised at how clearly I was able to see some underlying rationales for my intuitive liking of "Swastika." Applying the four utterance markers, I came to a number of conclusions, grouped around three central themes: (1) the primarily monologic qualities of the site, (2) the layers of opinion expressed on the site, and (3) the connection of the site to other activist enterprises "in real life."

Monologic Site Qualities

Several times I have mentioned that "Swastika" was rendered more in monological than dialogical terms. This is clear from the standard reading, which calls attention to the rather unusual arrangement of the pages as chapters, much as one would find in conventional (that is, monological) texts. This bookish approach to the kind of subject (social dysfunction) often approached in a less conventional (that is, dialogical) fashion on the Web was doubtless accentuated by the fact that "Swastika" was really a subsite of a larger site for a college of Judaic studies. Its inclusion on an educational site not only lent more credibility to the presentation of "Swastika," but academic conventions almost certainly dictated that this presentation would incline to the monological.

However, it is interesting that this "monologic" site quality was in fact accomplished dialogically. We can see this in one particularly striking way "Swastika" inclines to monologism: through its instantiation of OTHER MEANING. Frequently, this took the form of citing statistics and other supporting evidence much as one might do in conventional rhetoric (see, for example, Booth, Colomb, & Williams, 2003, esp. pt. 3, pp. 109–181). This reliance on traditional argumentation is unusual: as a rule, activist sites not only do not favor this kind of support, but the Net-savvy activist frequently seems to believe (as did the authors of Bush site version 3) that even a small amount of conventional evidence works against attracting the interest of the Web visitor. Moreover, "Swastika" made little effort to aid the visitor in processing arguments and evidence, as by placing them on the page in visually interesting or provocative ways. Yet by referencing conventional sources, in a conventional way, "Swastika" imported the kind of OTHER MEANING that imbued the site with enhanced credibility and gave it its distinctive flavor.

An example can be found in Chapter 8, the interview with Cindy Grossberg about her work as counselor for the Anti-Defamation League (ADL). Ms. Grossberg's office processed complaints to the ADL about anti-Semitic incidents. According to Grossberg, "Over 100 anti-Semitic incidents a year occur in the New England region, some of them more dramatic and scary than others. The Green case [an anti-Semitic letter, followed by a swastika burned on their lawn, followed by a second, more threatening letter] is middle level."

To me the most surprising aspect of this utterance is Grossberg's assertion that, among anti-Semitic incidents, the Green case is about "middle level" in terms of drama and "scariness." Considered monologically, this is a very matter-of-fact statement; considered dialogically, it is more startling, since it implies that, routinely, incidents that are more "dramatic and scary" are reported. Rhetorically, this formulation is effective, setting up tension between what, in conventional terms, seems to be the chief focus of the site, namely, the Green case (see the standard reading, especially discussion of the site title), and the "real" focus, which we learn about relatively later in the chapter sequence of pages: instances of anti-Semitism more serious than what happened to the Greens.

Even allowing for the idiosyncrasies of Internet discourse, this is a fascinating configuration of OTHER MEANING. Freeman and Grossberg obviously intended visitors to proceed through the site in a certain order. Apart from the sequence of chapters, there was also an obvious progression of chapter topics, beginning very locally with the Green incidents through ever more expansive domains to end with Lawrence Zeigler's reflections on his life and in general on the global problem of anti-Semitism. Yet evidence that the Green incident is only "moderately" frightening was left until the next to the last chapter. If more serious incidents existed, why not focus first on them, rather than the Greens?

Considering these references as OTHER MEANING results in three possible answers. First, the very locality (that is, immediacy) of the Greens' plight made what happened to them a good focal point to start an inquiry into anti-Semitism generally. Although there have been equally or more serious incidents (defacement of synagogues is certainly as ominous), that the Greens were a local family gave their story a human-interest quality that made it a good journalistic "lead." Some support for this interpretation is that the last image in the last chapter—Lawrence Zeigler's interview—and thus the closing element of the entire site—was a photograph of Zeigler addressing the Unity Rally precipitated by the incidents with the Greens. In terms of the dialogical reading, we can say that the designers of "Swastika" used OTHER MEANING strategically (more so, that is, than many other designers seem to) and consistently to paint a picture of a serious social problem that could best be combated by firm action undergirded by compassion and understanding, as is proposed in the most idealistic conceptions of democracy.

Second, an attack on a Jewish family in a predominantly Jewish suburban community is "news." Thus, although there may have been more serious incidents of anti-Semitism, these were, sad to say, more common than the kind of attack suffered by the Greens. As chronicled by the ADL, there have been multiple defacements of synagogues ("Selected Anti-Semitic Incidents," n.d.) and numerous conflicts involving

Jewish professors over the anti-Semitism of some Black Studies programs ("Schooled in Hate," n.d.). Hence, Ms. Grossberg's evaluation provided a sobering reminder to those who, after reading the first chapter, concluded that, because there were no more incidents after the rally, the vigil, and the second letter, matters were under control. Grossberg's reference to OTHER MEANING reminded visitors that they needed to see anti-Semitism as an ongoing problem that, though connected to the Green case, is far worse. Here, too, OTHER MEANING served to refocus the problem. Visitors probably would be expected to assume that the Green incidents represented among the worst of such episodes, and by implication, also assume that since the Green incident ended somewhat favorably, the problem had been significantly abated. Ms. Grossberg's invocation of OTHER MEANING dashed cold water on these assumptions.

Third, the Green incidents make a good beginning point because of how the family responded. How an event comes to affect people has a great deal to do with how they react to it. In other words, although menacing anti-Semitic incidents abound, few of them become a cause célèbre. As Grossberg, Daniel Green, and others point out throughout the site, one has a choice of ignoring hate incidents, reporting them to police, or making a more public declaration about what happened. The Greens chose the third alternative, pursuing an active agenda to publicize the incident and garner community support. The response to their pleas made the incident more well-known than it might have been otherwise and this may have been the key consideration for making it the focal point, even though Cindy Grossberg was obliged to remind visitors of the more troubling state of affairs. A key aspect of dialogism, as was shown in Chapter 2 of this volume, is that dialogic utterances are securely bound to what goes on in the world, whereas the monologic perspective encourages utterances that are disjunct from "messy" reality of the world. Utterance is "ideologically freighted" (Weiss, 1990) in that it "picks up" elements of meaning systems as it traverses through social life. Therefore, the swastika and the hate letter are merely moments in a continuing saga in the development of various meanings that will determine how they will be taken; they have no intrinsic meaning separate from the social fabric, but are, rather, points along trajectories taken by living participants in the drama, who will, along with others, actualize conditions that will frame meanings. The incidents that happened to the Greens take on the meanings they do because of what Daniel Green and his family chose to do in response to them, and how

others chose to respond to what they did. In the monologic interpretation, the dynamism and diversity of these complicated alternative
trajectories become, necessarily, flattened and homogenized; in the
dialogistic interpretation, however, they are foregrounded, emphasized,
and discussed as distinct from other paths of development.

Multifaceted Opinions

A second feature that made "Swastika" more effective than many
other social activist sites was that opinions on the site were multifaceted.
Intertwined with the reactions of anger and outrage one might expect
were other opinions (the majority, actually) and these were restrained,
optimistic, evenhanded, and tempered. In short, "Swastika," though
hewing to its clear, central theme (anti-Semitism in Massachusetts and
beyond) presented an impressive range of reactions.

We could see this by examining the range from less to more
contentious responses. One of the least quarrelsome responses is an example of OTHER CONCEPTION from Chapter 4, the interview with
M. Jonathon Weiss, rabbi of a local synagogue near Norton, concerning
desecration to the synagogue there. Rabbi Weiss even considered the
possibility that the desecration was not a true hate crime: "But everyone
said that half the people who commit these acts are not dangerous, that
they know the vulnerable spots and are just trying to get a rise out of
people, that swastikas get everybody upset. So I suspect it was just an
act of misguided vandalism by some kids" (Interview, para. 14). Weiss's
opinion is a sentiment expressed several times in "Swastika": it is important to guard against the tendency to overreact to what might simply
be childish pranks. Weiss invokes a specific kind of OTHER CONCEP-
TION here, in which he offers at least two ways (connections to two
systems of meaning) to view the desecrations: as hate crimes or as
pranks.[37] These specific types of OTHER CONCEPTION are quite in line
with the overall tone of "Swastika," which was firmly aimed at pre-
senting a balanced view, or at least a more balanced view than visitors
might expect from a site sponsored by a college of Judaic studies. The
alternative strategy, that of formulating his interpretation of the incident
to seem absolutely convinced these were racist hate crimes, would have
well served neither Rabbi Weiss nor the "Swastika" site as a whole.

However, if anyone has a right to be angry, it would certainly be
Daniel Green, whose family's property was defaced in a frightening
and grotesque way. It is therefore surprising to find from him this restrained instance illustrating multiple OTHER CONCEPTION: "No

one we know could possibly understand why it was us. We don't know if somebody hates us and expressed it with an anti-Semitic act, or whether we represent something that somebody doesn't like." Here, Mr. Green is at pains not to invoke an automatic attribution of widespread racial hatred through a more limited lens of OTHER CONCEPTION, just as Rabbi Weiss did; and, by extension, the same can be said of the site designers, since they incorporated these utterances. In this instance, once again, there is a divergence between what one might *expect* a victim of these incidents to say (monologic perspective), versus what he or she actually *does* say (dialogic). Obviously Mr. Green could have expressed himself in much stronger terms; yet here and elsewhere on the site, one cannot fail to be impressed with the equanimity with which these frightening events are recounted. There was nearly always emphasis on constructive dialogue, the formation of alliances among disparate groups, and the betterment of the community in which such unfortunate and damaging events occur. It was a specific strategy of OTHER CONCEPTION—that is, the way in which the perpetrators of the events in "Swastika" are portrayed—that enabled these goals to be accomplished. Both the interviewees, and the designers who wove their words into the site utterances, resisted a simple invocation of OTHER CONCEPTION in favor of a nuanced presentation in which dialogic alternatives were proposed.

The overall impression of hope and inspiration that characterized some of the pages of "Swastika" was evident in another example of EFFORT AT SHARING, from Chapter 9, featuring the interview with Lawrence Zeigler. Zeigler drew together a number of different strands of commentary to portray the whole situation in a much more hopeful and positive light:

> I met the other day with the head of the Lutheran community here whose namesake is Martin Luther, who was one of the most virulent anti-Semites in history, whose writings were used to justify Hitler. And just two years ago this guy from Woburn pens a resolution apologizing for the thousand years of Martin Luther's anti-Semitism, and it is passed by the National Lutheran Assembly. We are meeting with him here in Boston. The relevance of it is at University of Massachusetts Amherst, when [Louis] Farrakhan was speaking. He [Farrakhan] was quoting Martin Luther. Now we have the Lutheran Church saying we condemn what Luther said. Now what turned the Lutheran minister on to that? He told us. He had seen some incidents around. He had seen what was going on here. The Holocaust Museum

opened. I mean you don't know what idea is going to set off a stream
of consciousness in somebody.

The key to perceiving, and from perceiving to propagating, a
successful instance of EFFORT AT SHARING lies in creating a new
situation, not extant prior to melding various meaning systems together; this situation is similar to the one Vygotsky spoke of in
defining the zone of proximal development (see Chapter 2 this volume). We can view Zeigler's fusion of accounts concerning Martin
Luther, Louis Farrakhan, and the National Lutheran Assembly as
"new territory," and we can characterize this blending as unantici-
pated. Monologically, the realms of meaning seem to be separate from
one another and for this reason had to be tied together in Zeigler's utterance. Thus connected, however, they interanimate each other to
achieve Zeigler's persuasive goal.

As a further example of EFFORT AT SHARING, the reporting by
Freeman and Grossberg of Zeigler's remarks in the context of
"Swastika" performed a similar function. Coming in the last chapter, it
reflected what the composers wanted visitors to take from the site.
However, the quoting of Zeigler's remark did more toward unifying
perspectives. First, it emphasized Zeigler's interfaith initiatives, a major
part of his lifework. This was persuasive, as it emphasized that these
problems are not of concern only to those who practice Judaism.

Second, Zeigler's utterance drew attention back to other parts of the
site. Disputes with the Nation of Islam and Louis Farrakhan are significant features in chapters dealing with Professors Leopold and Castell
(Chapters 5 and 6, respectively). By conflating this contentious issue with
discussion of the achievements of his interfaith initiatives, Zeigler resitu-
ated it, and portrayed it not as a catastrophe, but as an example that runs
counter to other, potentially more fruitful, possibilities for achieving reconciliation with the "real" authorities on Lutheranism (the Lutheran
Assembly). This melding of alternatives represented some of the ideals of
dialogism, expressed as EFFORT AT SHARING, as Zeigler pointed out
what people of different groups have in common, rather than how they
disagree. In a dramatic confirmation of dialogism's multidimensionality,
this EFFORT AT SHARING turned out, in a very circuitous way, to have
been an example of CONTESTING OWNERSHIP, since the totality of its
impact served to advance an alternative to the view that groups pursue
separate goals and aims, rather than trying to find a creative way to
explain how they share these same goals and aims.

However, there was one more kind of voice to be heard in the chorus commenting on anti-Semitism via "Swastika on the Lawn." This rather less optimistic account, also conveyed through OTHER CONCEPTION, was from Chapter 6, which reported interviews with Randall Castell, professor of economics at the University of Massachusetts–Edgarton. Castell's tone was different from that of most of the people in "Swastika." He was seldom conciliatory, and often fiery and confrontational. An example of how this style affects his OTHER CONCEPTION of his university's administration is the following:

> Although some legal issues are unresolved, the Administration could certainly exercise more principled leadership before even getting to the legally contested areas. However, the Administration seems to have been cowed and paralyzed by its inability or unwillingness to distinguish between the First Amendment right of student groups to bring noxious ideas to campus, and those groups' non-existent right to receive administration neutrality about these speeches.

In Castell's interview, one found few positive references (except toward the very end of his chapter's rather lengthy page, and then somewhat reluctantly). Castell's portrayal certainly did not have the hopeful tenor found in Lawrence Zeigler's wide-ranging (and dialogical) descriptions. To the contrary, Castell's values tended more toward the monological, being primarily focused on hard research and facts. He was relentless in insisting, for example, in calling his university's administration to account for using student funds to bring to the campus speakers associated with the Nation of Islam. Moreover, he was eager to refer overtly to weaknesses by the university administration in discharging what Castell saw as their responsibilities.

At first glance, Castell's position might seem out of line with the goals of the site, which in the main promoted a more hopeful view. However, the marked emphasis placed by site composers on Castell could not have been accidental. Data obtained from Netscape's "Page Info" feature revealed that Castell's page was the longest on the site (53,569Kb), more than twice the average length of the remainder of the pages (about 25,600Kb). Moreover, apart from its quantitative significance, it was also probably the most extensively researched of the pages, not excepting even the thoroughly documented introduction page with its detailed account of the history and extent of anti-Semitism in America. Castell's narrative was not only backed with sources (it was one of the few pages on "Swastika" to be footnoted), but had a wealth of precise details concerning specific incidents of anti-Semitism at Edgarton.

Knowing the degree of importance site composers assigned to Castell's views, we must assume that these, too, were in line with site goals. This insight leads us to look more closely at how others are depicted on the site, in portrayals that might, on the surface, be taken as largely positive. We could see beneath the calls for unity and conciliation a true anger and resentment over hate crimes and other acts of anti-Semitism, and realize that while contributors were more than willing to cooperate in making accommodations, they did not intend to be victims. The inclusion—indeed, the elevation—of Castell's view confirmed this, and as such, pointed to an alternative motivation for site designers.

The inclusion of Castell's somewhat different view of the situation showed that the designers of "Swastika" realized the advantages of dialogue, as opposed to monologue. They clearly understood that, to fully explore the problem of anti-Semitism, they could not focus only, or even primarily, on positive experiences such as the Unity Rally, or dramatic accounts of hooliganism such as those that happened to the Greens. Furthermore, it was necessary to hear confrontative as well as placative voices. While according to conventional (monologic) journalistic procedures about what should occur in a story and when, it made sense to have Castell's more combative report come later in the sequence of pages (that is, after establishing the predominant tone of community unification), it was also understandable in a dialogical sense to accord Castell more space to make his points. The dialogistic perspective privileges the inclusion of alternative representations, and also utilizes material gleaned from sociohistorical context to highlight, or in some cases, de-emphasizes the utterances these voices formulate. It might be useful to visualize the process of answering different audiences with different needs in terms of Bakhtin's fascinating notion of the "superaddressee" (Bakhtin, 1986) or the internal idealized and imaginary entity that will perfectly understand and empathize with one's utterance. Although the designers of "Swastika" seemed to be answering to a superaddressee who respects Judaic traditions that elevate reason and public discourse, they also answered to another who insists that wrongs against the Jewish people cannot be forgotten.

Site and Activism "In Real Life"

A third feature of "Swastika" that contributed to its effectiveness was that the site's utterances were firmly situated in and connected to other activities "in real life," that is, explicitly not associated with cyberspace. While cyberspace is "real" in terms of how it is experienced by Internet users, its evanescent qualities (such as impermanence, a sense on the part of the user of being adrift) make it a particular fertile context for the importation of material from "real life"; indeed, as I have already noted (Chapter 1), it is not simply a convenience to import knowledge to "flesh out" entities one encounters in cyberspace. Given that one has so little information about one's interlocutors, it is essential to do so.

Thus, in "Swastika," the way site utterances were framed, and responded to, both had a great deal to do with events in Norton and elsewhere in Massachusetts. According to the dialogic approach, communication cannot be divorced from social context, but both drives it and in turn is driven by it. We already saw an example of this in Lawrence Zeigler's interfaith initiatives, which tied together his utterances in the final chapter with his interactions with religious leaders. This interconnection among a number of social reform activities, of which the Web site is only one, was a signature feature of "Swastika" (as we saw through defining the connection between Daniel Green's utterances in Chapter 1 and the involvement of the community in the Greens' problems).

Another example of this "cybersocial" fusion, indicated through considering CONTESTING OWNERSHIP, is Phyllis Feingold's parsing of passages from curricular materials examined by the Hadassah-sponsored organization she heads, Curriculum Watch. Feingold's complaint about some passages in textbooks was they presented sanitized descriptions of anti-Israel terrorist groups, such as Hamas. In the following quotation, Feingold objected to a definition in a glossary for a textbook that mentioned the terrorist group Black September:

> In the glossary, Black September is defined as "the name of the PLO organization responsible for holding Israeli athletes hostage at the 1972 Olympics. They took their name from the month of 1970 during which the Jordanian army ousted the PLO from Jordan after their repeated attacks against Israel threatened the power of King Hussein." Note how it says "responsible for holding Israeli athletes hostage," without mentioning the assassinations and campaigns of terror.

At these and other points, Feingold described how her organization's interpretation of passages about Jews and Israel, and related matters, had resulted in negotiations with publishers, leading in some cases to changes in these representations.

Feingold's interpretation of the textbook passage was dialogistic. By their nature, textbook utterances are often assumed officially sanctioned, in part because they are used in the context of the classroom, where the environment gives the textbook a degree of authority. Feingold's act of questioning the validity of these representations was in fact a way of challenging the authority of their composers' purported ownership of them. By so doing, Feingold asserted, in the name of the Jewish people she represents, that the recounted events have another explanation. Were it not for Feingold's reading of the state of affairs described by the passage, it might have passed for being evenhanded. However, when one dialogically unfolds the textbook utterance, what it communicates becomes more suspect.

This fact aside, however, Feingold's observation reinforced what appeared to be the more general persuasive goal of "Swastika": to establish the pervasiveness of anti-Semitism, beyond what was involved in the Green incidents. Its placement was therefore interesting. Instead of referring, comparatively earlier in the site, to Feingold's reading of the textbook passages, the authors chose to begin with the significantly less ambiguous incident of harassment directed toward the Greens. Although there may be some debate about how textbook passages are parsed by Feingold and her colleagues, one cannot dispute that what happened to the Greens is well beyond what is tolerable in civil society. In other words, site designers began with what is less ambiguous and progressed to areas where the arguments depend more on interpretation. This is also a clue to the fact that they knew the way to best employ dialogical approaches to communication. They began with what is less debatable (that is, the hate crime, which allowed less room for alternative interpretations) and, having established that, moved on to areas where alternative interpretations were not only available, but necessary, to grasp the authors' points.

From incidents of thuggery, the authors then moved through interviews with several rabbis concerning desecration to temples and religious objects such as the Menorah to anti-Semitism in academia. Through the account of this progression, all of which was related prior to the page containing Feingold's interview, the case for anti-Semitism was well established before the comparatively more controversial issue of interpreting textbook passages was brought out. Presuming one progressed through the site in the order intended by its composers, Feingold's CONTESTING OWNERSHIP became less controversial, in line with Bakhtin's principle that utterance draws on previous utterance to establish its meaning.

Finally, we should note that "Swastika," despite its largely conventional rhetorical mode of expression, relied for material to inform its utterances on sources not explicitly written or even spoken. Rather, frequently OTHER MEANING came from the lived experiences of Jews in Massachusetts. An example was Lawrence Zeigler's account of his experiences growing up as the only Jewish student in his elementary school. Zeigler's story offered a sociohistorically specific interpretation that helped put current anti-Semitic activity in perspective. It recalls Vico's argument that, to understand what was happening in a historical period, one must seek answers in the utterances of those who lived during that period. Although we saw Zeigler's experiences only through written utterances, based on what he spoke in interviews, it was clear that the people responsible for constructing and posting the site intended it to intersect with the cultural experience of being Jewish in America.

Summary

As was the case with the Bush and Gore campaign sites, the utterance reading of "Swastika" dialogically opened up a vista of interpretations that elaborate, and in some cases contradict, impressions gained from a standard (conventional) reading. Like all Web sites, "Swastika" presented at least two faces, depending on whether it was viewed in monological or dialogical terms. The results of the dual reading of "Swastika" are particularly beneficial in unfolding the forces underlying the surface impressions that might lead one to think of it as a simple, straightforward, even boring site. Not only do dialogical insights lead us to appreciate "Swastika," but they also point out important qualities of effective activist sites that can be emulated by others who want to use Web utterance to aid in social reform.

"Swastika on the Lawn" treated its subject seriously and relied on knowledge and evidence; grounded most of that evidence, not in abstraction, but in the experiences and thoughts of living human beings;

and respected its readers in that it did not prematurely breach their sensibilities with exaggerated claims before laying the groundwork for its more controversial assertions. In many ways, "Swastika" was a good union of noticeably monologic qualities (such as the conventional narrative, reportorial style) together with dialogic elements (such as the firm grounding in sociohistorically specific circumstance).

CONCLUSION

The dual readings of the sites of the U.S. presidential candidates and "Swastika" have pointed the way to achieve a fuller understanding of Web pages/sites as vehicles of political communication. Despite some significant differences in the sites that serve as data for these two case studies, a comparison of findings reveals some important areas of similarity, both those cited in this chapter and others I am sure will come to fruition as further research is done using the dual reading method. The great value of dual reading is that, by following the process, which entails recognition of the inherent monological and dialogical qualities of language, one can confront pages/sites that at first seem impenetrable owing to their impossible vastness and diversity, and render them not only manageable, but also configured in ways that repeatedly generate progressively deeper insight. This inviting of different viewpoints, the essence of dialogism, and the continual learning from the interanimation of these views, must lead eventually to a better understanding of Web pages as forms of civic discourse.

The design of Web sites for propagating civic and political messages presents challenges having to do with the Web in its current state and what we can expect it to be in the future. Because the Internet and the Web are relatively undeveloped (compared to other mass media), significant problems must be overcome, and by contemplating these we can devise next steps to help realize the Internet's potential for wide-ranging civic discourse.

NOTES

1. "Java is a high level programming language developed by James Gosling and others at Sun Microsystems, mainly since 1995, when it became popular for Internet programming" (Thimbleby, 2000, p. 937). Small Java programs called "applets" that run within a Web browser are enormously popular in

designing Internet pages and sites, providing animation and other features. JavaScript is "a popular scripting language that is widely supported in Web browsers and other Web tools. It is easier to use than Java, but not as powerful and deals mainly with the elements on the Web page" (Freedman, 2001b, p. 208).

2. As one of many examples, Angelfire (www.angelfire.lycos.com) offers free Web space, and a twelve-step process of filling in blanks to make one's own page. As a test, I signed on to Angelfire, went to their Web shell and completed a reasonably professional test page in about 15 minutes. While I do have some experience in Web design, and therefore was more familiar with the terminology than a beginner might be, the procedure is so simple and straightforward that any computer user could become familiar with it in a very short time. Moreover, the Angelfire site, like others of this type, provides the capability to add on many features, available on the Web for free. We should remember that a rapidly composed page like my test case merely establishes presence on the Web; from there the page can be easily modified to be as complex as the designer wishes.

3. A good example is the chapter arrangement of "Swastika on the Lawn," analyzed later in this chapter.

4. Sites discussed in the cited research are those of conventional political party candidates and do not include many other types that could carry political messages.

5. Sterne (1997) offers a somewhat different opinion, emphasizing factors such as limited canvas area, and a color palette that, if one wants to display colors that will be seen on all monitors, is limited to only 256 colors (the so-called color-safe palette). Sterne quotes one marketing expert as saying that "the Web is one of the most restrictive canvases ever offered to an artist" (p. 258). However, this claim is made preparatory to asserting that these restrictions will lead to a rebirth of "pure style" in design and thus a realization of a greater range of possibilities.

6. Here I refer to category systems, as applied to the finished product. Of course these categories are described in great detail in the markup and other languages (coding), such as HTML, that render the page for viewing in the browser.

7. Inevitably, in discussing candidate Web sites, one has to confront the question of whether Web sites are demonstrably useful in the campaign or whether they are merely window dressing used to show how up to date the candidate is. In the absence of publicly available information to verify this, I rely on (I admit) the cynical view: Web sites are very popular among candidates, and they would not be if they did not have some benefit for the campaign. With regard to presidential campaigns, there is some anecdotal evidence to suggest that both the Bush and the Gore campaigns in 2000 were not strongly attached to the Web as a campaign tool (King, n.d.). However, it is unclear whether their ambivalence was due to an intrinsic aversion to the Internet or unfamiliarity with

how it works (my analysis of the development of both candidates' Web sites seems to indicate the latter). The Internet has two qualities that might lead a campaign staff—particularly an experienced staff—to be hesitant to use it. First, because the Internet has been widely available only relatively recently (roughly the early 1990s), there have been only three presidential campaigns in which it has been used—two, really (1996 and 2000), since the use of the Internet in the 1992 campaign was minimal. Second, technological innovation involving elements of the Internet continues to accelerate rapidly, so that it is difficult for those who wish to use it to keep current with its capabilities and potentials. Clearly, candidate Web sites continue to grow in number and size, as well as sophistication. An excellent example is the use by 2004 Democratic candidate Howard Dean of the Internet as a highly effective fund-raising tool and as a channel (simulcast on television) of his announcement of his candidacy.

8. Data was originally gathered only on candidates from the two major U.S. political parties (Democrats and Republicans). Hence, Pat Buchanan's site was included, though he later switched from the Republican to the Reform Party.

9. Another question that inevitably comes up in connection with candidate Web sites is whether it is the candidate, the campaign staff, paid consultants, or some combination of these who stand responsible for what is represented on the candidate's site. My position is that the responsibility rests with some combination of these individuals or constituencies; however, the decision about how the site will appear ultimately rests with the candidate or someone on the staff he or she trusts. Appearance and image are too important in politics for them to be left to the decision of hired designers with no connection to the campaign. Moreover, I stand by my analysis of the Bush and Gore sites presented in this chapter. It is very clear to me that the sites (particularly as they develop over time) carry the stamp of their respective candidates, both their strengths and their weaknesses. Whether this is due to the candidate's personal inclinations or decisions made by the staff or Web designers (who are in some sense extensions of the candidate) based on what they think the candidate's preferences are, the Web site is part of the image of the candidate in the public arena as surely as a television appearance or public speech. Hence, it can be analyzed as a form of expression, in and of itself, whether it satisfies some monologic conception of whether there is a "direct line" between the candidate and the final product or not. In fact, dialogism is concerned with destabilizing linear connections such as these.

10. Actually, the designers of version 1 apparently intended to use sans serif type, but due to an error in the HTML coding language for the home page (version retrieved October 25, 1999), the text is displayed in the font specified by the user's browser. It should also be noted that there is no way that a designer can specify the exact fonts to render a page on a user's screen; the designer can merely specify a number of fonts (in the case of versions 1 and 2,

these very similar fonts are Verdana, Arial, Helvetica, and Sans). In the vast majority of cases, the user's computer will have one of these fonts.

11. "A web page that allows users to enter data, which can then be sent back to the server" (Downing, Covington, & Covington, 2003, p. 201). Among specific features of forms that can be generated by HTML and other code, the authors include text fields, list boxes, radio buttons, and check boxes.

12. A pull-down menu is a menu of choices that can be pulled down from the menu bar (or other location) by a mouse click and is available as long as the user keeps it open (that is, by holding down on the mouse).

13. There are three, very minor, instances of one graphic missing from this page rendering. The graphic is an arrow in the form of a doubled carat—">>"—to show where to activate a pull-down menu. Apparently, this graphic is not in the directory file with the rest of the graphics for the page, but is imported from some other source. Rather than try to reconstruct the image (which is very small) from the screen snapshot, I just filled in the image with appropriate background color. Another slight adjustment made in the image was the coloring-in of the small letter menu on the left side, using lighter colors, so it would be visible. Against the black background, the red color I have set on my browser for followed links is barely visible.

14. For the 2004 election, Howard Dean has already used his Web site to simulcast the speech in which he declared his candidacy and has taken the lead in fund-raising due largely to online contributions.

15. There is an item on one pull-down menu that allows the visitor to "search the issues," but it is not easy to find. The menu is in the top right area of the page: the displayed choice is "Search News," with two other choices displayed when one presses the button: "Search Issues" and "Search Entire Site." The "Issues" page (linked from the home page) is extraordinarily sparse, with only two links to tertiary pages ("FAQ" and "Issue Breakdown"). Indeed, like the home page, most of the "Issues" page (the main text area) is devoted to promotional messages/links (for example, "Join the Revolution" and "Download Some Free Stuff").

16. Here the Bush team pays a price for its decision to use a black background: many colors to indicate followed links (these are set by the user in the browser preferences) are nearly invisible against a black background.

17. Cheney does appear, with Bush, on the main page logo, but this did not happen until several iterations of version 3 later. Lynne Cheney is never prominently featured.

18. There is as yet no evidence that the approach taken by the Bush team toward its Web site gained them any advantage in terms of votes, although Ben-Ur and Newman (2002) note that "[b]ecause the election yielded such close results, every corrective strategy could have contributed significantly" (p. 1062).

19. However, it must be noted that the Bush site is the only one in the database to extensively change twice, and the first revision of the site was no doubt

necessitated by the fact that version 1 was so ineptly executed (see standard reading). Of the remaining candidates, few lasted long enough for there to be a need to revise the sites, based on reconceptualizing the audience or anything else.

20. The connection between this indication and, for example, Bush's conduct of the Iraq war is much too obvious to be coincidental.

21. PDF is "a file format that has captured all the elements of a printed document as an electronic image that you can view, navigate, print, or forward to someone else. PDF files are created using Adobe Acrobat, Acrobat Capture, or similar products. To view and use the files, you need the free Acrobat Reader" (Thing, 2002, p. 522).

22. "CGI defines an interface for running external applications and programs on behalf of a Web server" (Tittel, Gaither, Hassinger, & Erwin, 1996, p. 14). The key element in CGI operation is the gateway: "Gateways are really applications that handle information requests on a server's behalf. The server hands client requests off to referenced CGI applications, including the appropriate data from the requesting client. The CGI application executes using this input data, and returns its results back to the server. The server, in turn, passes this back to the requesting client" (Tittel et al., 1996, pp. 14–15). This technology is used when site visitors fill out a form (as they do, for example, on candidate pages to subscribe to a newsletter). For CGI to work, it must connect to databases. In other words, CGI scripting shows an increase in site complexity.

23. Obviously there are exceptions—for example, Steve Forbes, who also had one of the most extensive Web presences of any candidate.

24. At least, not by users reading them with Acrobat Reader; the full version of Acrobat will allow users to modify PDF documents, but of course the full version is not free and therefore is not available to all users, as Acrobat Reader is.

25. In a comprehensive survey of campaign site elements, Benoit and Benoit (2000) judged the Gore site to be one of the top two.

26. "(PIX [picture] element) The smallest element on a video display screen. A screen is broken up into thousands of tiny dots, and a pixel is one or more dots that are treated as a unit. A pixel can be one dot on a monochrome screen, three dots (red, green and blue) on a color screen, or clusters of these dots" (Freedman, 2001b, p. 300).

27. "GIF, or CompuServe GIF, is the most widely used graphics format on the Web today. GIF stands for Graphics Interchange Format and was developed by CompuServe to fill the need for a cross-platform image format" (Lemay, 1996, p. 208). Animated GIFs "embed multiple GIF images into a single file for animation" (Siegel, 1997); when activated, the animated GIF can replay, at different speeds, a series of still-picture GIFs, and can thereby create the illusion of motion (animation). Animated GIFs are one of the most basic and cheapest forms of animation, and due to the need of Web sites to attract attention, have become extremely popular (Sterne, 1997).

28. The symbols used here designate the hexadecimal code for the color, each pair representing, respectively, the amount of red, green, and blue in the color ("violet dusk-ish" has equal amounts of red and green, and quite a bit more blue) (Musciano & Kennedy, 2002, pp. 617–620). There are 256 colors designated as color safe, that is, that will be displayed more or less accurately on any computer monitor.

29. RealPlayer is "an Internet media player and browser plug-in development by RealNetworks, Inc., that supports playback of RealAudio and RealVideo, as well as certain other formats" (Microsoft Corporation, 2002, p. 441).

30. In HTML coding, this is often done, as it is here, by defining a table and putting the information in a cell of that table. If one sets the table border to zero, then it will not look onscreen as if there is a table, but only as if the displayed information is limited to a certain width.

31. Unlike version 1, the page background color is specified in the HTML coding.

32. "Page Info" is a choice on the "View" menu in Netscape Communicator (I used version 4.7.1) that causes a pop-up window to display information about all the elements on a page, including graphics, CGI scripts, and so on, as well as when the page, and each element of it, was last modified.

33. The fact that the photos are of equal size indicates egalitarianism, not only between the candidates, but also between the candidates and their spouses.

34. There is considerable ethnocentrism in the "rules" for good site design. The conventional wisdom about effective Web design holds true for Western cultures (the vast majority of Web users are in the United States and Europe), but as I showed in a case study of a touristic site in Chinese and English (Holt, 2003b), these rules do not necessarily apply in an Eastern culture.

35. I refer to "Swastika on the Lawn" in the past tense, since it was recently removed from the site of the college that sponsored it. That "Swastika" worked so well in accomplishing its goals, yet now is no longer on the Web, is testimony to the unique nature of Internet utterance.

36. As previously, the names of these individuals have been changed, but are similar in structure to the names used to identify the individuals mentioned on the site.

37. On the other hand, one could see this as CONTESTING OWNERSHIP. Rabbi Weiss poses a challenge by offering an alternative explanation to those who view such incidents as hate crimes.

Chapter 5

Conclusion

As noted in Chapter 1, the goal of comprehending both the monologic and dialogic approaches to thought and language, and their combined use in dual reading, is to improve our understanding of the Internet as a tool of civic discourse. In this final chapter, I revisit issues posed in Chapter 1, drawing together numerous findings to assess the promises and possible limitations of Internet communication as a channel for civic discourse in the third millennium, as well as suggesting some ways its potential could be more effectively exploited.

DUAL READING IN THE STUDY OF INTERNET DISCOURSE: SOME METHODOLOGICAL REFLECTIONS

Throughout this book I have pointed to the Internet's size and diversity as factors that make Internet communication particularly difficult to analyze. Given this scope, and the vast number of intercombinations of elements it leads to, we can expect forms of Internet utterance to increase. Unfortunately, in devising ways to accommodate this diversity, we already lag behind, and I contend that so long as we do not acquaint ourselves with the dual qualities of Internet discourse, our attempts to understand will lag still further. One consequence of this situation, unfortunately, may be that we also fail to realize the Internet's potential as a way of communicating in the civic and public sphere.

However, as we have seen (through the analyses in Chapters 3 and 4), the Internet's vast size and relentless diversity need not prevent us from understanding its two most frequent forms of discourse. As explained in Chapter 2, the complex roots of dialogism make of dual reading an extraordinarily productive way to look not simply at Internet communication but all discourse. The dual reading method, and the dialogical view on which it is based, remain open to the Internet's vastness through not rejecting a multiplicity of possible interpretations for any given Internet utterance. In this section, I summarize and extend discussion in previous chapters concerning the insights dual reading offers as well as its potential limitations.

Dual Reading: Insights Provided

How does dual reading help us better understand Internet utterance? First, it helps us move beyond the limitations of formal theory. One difficulty that keeps communication scholars from making full use of the Internet as a tool of civic discourse is their tendency to try to understand communication the way it has always been understood—by means of formal theory. Yet we should ask ourselves if formal theoretical (that is, primarily monologic) systems should be the preferred goal of Internet communication research. Although even dual reading is to some extent theoretical (in that it makes general statements about specific instances of discourse), the great majority of communication research to date has been built on formal theory that, being primarily empirical and quantitative, aims at homogenizing sociohistorically specific information into general statements.

The limits of formal theory in analyzing Internet discourse are analogous to the limits demonstrated in Chapters 3 and 4 for standard readings of EDMs and Web pages/sites. The standard reading only takes the researcher so far into the substance of Internet utterance. As we saw in Chapter 4, for example, standard readings of the candidates' Web sites left us with significant unresolved questions concerning the strategies of campaign site designers; likewise, standard readings of EDM threads (Chapter 3) failed to explain the subtleties of the underlying dynamics (such as the "identity" of Jerry Chen) of the utterances that comprised them. Similarly, theory that assumes a primarily monologic perspective generalizes about specific instances of communication in such a way that it gives us only a partial picture of Internet discourse.

Given these circumstances, it is time we moved beyond primarily monologic conceptions of theory and, as it were, give up attempts to construct formal, conventional theories about the meaning of Internet discourse. Instead, we should embrace enthusiastically the "new" and celebrate, rather than bemoan, the scope and diversity of Internet discourse. In the words of Weinberger (2002), quoted earlier in Chapter 1, we should "savor the rush" that comes from realizing the old forms of identity and communication—and, one could add, the communication theories by which we sought to understand them—no longer play as significant a role in this new form of communication. Indeed, the open-ended quality of Internet utterance is the factor that most surely confirms its potential as playing a role in civic society. Perhaps the day we should dread is when we actually do have a firm, reliable (that is, monologic) system to theorize about Internet utterances. On that day we will have, to appropriate a memorable Bakhtinian metaphor, laid out Internet communication "for burial," having taken it from the realm of living language and into the realm of abstraction, as the historians of Vico's day did with the visceral, immediate expressions of writers such as Homer.

Closely related to the size and multiplicity of Internet discourse is another problem brought up in Chapter 1: how difficult it can be to "get a grip" on Internet discourse. Confronting Internet utterance in civic society with the intent of probing its underlying meaning is often a very daunting process; where does one begin? Here, too, dual reading makes a valuable contribution, in both monologic and dialogic terms. On the monologic side, dual reading gives the structural-functional analysis a "new lease on life." Although there may never be an overarching monological theory/classification system for Internet discourse, we cannot entirely jettison the monologic view, since it is inevitably a part of living language. Rather, like dialogism, structural-functional analysis can and should be updated and attuned more flexibly to Internet utterance. Standard reading allows the analyst more freedom to choose from a number of structural-functional models to suit the nature of the discourse being analyzed. This is because the standard portion of dual reading avoids a "one-size-fits-all" approach, in favor of a more flexible range of choices that better adapt to the wide diversity in Internet discourse.

On the other hand, dual reading results in benefits for interpretive approaches as well. As noted repeatedly, once one starts to look at an utterance dialogically, one's degree of insight is significantly increased—more, perhaps than one is comfortable with. The potential for expanding the problem space in utterance reading is infinite, because the details of the world that can be brought into Internet utterance to inform its meaning are limitless. However, because the utterance portion of dual reading involves a limited number (four) of the more commonly used elements whereby the world is brought into the post and the page, the analyst has a way of controlling the unimaginable variability in possible dialogic insights revealed by the utterance reading.[1] Aside from that, of course, these four elements are hardly precisely defined, being broad enough to allow the individual analyst's view to manifest itself in the conception of the utterance in question. In Chapters 3 and 4, I concentrated only on the most interesting of these alternative readings. However, as is the case with all dialogical inquiry, I had to generate more alternative readings than I ended up using. Dual reading is ideal for generating such alternatives.

I should also mention that this necessary limitation in ways to conceptualize sociohistorical variety is not a drawback. The goal of dialogism, and the utterance reading it informs, has never been to exhaustively describe the infinitely multifaceted reality it insists we acknowledge. The human mind cannot encompass, nor human language express, such vast knowledge. Since we know that we must express sociohistorical specificity using imperfect ("imperfect," according to monological standards) processes of language and thought, we are in effect imprisoned by words and the concepts on which they are based. Knowing this, we can visualize the analysis of Internet discourse as pursuing a different goal. It is less a question of how the method describes reality than with (as was the case with pragmatism) how it can lead the reflective human consciousness in the direction of a reality that remains forever tantalizingly beyond thought and language. Monological perspectives, as we have seen, are ill-equipped to accomplish this task. However, because it is necessary that so-called dialogical thought be expressed in conventional language, dialogism is equally ill-prepared to lead us toward the real, at least not without first being reframed in conjunction with analysis based on primarily monologic assumptions.

The repeated use of monological and dialogical perspectives, and especially shuttling between them, generates an extraordinary number and variety of insights. This works to considerably expand the problem space involved in the analysis of Internet utterance. An analogy to this process is to be found in the field of conversation analysis (Psathas, 1995), another area in which monological and dialogical perspectives on language both inevitably play a part (Holt, 2003a). According to Schegloff (1991), a pioneer in conversation analysis, the inspiration to probe human talk comes from discovering how to convert insistent intuition into empirically detailed analysis (p. 66). In Internet discourse, insistent intuition is roughly analogous to dialogism, empirical analysis to monologism. In other words, both modes of inquiry need to be fused in order to provide an adequately nuanced, yet consistent, account of discourse.

Simply put, dual reading allows for greater flexibility in approaching persistent problems of analyzing Internet utterance. The range of alternative readings presented by dual reading allow the analyst to devise an appropriate strategy for the standard reading (choosing among many templates available from monological systems of thought) and yet have a manageable approach to utterance reading (conceptualizing importation of sociohistorical specificity in four flexible, yet rich, indicators found in all discourse). This de facto recognition of the breathtaking variety in Internet utterance is both more realistic and more able to generate insight than is possible using the methods in conventional theories.

Dual reading also helps keep separate the conceptual distinction between monologism and dialogism (keeping in mind this is a conceptual, not a real, distinction). The "dual" reading in fact involves three activities, pursued more or less simultaneously: the standard reading, the utterance reading, and the comparison between the two. As dialogically inclined thinkers remind us, neither life nor the processes by which we look at it can be neatly categorized, but rather involve a dynamic, ongoing shifting back and forth between modes of thought, with each "pass" across data resulting not merely in a change in how the data is conceived, but in the *consciousness of the researcher*. One difference between monologism and dialogism is that, in the former, comparatively little attention is paid to changes in investigator consciousness (with corresponding changes in how the data is conceived [see Chapter 2, particularly the discussion of the move from mind-body dualism]), whereas in the latter it is a chief point of concern. The advantage of dual reading is that, in moving back and forth between the two ways of looking at the data, one is kept constantly in mind of the assumptions one is using.

Dual reading also helps the investigator avoid falling into too-rigid analytical habits. A persistent problem in the analysis of any utterance is the tendency of the analyst to lapse into routine practices, using what consistently "works," and thereby remaining closed to other approaches. This is often more a problem with monological perspectives, which can gain the prominence they do because they are largely unquestioned.

However, in dialogical approaches, another danger arises from widening, rather than narrowing, one's perspective. Because using the dialogical mode can be such a liberating experience, one can be led to think that unlimited multiplicity means all monological perspectives (which restrict multiple interpretations) are invalid. This can lead not to making analysis of utterance clear but irretrievably murky.

The best approach is one in which the analyst is kept constantly in mind of the ongoing need to confront the assumptions of both monologism and dialogism, both always part of language, and each offering advantages and disadvantages. Dual reading keeps such assumptions in the forefront of the analyst's mind. The shifting back and forth between modes of analytical consciousness can help one avoid falling into predictable patterns of thinking, through constant refreshment of one's analytical perspective.

A related advantage is that dual reading tends to mitigate extreme formulations, whether they are cast in primarily monologic or dialogic terms. With dual reading, one need not surrender to the limitations of the monological perspective, with its strict constraints on what is "acceptable." On the other hand, dual reading helps one avoid the unnerving chasm of limitless alternative interpretations that arise from taking an unreservedly dialogical position. It can be as incapacitating to function under far-reaching freedom as under far-reaching restraint, since to insist that one must have extreme freedom is itself a form of extreme restraint. Students of Internet utterance would do well to heed Chinese philosophers, who have said for centuries that the best approach to life lies in embracing the "Golden Mean," avoiding excess and seeking unity and completion rather than division and separation.

A final notable benefit of dual reading, in both its standard and utterance modes, is that it refocuses analytical attention toward the human being and away from technology. Whether attempting to understand the world primarily in the monologic or the dialogic mode, the individual in civic culture has the responsibility to construe the world in terms of how it functions and what it means. In discussions of Internet communication, too often the focus is on technological acceleration, on human–machine interface, on the broad sweep of globalization—in short, on almost anything but the locus at which technological practice and all other facets of culture are actualized, the individual human being. Despite the ever-accelerating pace of technological change, it is human consciousness that forges the frameworks according to which utterance will be interpreted. Dialogism tells us it is impossible to render our magnificently complicated world into neat categories. The real reason for this is that the individual human being is too complex to be depicted in simplified terms and it is this individual social actor who, acting in collaboration with others, has the resources to interpret any utterance.

Dual Reading: Limitations to Keep in Mind

Despite the promises noted in the previous section, there are a number of possible limitations to keep in mind when using dual reading. While these certainly do not invalidate the method's utility, they do need to be acknowledged if one is to make optimal use of it.

First, and most obviously, it is possible to take only one perspective—either primarily monological or dialogical—at a time. I have encountered this problem since my early studies of Taoism and human communication (see, for example, Holt, Chang, & Steingard, 1990), long before I encountered Bakhtin; I have also confronted it in studies of collaborative storytelling and conversation (see, for example, Holt, 1989, 2003a). In the analysis of discourse, taking a primarily monological point of view predisposes one to put the dialogical perspective into the background, and vice versa. Nevertheless, even though it is not possible to take both perspectives simultaneously, dual reading offers the next best thing: an integrated process by which one can assume each perspective, one at a time, and compare them.

The key idea that should be cultivated by the analyst of Internet utterance is that language always has elements of both monologism and dialogism. In my opinion, this realization is the single most important prerequisite for achieving understanding of living language. Proceeding from this basis, one comes to realize that the ideal situation (presumably involving some gestalt act of grasping the totality of language in all its aspects) is impossible, given humanity's current state of cognitive evolution. Thus, while taking monological and dialogical perspectives "one at a time" may not be ideal, such a procedure is a good place to begin.

A second potential limitation of dual reading, closely related to the one I have just described, is that, ironically, one could say that at its root the entire approach is monological. Dual reading does not really permit the analyst to step outside the restraints of monologism. In the standard reading, obviously, the monological perspective predominates. In the utterance reading, however, we also take a monological approach, at least to the extent of viewing infinitely varied sociohistorical circumstance according to four utterance elements, said to be appropriate no matter which sample of Internet discourse one applies them to. This range of applicability is confirmed in the marked qualitative differences in the data for the four case studies in Chapters 3 and 4. Thus, paradoxically, the so-called utterance reading is also, to some extent, monologic.

Indeed, even if one takes a dialogical view, one still must express insight gained thereby in monological terms. Sociocultural practices governing this predisposition to monologism include many conventional understandings related to making linguistic expressions predictable and standardized. All accounts, even those informed by the dialogic mode of thought, must be presented in such a way that it appeals to the shared understanding of readers. As Bakhtin emphasized, and I have reiterated throughout this book, conventional (centripetal) understandings such as these are essential if language is to serve as the basis of widely understood utterances, limited as these understandings may be when held up against the richness of dialogical alternatives.

However, the need to express a view informed by dialogical insight in monological terms does not present a serious problem, so long as the analyst knows it exists and why. To reiterate: the purpose of dialogism is not to grant complete understanding of language and thought in all its manifestations—on the grounds of human cognitive limitations alone, this goal is absurd. Rather, the goal is to lead human consciousness in the direction of more complete realization of the various meanings of Internet utterance, and in the process provide alternatives to monological positions one might not otherwise have been inclined to question. A dialogical "purist" might scoff at having to thus compromise the integrity of the dialogic position; however, in my opinion the "pure dialogist" (should there be such an entity) would be as dangerous as a "pure monologist." To rephrase a common saying, it is not patriotism that is the last refuge of scoundrels, but methodological purity.

The final possible limitation to dual reading is that it simplifies—down to four—the elements to be used to think about sociohistorical circumstance in the utterance reading. These four categories represent the broadest possible ways to talk about some—only some—of the basic types of knowledge involved in formulating and understanding Internet discourse. I chose these four after analyzing numerous EDM threads and asking myself what aspects of the world were seemingly brought into play by the discussants on these lists.[2] Once I formulated these four concepts, however, I realized how useful they were, as indicators of four kinds of basic knowledge, in exploring how both composers and perceivers of Internet utterance communicate with each other. I would like these four elements to be seen, not as ends in themselves, but as stepping-off points to generate insights about how the world is brought into the post and the page. As I have pointed out repeatedly, the process of dialogical inquiry generates momentum: once begun, insights lead to further insights, and these to still further insights. As this approach is used with other Internet utterances, I look forward to fruitful and productive work about and beyond these elements that will lead to further refinement of their applicability and usefulness.

To summarize, despite these limitations, dual reading offers a powerful tool to approach what initially appears overwhelming: the scope and diversity of Internet utterance. The standard reading makes it easier to disentangle functional elements of EDMs and Web pages/sites, so that what might seem chaotic can be sorted into patterns that form coherent backdrops against which to view dialogic alternatives. At the same time, exploration of utterance and the context in which it achieves meaning (through the four elements) opens up many different alternative readings for a given utterance. Thus, dual reading acknowledges the futility of attempting to devise an encompassing classification system to categorize widely disparate elements of Internet discourse while at the same time recognizing the need for humans to understand utterances according to their monologic qualities, thereby accommodating the regularities in expression according to which humans fashion shared sociocultural understandings.

DIALOGISM AND THE INTERNET IN CIVIC DISCOURSE: SUGGESTIONS FOR FUTURE DEVELOPMENT

Having realized the need for a manageable yet textured reading of Internet utterance, and having also devised a method for achieving it, we have taken important steps toward our eventual goal of more fully utilizing the Internet in the practice of civic discourse. We are now prepared to address what can be done to bring the Internet into civic discourse. I should caution that my subsequent suggestions will not comprise firm guidelines for what is to be done next, still less a program of definite steps to be pursued. The difficulties of understanding Internet utterance discussed previously also unfortunately prevent us from formulating precise courses of action. Nevertheless, the important initial obstacle—realizing the nature of Internet discourse—is, through dual reading, at least within our grasp. This is a liberating achievement; at the outset of this project, I was prone, as I would guess many are, to see the Internet as a promising mode of communication for the propagation of civic discourse, but overwhelming in terms of what it is and what it can be.

As a rubric for discussing how the findings from analyses presented in this book help us understand and improve EDM threads and political/ideological Web sites, I return to the four principles enunciated by Dahl (1989) as qualities of ideal (Concept 1) democracy (see Chapter 1). Each participant should be able to experience *effective participation*, have *voting equality* at the decisive stage, have *enlightened understanding*, and have *control of the agenda*. As I have said, it is this loftier conception of democracy that should inspire us as we talk about bringing the Internet into greater use in civic discourse. By considering Dahl's four elements of ideal democracy, we can perhaps understand how some features of Internet discourse, which may at first seem irrelevant to the ideals of democracy, can be reconfigured in a democratic system to take advantage of the idiosyncratic features of this new medium. Indeed, one could visualize the distance between the ideal of democratic participation in Internet discourse and the less-than-perfect manifestation according to which we now operate as a Vygotskian zone of proximal development (see Chapter 2). The unrealized goal of what we wish to achieve—that is, an optimal intersection between civic society and Internet—is probably something of which we are only dimly aware. However, this fact is to our benefit as it causes us to rethink the traditions of democracy in light of what we have learned throughout this book. In the following I consider some ways "classical" democracy and new technology intersect. I will then expand beyond Dahl's four principles to address issues involved as individuals use the Internet for propagating political messages beyond boundaries once imposed by cultural practices "in real life."

Effective Participation

Dahl's first principle has to do with the necessity for people to participate in democratic government in such a way that their participation makes a difference. As we have seen, the Internet is more open to free formulation of utterance than perhaps any other form of mass communication. We have seen how access to the Internet, though presently most extensive in the United States and Europe, continues to offer increasingly greater and more widespread resources to computer users to participate in composing and reading EDMs, and in constructing and interpreting Web pages/sites. Apart from constraints on the use of computers, arising from lagging technological development and differences in socioeconomic status among users (and potential users), seldom has humanity witnessed a more "democratic" form of communication than the Internet.

Yet the notion of participation on the Internet, and participation "in real life," can be quite different. As we saw in examining "Wen Ho Lee," dual reading permits one to probe beneath the surface of civic participation via Internet utterance. The utterance reading of that thread pointed to a way of unravelling the puzzle of Jerry Chen's identity, and thus to clarify the connection between what was being said about Chen and about Wen Ho Lee. Similar observations were made about the "Carnival" thread, where it was shown that participants fashioned identity through a form of participation driven by a desire to elevate themselves with respect to a media icon claiming the moral superiority to judge them. The dynamics of interaction in "Wen Ho Lee" and "Carnival" shows us that the definition of *participation* changes considerably when examined in the context of Internet communication.

When Dahl speaks of participation, he refers primarily to activities defined through formal mechanisms of society, such as voting, political conventions, town hall meetings, letters to the editor, and so on. One doubts he was referring to a medium of interaction such as the Internet where one could engage in all sorts of activities impossible in face-to-face communication episodes, such as creating an alternate persona and then communicating through this entity to make differences in an on-line discussion, thereby presumably affecting the "real lives" of others who "participated" in the discussion. Ideal democracy has traditionally involved face-to-face communication and interaction. Nevertheless, we saw (particularly in Chapter 3) that people can "participate" in Internet communication without any interaction, as that term has been traditionally conceived (in the sense that no empirically verifiable information is shared by one interactant with the other). Indeed, findings in Chapter 3 revealed that the most important forms of participation can come from surrogate entities manufactured out of poster utterances. Does "Jerry Chen" "participate" in discussing Wen Ho Lee? How could one ever tell?

The utterance component of dual reading offers information about the multifaceted, often confusing, forms of participation on the Internet. This is more evident in communicating via EDMs. Equipped with a more thorough knowledge about who is participating and how, contributors, recipients, and list managers might be better prepared to understand the dynamics involved in the shuttling back and forth among utterances in list exchanges. This potential for expanding the problem space of discussion in democratic forums is in line with what has traditionally been considered perhaps the core advantage of civic discourse: if enough alternative representations are generated, there is a better chance of choosing among them to fashion more effective and appropriate thoughts and utterances. The process of changing the quality of EDM discourse is a matter, first, of recognizing that more effective discourse is possible, and second, awakening users to the subtleties of EDM communication. All of this activity, it should be noted, involves increased participation by both the propagators and the perceivers of Internet utterance, much the same as it would be for people (as in "classic" democracy) to come up with a constitution and then debate it face to face. Both Internet and face-to-face channels involve ongoing, active, effortful reformulation of positions, the very essence of the "classic" conception of participation.

Improving the process of constructing and maintaining Web sites presents somewhat different challenges. To manage Web pages/sites, designers have to go through a complicated, if often unsystematic, process of education that keeps them constantly in mind of their responsibilities to the Internet community. They learn, among other things, the following: they can be held liable for some damages incurred from using their sites; they must be aware of issues such as security, copyright protection, and the like; they must be cognizant of the limitations in the parameters of computers and servers, such as restrictions in bandwidth; they must attend to keeping their links up to date; and much more. Thus, if one formulates and maintains a political Web site, particularly an active one, one will be well educated in a number of cultural precepts of Internet life. Moreover, unlike list management, there are a number of programs that lead to certification as a Webmaster.

It is evident that this level of involvement demands participation in Internet discourse, just as surely as it does in the case of EDM threads. Similar to the process of consciousness transformation that occurs when one assumes the dialogic perspective, when the Webmaster imports the various kinds of knowledge mentioned above, the conception of the communicative relationship between designer and visitor is altered, leading in turn to alteration of the product (that is, the Web page/site), and thus to alteration of the perception of the visitor. This is an illustration of the dialogic move from passivity to activity (Chapter 2). Neither the formulator nor the perceiver of the Web page/site utterance can function without active, ongoing, effortful participation, of exactly the kind that Dahl referred to in describing "classic" democracy. Indeed, it could be argued that in some ways the kind of participation needed to construct Web sites and ensure they are placed in the stream of Internet communication is an even more intensive form of participation, involving not just communicative skills but technical expertise as well. This was dramatically illustrated in the drastic shifts in the final versions of the Bush and Gore sites (see Chapter 4).

Voting Equality

On the Internet, an analogue to voting equality would likely be free participation in the construction of political utterances. In other words, if there were equality, people would get to "vote" on content. Obviously, this is hardly an issue with EDMs, where, particularly on unmoderated lists, participants all have an equal chance to say pretty much what they want, in effect casting a "vote" (or many votes) on what will comprise the "sense of the list." This access and availability could be still further improved by augmenting list messages with other means to assess the shared perceptions of list members. For example, one could provide links in messages to Web sites that could describe key issues and make it easy for users to quickly complete questionnaire items.[3] The people who oversee the site that sponsors the list that gave us "Laura at the Carnival" (Chapter 3), although not having a questionnaire page, provide several pages that report on FAQs (frequently asked questions), provide biographical data on list members, inform visitors of news concerning gays/lesbians, call attention to notably witty posts, commemorate list members who have passed away, and so on. At present, these and similar pages serve a primarily reportorial function; however, they could be easily modified in the directions suggested above to actualize even greater participation. If this were done, it would be easy to both communicate the sense of the list to members and allow them to express an opinion on that sense—in effect, allowing them to vote equally, both with their individual posts and with respect to the content of the Web pages/sites that provide a context for EDMs.

"Voting equality" with respect to Web pages/sites is a more difficult issue, since input from visitors concerning content is very rare, perhaps because, despite strides in making page/site construction more accessible (see Chapter 1), the manner in which sites are constructed is still considered mysterious by the majority of the "surfing public." In addition, Webmasters can be very protective of their creations and reluctant to solicit suggestions on how they can be improved.

Still, if we are to dislodge the grip of monological views on site design, the first priority should be to expand the range of alternatives. Therefore, in addition to regularly seeking input from visitors (who are often highly reluctant to offer feedback), site designers should present alternatives. At the outset, these could be very basic, involving variations in such elements as background and text color, arrangement of text, and placement of graphics; later, alternatives for more subtle elements (such as verbal content) could be introduced.[4] Using a site questionnaire mechanism such as the one I just proposed for EDMs, Webmasters could get input on how people want to see the page displayed. Here, too, I envision the potential effect of these changes to be incremental and accumulative; as more people use mechanisms to gather feedback (or present alternatives), the sophistication of resources to aid in gathering this information might also improve.[5] For example, there could be a time when page construction software would include a component that would allow its users to devise feedback pages, as a routine part of constructing a site.

Of course, this is all possible now, provided one is willing to go to the frequently strenuous effort of cobbling the project together from disparate sources on the Web. However, most people are unwilling to exert this kind of effort. At every opportunity, the Internet community should be reminded of the importance of opening up pages/sites to suggestions by visitors, and in that way we may be able to avoid some of the errors that attend the current hit-and-miss guesstimation methods of ascertaining visitor response that we have today.

If the Web page/site is to live up to its potential as a tool of civic discourse, it must be seen as something other than the product of the highly trained elite. As an added benefit, the more alternatives Webmasters generate to present as choices for visitors, the greater will be the expansion of the problem space for effective presentation, and the higher the ultimate quality of the product. Solicitation of feedback will thus increase the effectiveness of the designer and the perceptiveness of the visitor. Thus, even though the presentation of Web pages/sites may currently be seen as principally "one-way" communication (designer to visitor) the suggestions presented above for permitting the visitor to exercise a "vote" (that is, a more equal choice) in how these page/site utterances are presented would make of the process a more appropriate tool of civic discourse.

Enlightened Understanding

Clearly, for both EDMs and Web pages/sites, the key to greater understanding lies, as the pragmatist John Dewey often said, in education. Education in Internet political discourse has to do both with knowledge about how Internet messages are fashioned and conceived, and also with the ways in which the idiosyncratic qualities of the medium work in aiding or hindering these processes. The analyses in Chapters 3 and 4 clearly showed the need for both kinds of understanding. An expanded conception of what is involved in Internet utterance helped provide an awareness of the nuances of messages (as in the expansion of problem space in the utterance readings). At the same time, the analytical path followed in those analyses frequently made use of technical information about computers and the Internet to clarify the possible reasons why Internet utterances are fashioned in the way they are (as in use of the e-mail mechanism for quoting entire magazine articles that we saw in "Wen Ho Lee" [Chapter 3] or the technical enhancements that assumed an increasingly prominent place in the sites for candidates Bush and Gore [Chapter 4]). Taking advantage of our understanding of computers, we are thus provided with material to construct a more useful framework for the depth interpretation of the utterance. In civic culture, enlightened understanding arises from access to knowledge, achieved through an ongoing process of education.

To achieve enlightened understanding in the sense proposed by Dahl (1989, 1998), we will have to rely on education to teach us more about both Internet utterances and about the mechanisms through which they are communicated. Education in the former domain could begin with an approach such as the one outlined in this book and with a thorough comparative analysis of results thereby obtained with those gained using other methods used in the rapidly accumulating body of research into Internet communication. However, to conduct such meta-analyses requires that we also understand key aspects of the second knowledge domain, namely, computers and technology. In fact, as scholars, we should ensure that our work is based not only on knowledge of theories from communication and related fields. We should be certain our analyses are also based on sound knowledge of the technology that imbues Internet communication with its unique qualities. In this way, we can unite the two domains of understanding needed to interpret Internet utterances. This book, which is unashamedly grounded in knowledge relating as much to technology as to communication and allied areas, is an example of this kind of productive melding of two domains that interact with one another all too infrequently.

Unfortunately, the great majority of formal educational training in page/site design (training in EDMs and list management is nearly non-existent) is centered in departments of computer science and related disciplines. Nevertheless, one point made overwhelmingly clear throughout this book is that the scientific, nearly always monological, approaches favored by computer scientists can explicate only part of the meaning of a message or a page/site. Those elements of Internet communication that yield the highly textured interpretations we saw in Chapters 3 and 4 are typically studied, not by engineers, but those in other fields, such as rhetoric, communication, history, political science, and even the arts. Achieving enlightened understanding, therefore, will require more interdisciplinary cooperation among fields that may at this time see themselves as separate from one another. Communication studies, with its roots in both social science and rhetoric, may be in an optimal position to lead the way in forging an eclectic view of Internet political discourse.

Control of the Agenda

For Dahl's final requirement for ideal democracy, the notion that the individual participant should have some voice in controlling "the agenda," I am afraid that I have little to suggest, beyond very general reiterations of points made throughout this book. To complete the ana-logue to Internet communication, "the agenda" could be taken to relate to the direction in which Internet communication can be expected to develop. Simply put: I do not think we know enough about the Inter-net to confidently predict, far less debate or in some other way try to control, the development of communication on it. As I have said re-peatedly, we do not yet know what the Internet is; thus it would be presumptuous to try to define an agenda and still more brazen to prescribe means for individuals to participate (have "a voice").

Still, the approach I take to the Internet is the one that guided it in its earliest days and the one many developers still believe in. This view sees the Internet as an open vista of possibilities for people to realize their potential as communicators, and moreover, as up to them to de-termine whether that potential will come to fruition. With a more thorough understanding of Internet utterance, we can at least gain a clearer grasp of both the potentials and the pitfalls that may arise as

Internet political utterances join the onrushing stream of technological innovation and cultural upheaval in the third millennium. We may thus be prepared to harvest the fruits that will eventually result from planting the seeds of a new, more humane approach to Internet communication. Computer-mediated communication has the popular image of being more impersonal than other types; what I have suggested throughout this book is that when we turn our focus toward humans, and away from technical considerations, this "impersonal" communication is seen to be inextricably linked to the chaotic, unpredictable, "messy," and, thus, ultimately more human world.

We cannot expect changes such as the ones referred to in this discussion to have an instantaneous, or even a short-term effect. To realize the potential of the Internet as a tool of civic discourse, we must think, not in terms of our limited lifetimes, but in terms of successive generations. Moreover, true to the process of interanimation realized in the dialogical perspective, we can also expect the development of Internet communication to have additive effects that cannot at present be predicted.

I confidently expect the evolution of Internet political discourse to follow the same pattern that has occurred in many other types of evolution of the Internet and similar technological domains: because of unexpected permutations in which growth in one area unexpectedly accelerates growth elsewhere, the gestalt of the future states of Internet political discourse is nearly certain to be something that we cannot at this moment conceive. Absent the complete understanding of the Internet that, some say, we will never achieve, the best we can do is sharpen our perception of Internet discourse, and be prepared to adopt perspectives that are sufficiently sensitive to both the monologic and the dialogic aspects present in all utterance. I believe that very positive results will be obtained simply by making these issues part of the agenda of the Internet community.

BEYOND THE WORLD AS ONE SEES IT: ISSUES CONCERNING CIVIC DISCOURSE AND THE EXTENT OF THE INTERNET

While Dahl's four requirements for ideal democracy provide a great deal of insight, there remain some additional issues of concern about the future of Internet communication as civic discourse. Of these the most pressing have to do with the capability of the Internet to propagate political messages that extend far beyond the traditional boundaries of one's culture and circumstances of daily living. Taking the realistic tack, it might be well to close our discussion with some considerations about the obstacles that face us in bringing Internet utterance to full flower as a means of communicating political thought. In the following I address concerns related to using the Internet and the Web for civic/political messages.

First, despite the enthusiastic trumpeting of the Internet as a new, promising, and indeed potentially revolutionary form of communication (Grossman, 1995), promotion strategies to Internet audiences seem driven by stereotypes that mire current thinking about the civic participants (Bimber, 1998; Margolis & Resnick, 2000). Absent knowledge about real differences and similarities between participants in the political process, the makers of Internet utterances frequently cast messages by appeal to stereotypes, though this is of course a persistent problem with all media representations, not just those on the Internet. The chief difference perhaps is that, given the scope of the Internet and the Web, the range over which the negative effects of such stereotypes can manifest is drastically increased and because much of what is expressed as Internet utterance stays on the Internet (in the case of EDMs, messages are often archived, and Web pages/sites often continue on the Web because their original propagators have forgotten about them), utterances manifesting stereotypes remain in the public discursive sphere for long periods of time. Such stereotypes are evident in many Web utterances, as illustrated in the frequent use of conventional political representations on the sites of presidential candidates (that is, the emphasis on conventional political symbology [for example, stars and stripes], or the inclusion of conventional political utterances, such as candidate positions on issues, accounts of the candidate's family life, or provision of alternate sites in Spanish). Although such stereotypical representations work by appealing to features of visitor consciousness that are expected, and hence not so different as to be jarring to their sensibilities, they also work to perhaps unreasonably restrict the conception of the audience. Hence, when a campaign team chooses to step outside the expectations of these stereotypes (as the Bush team did with version 3 of their site), the persuasive effect can be quite dramatic.

If the promise of new technology to present ideological and cultural views to one another is to be realized, one must see Internet communication as more than yet another communication venue where stereotypes affect message production. Rather, it should be seen as a unique form of communication in which such variables as range, potential audience, and possible content are greatly changed and the effects of all these and other characteristics of communication are accentuated.

Second, although the potential for the Internet and the Web to influence civic discourse has sometimes been conceived in international, cross-cultural terms (Halavais, 2000), expertise about how to effectively design messages and pages/sites remains inadequate to the demands of intercultural representation. With Web pages/sites, for example, little is understood about effective design even when it comes to pages in English (the predominant language in which the Web is expressed), still less so in languages other than English (or where pages are constructed in non-Western cultures where English is the predominant language [Holt, 2003b]). What designers of Web pages/sites in the West think they are communicating to people who speak other languages or who live in other cultures may be inappropriate, since it is based on inadequate understanding of these individuals' lives.[6] For the kind of sites analyzed in previous chapters (formal campaign and activist sites), this is of less concern, since their apparent target audiences are in the West and speak English.[7] However, for sites to fulfill their promise in civic discourse, linguistic and cultural particularity will have to be dealt with.

Specifically, given the increasingly central role played by the Internet and the Web in civic/public discourse, and the likelihood that both Internet and Web use will continue to expand, we need to be aware of, and think of ways to deal with, three specific issues. Each of these issues has to do with the conflict between the ideal of Internet communication as a tool for all, versus the specificity of its cultural underpinnings.

The first issue concerns ethnocentrism in Web design. Not only is there almost no research comparing cultural and linguistic assumptions of designers of Web sites propagating civic ideas in different cultures, assumptions about Web design are so ingrained one fears the question may not even have occurred to most designers and analysts. Nor is there likely to be improvement until we acknowledge the overwhelming emphasis on the English language and Western cultural assumptions in the formulation of pages/sites. A significant impediment to this realization is that one seldom visits a site in a language one does not understand, and beyond merely the language barrier, one might find the subtleties of representation defined by the culture's rules even harder to grasp. If the Internet is to fulfill its considerable promise as an instrument of civic discourse, this limitation in visualizing others—which works to distort representations in precisely the ways that limit full participation in civic life—must be overcome.

A second issue has to do with the fact that, because the Internet was developed in the United States, it involves cultural ideals about democracy and free expression not necessarily part of many of the world's other cultures. The presidential campaign Web site (Chapter 4), for example, is built on the idea of free election of governing representatives, a characteristic not shared in many cultures where the Internet is available (Graham, 1999). As an example of a social activism site, "Swastika on the Lawn" (Chapter 4) contains utterances best matched to a cultural system with freedom of expression in education (the site was hosted by a college of Judaic studies) and social and political life (it had numerous controversial statements about groups and people who hold different opinions). Indeed, a central theme of "Swastika" is that academic environments must find ways to accommodate differing points of view. These utterances are propagated freely in a democracy, but may be more difficult to understand in cultures where such ideals are not shared. Thus, the important and effective message of tolerance and forbearance in the face of hatred of "Swastika" could be lost simply because visitors do not begin with the same assumptions the designers do. Just because we can "look through the window" of our computer screen at other parts of the world does not mean we will understand what we are looking at—in civic discourse, awareness is merely a preliminary step to achieving understanding.

The third issue concerns the fact that Web communication is not equally available to potential participants in civic discourse:

> While everything that has been said so far is true of many citizens of North America and Western Europe, it is far from true of all the citizens in these places, still less true of Eastern Europe, and hardly true at all in, say, Africa, the Indian subcontinent or Central Asia. (Graham, 1999, p. 70)

For cultures labeled "less developed," making information technology available may be of much lower priority, perhaps not a priority at all. Furthermore, even granting computers could be made available in such cultures, the electronic communication infrastructure (such as telephone lines) can be wanting, so even if the computer is available, it might not be connected to the Internet. In such cases, physical constraints inhibit the potential for the Internet to be used in civic discourse.

These barriers are formidable and it may take years or decades to address them. Nevertheless, because technology will continue to develop at its own ever-accelerating pace (Gilder, 2000; Gleick, 1999), there is a special urgency to the task of ensuring that the evolution of technology will not outpace the evolution of civic discourse. We must dialogically link civic discourse to computer-mediated communication and to give to the former the same enthusiastic attention we customarily give to the latter. Civic discourse can be fully ushered into the computer age, but only if its special characteristics are clearly seen and our models of communication are sufficiently sensitive to the unique qualities of the new medium.

SOME FINAL THOUGHTS

In this book, true to the spirit of dialogical inquiry, I have tried to bring together what at first appears to be separate. Beginning with a description of the technological and political landscape, I moved from an introduction of two very broad perspectives on human cognition and language—monologism and dialogism—demonstrating how the dialogic perspective has emerged in roughly the past three centuries to offer a haven from the restrictions of the monologic view. At the same time, it proved necessary to acknowledge, as Bakhtin reminded us, that all living language embodies both monologic and dialogic elements. I then explored four specific samples of Internet political/ideological discourse, expressed as the two most common forms of Internet utterance, EDMs and Web pages/sites, finding dramatic confirmation of the power of dialogic inquiry, particularly when coupled with, and compared and contrasted to, the monologic framework. I concluded with a discussion of some of the issues that must be taken into account if Internet discourse is to be more fully utilized in the conduct of civic life. I conclude that despite significant obstacles to be overcome, Internet utterance stands a very good chance of becoming the instrument of democratic civic participation that it was envisioned to be in those early days of its introduction as a widespread means of communication among people from different cultures and in widely divergent parts of the world.

Yet both the dialogic approach to thought and communication, together with new forms of discourse engendered by the Internet, work in tandem to offer us a way out of current dilemmas in studying computer-mediated communication. Perhaps the key idiosyncratic feature of the dialogical approach is the realization that the first step in dislodging the grip of monologism is to call attention to its existence. Despite monologism's necessity as a feature of human thought and living language, unrestrained endorsement of monologic views leads to illusion. Moreover, belief in viewpoints that are principally monological is a form of intellectual sleep. To realize the possibilities of the Internet as a tool of civic discourse, one must rouse oneself from what one might call the comfort of monological views. The effects of monologism are not by themselves unreservedly deleterious. However, over time, monologism provides the widely, sometimes nearly universally, agreed-upon perspectives that humans, out of passivity, appear not to think it important to question: they become "Truth" with a capital "T" because they are so widely believed. To learn to question these "certainties" is the first step toward showing them in a more realistic relationship to the phenomena they describe; likewise, to challenge entrenched ideas and practices is also the most cherished ideal of civic discourse. The Internet presents us with a way to fashion a vision of democracy and civic participation more appropriate to the times in which we live, and in the future as well. It is hoped that the methods and suggestions proposed in this book will provide some inspiration to take the first step in that direction.

NOTES

1. I focused on only four elements that indicate how sociohistorical knowledge is imported to aid in the composition and interpretation of Internet utterance. Anyone thinking in the dialogical mode should never be deluded that it is possible to account for all the ways sociohistorical knowledge can inform the utterance reading.

2. For the record, dual reading was first developed for EDM threads (Holt, 1999) and later applied to Web pages/sites (Holt, 2001).

3. In my experience, asking list members to reply by self-initiated e-mail garners very few responses. A quick questionnaire with five items, four choices each, on a Web page where one can click one's responses, usually generates greater response.

4. As noted in Chapter 4, the presidential candidates have already started this process through offering site visitors the capability to "personalize" the Web site to suit their particular needs.

5. One could easily envision the widespread use of either client- or server-side software that would automatically generate alternatives to site designs and present the user with a variety of reformulations of the page/site utterance from which to choose.

6. The "translation" features of search engines such as Google are no remedy, either. For one thing, the word-for-word translation of pages not in English is frequently hilarious; for another, even a good translation (which Google's certainly is not) does not address the underlying cultural ethos behind the page's presentation.

7. The emphasis on English is true for the most part, though, as we have seen, presidential candidates have made great efforts to gain support of Spanish-speaking electorate by providing versions of their sites in Spanish.

References

Addams, J. (1902). *The spirit of youth and the city streets*. New York: Macmillan.

Addams, J. (1912). *Democracy and social ethics*. New York: Macmillan.

Albert, D. Z. (1992). *Quantum mechanics and experience*. Cambridge, MA: Harvard University Press.

Anderson, B. (1991). *Imagined communities: Reflections on the origin and spread of nationalism* (rev. and ext. ed.). London: Verso.

Argyle, K. (1996). Life after death. In R. Shields (Ed.), *Cultures of Internet: Virtual spaces, real histories, living bodies* (pp. 133–142). London: Sage.

Bakhtin, M. M. (1981). Discourse in the novel. In C. Emerson & M. Holquist (Eds.), *The dialogic imagination: Four essays by M. M. Bakhtin* (pp. 259–422). Austin: University of Texas Press.

Bakhtin, M. M. (1984a). *Problems of Dostoevsky's poetics* (C. Emerson, Ed. and Trans.). Minneapolis: University of Minnesota Press.

Bakhtin, M. M. (1984b). *Rabelais and his world* (H. Iswolsky, Trans.). Bloomington: Indiana University Press.

Bakhtin, M. M. (1986a). The problem of speech genres (V. McGee, Trans.). In C. Emerson & M. Holquist (Eds.), *Speech genres and other late essays* (pp. 60–102). Austin: University of Texas Press.

Bakhtin, M. M. (1986b). The problem of the text (V. W. McGee, Trans.). In C. Emerson & M. Holquist (Eds.), *Speech genres and other late essays* (pp. 103–131). Austin: University of Texas Press.

Bakhurst, D. (1988). Activity, consciousness, and communication. *The Quarterly Newsletter of the Laboratory of Comparative Human Cognition, 10*, 31–39.

Ballestero, D. (2000, November). Breaking ground. *Hispanic Magazine.* Retrieved November 11, 2003, from http://www.hispanicmagazine.com/2000/nov/CoverStory/.

Bane, V. (1999). *Dr. Laura: The unauthorized biography.* New York: St. Martin's Press.

Baym, N. K. (1995a). The emergence of community in computer-mediated communication. In S. G. Jones (Ed.), *CyberSociety: Computer-mediated communication and community* (pp. 138–163). Thousand Oaks, CA: Sage.

Baym, N. K. (1995b). From practice to culture on the Internet. In S. L. Star (Ed.), *The cultures of computing* (pp. 27–52). Oxford, England: Blackwell.

Bell, J. S. (1987). *The speakable and unspeakable in quantum mechanics.* Cambridge, England: Cambridge University Press.

Benedict, R. (1934). *Patterns of culture.* Boston: Houghton Mifflin.

Bennetts, L. (1998, September). Diagnosing Dr. Laura. *Vanity Fair, 457,* 306–312.

Benoit,W. J., & Benoit, P. J. (2000). The virtual campaign: Presidential primary websites in campaign 2000. *American Communication Journal, 3,* 3. Retrieved November 11, 2003, from http://acjournal.org/holdings/vol3/Iss3/rogue4/benoit.html.

Ben-Ur, J., & Newman, B. I. (2002). Motives, perceptions, and voting intention of voters in the 2000 U.S. presidential election. *Psychology and Marketing, 19,* 1047–1065.

Berger, P. L., & Luckmann, T. (1966). *The social construction of reality.* New York: Doubleday.

Berlin, I. (1979a). Vico and the ideal of the Enlightenment. *Against the current: Essays in the history of ideas* (H. Hardy, Ed.) (pp. 120–129). Princeton, NJ: Princeton University Press.

Berlin, I. (1979b). Vico's concept of knowledge. *Against the current: Essays in the history of ideas* (H. Hardy, Ed.) (pp. 111–119). Princeton, NJ: Princeton University Press.

Bimber, B. (1998). The Internet and political transformation: Populism, community, and accelerated pluralism. *Polity, 31,* 133–160.

Biography of Lynne V. Cheney. (n.d.). Retrieved June 27, 2003, from http://www.whitehouse.gov/mrscheney/bio.html.

Bonchek, M. S. (1997). *From broadcast to Netcast: The Internet and the flow of political information.* Unpublished doctoral dissertation, Harvard University, Cambridge, MA.

Booth, W. C., Colomb, G. G., & Williams, J. M. (2003). *The craft of research* (2nd ed.). Chicago: University of Chicago Press.

Brown, J. S., & Duguid, P. (2000). *The social life of information.* Cambridge, MA: Harvard Business School Press.

Bruner, E., & Gorfain, P. (1984). Dialogic narration and the paradoxes of Masada. In E. M. Bruner (Ed.), *Text, play, and story: The construction and reconstruction of self and society* (pp. 56–79). Prospect Heights, IL: Waveland Press.

Bruni, F. (2000, September 8). Bush suggests willingness to move on debate issue. *The New York Times*, p. 16.

Bucy, E. P., D'Angelo, P., & Newhagen, J. E. (1999). The engaged electorate: New media use as political participation. In L. L. Kaid & D. G. Bystrom (Eds.), *The electronic election: Perspectives on the 1996 campaign communication* (pp. 335–347). Mahwah, NJ: Erlbaum.

Bucy, E. P., & Gregson, K. S. (2001). Media participation: A legitimizing mechanism of mass communication. *New Media and Society, 3*, 357–380.

Bush ads aim for big share of Hispanic vote. (1998, August 15). *Houston Chronicle*, p. A33.

Cassidy, J. (2002). *dot.con: How America lost its mind and money in the Internet era*. New York: HarperCollins.

Castells, M. (1997). *The power of identity*. Oxford, England: Blackwell.

Castells, M. (2001). *The Internet galaxy: Reflections on the Internet, business, and society*. Oxford, England: Oxford University Press.

Caywood, C. L. (Ed.) (1997). *The handbook of strategic public relations and integrated communications*. New York: McGraw-Hill.

Chan, W.-t. (1963). *The way of Lao Tzu (Tao-te ching)*. Indianapolis, IN: Bobbs-Merrill.

Cooperative Extension, University of Nebraska–Lincoln. (2001). E-mail glossary of terms, NF01–45L. Retrieved April 9, 2004, from http://ianrpubs.unl.edu/consumered/nf456.htm.

Corrado, A. (2000). *Campaigns in cyberspace: Toward a new regulatory approach*. Washington, DC: Aspen Institute.

Corrado, A., & Firestone, C. M. (Eds.). (1996). *Elections in cyberspace: Toward a new era in American politics*. Washington, DC: Aspen Institute.

Craig, J., & Bevington, W. (1999). *Designing with type: A basic course in typography* (4th ed.). New York: Watson-Guptill Publications.

Crapanzano, V. (1990). On dialogue. In T. Maranhão (Ed.), *The interpretation of dialogue* (pp. 269–291). Chicago: University of Chicago Press.

Cuprisin, T. (2002, March 15). No surprise: WISN radio dropping "Dr. Laura." *Milwaukee Journal Sentinel*, p. 08B.

Cushing, J. T., & McMullin, E. (Eds.). (1989). *Philosophical consequences of quantum theory: Reflections on Bell's theorem*. Notre Dame, IN: University of Notre Dame Press.

Dahl, R. A. (1989). *Democracy and its critics*. New Haven, CT: Yale University Press.

Dahl, R. A. (1998). *On democracy*. New Haven, CT: Yale University Press.

D'Alessio, D. (2000). Adoption of the World Wide Web by American political candidates, 1996–1998. *Journal of Broadcasting and Electronic Media, 44*, 556–568.

Davis, R. (1999). *The Web of politics: The Internet's impact on the American political system*. New York: Oxford University Press.

Demetriou, C., & Silke, A. (2003). A criminological Internet sting: Experimental evidence of illegal and deviant visits to a website trap. *British Journal of Criminology, 43,* 213–222.

Dershowitz, A. M. (2001). *Supreme injustice: How the high court hijacked election 2000.* New York: Oxford University Press.

Descartes, R. (2000). *Meditations and other metaphysical writings* (D. M. Clarke, Trans.). London: Penguin Books.

Dewey, J. (1903). *Studies in logical theory.* Chicago: University of Chicago Press.

Dilthey, W. (1988). *Introduction to the human sciences: An attempt to lay a foundation for the study of society and history* (R. J. Betanzos, Ed. and Trans.). Detroit, MI: Wayne State University Press.

Downing, D., Covington, M., & Covington, M. M. (2003). *Dictionary of computer and Internet terms* (8th ed.). New York: Barron's.

Dr. Laura wants you to stop whining. (1998, January/February). *Psychology Today, 31,* 28–34.

Duranti, A., & Goodwin, C. (Eds.). (1992). *Rethinking context: Language as an interactive phenomenon.* Cambridge, England: Cambridge University Press.

Eccles, J. C. (1989). *Evolution of the brain: Creation of the self.* London: Routledge.

Edwards, D., & Middleton, D. (1986). Constructing an account of shared experience through conversational discourse. *Discourse Processes, 9,* 423–459.

Elber, L. (2001, March 30). Controversial "Dr. Laura" TV show cancelled. *Associated Press,* BC cycle.

Engeström, Y. (1987). *Learning by expanding: An activity-theoretical approach to developmental research.* Helsinki, Finland: Orienta-Konsultit Oy.

Ermarth, M. (1981). *Wilhelm Dilthey: The critique of historical reason.* Chicago: University of Chicago Press.

Frank, R. (2003, June 15). How 15 minutes became 5 weeks. *The New York Times,* sec. 2, p. 1.

Freedman, A. (2001a). *Computer desktop encyclopedia* (9th ed.). New York: McGraw-Hill.

Freedman, A. (2001b). *The computer glossary: The complete illustrated dictionary* (9th ed.). New York: AMACOM.

Garfinkel, H. (1967). *Studies in ethnomethodology.* Englewood Cliffs, NJ: Prentice-Hall.

Garfinkel, S. (2001). *Database nation: The death of privacy in the 21st century.* Beijing, China: O'Reilly.

Gilder, G. (2000). *Telecosm: How infinite bandwidth will revolutionize our world.* New York: Free Press.

Gleick, J. (1999). *Faster: The acceleration of just about everything.* New York: Pantheon Books.

Goodman, M., & Griffiths, J. (1994). Don't blame your flame. *People Weekly, 42*(2), 93–94.

Graber, D. (2003). The media and democracy: Beyond myths and stereotypes. *Annual Review of Political Science, 6,* 139–160.

Graham, G. (1999). *The Internet: A philosophical inquiry.* London: Routledge.

Grice, H. P. (1975). Logic and conversation. In P. Cole & J. Morgan (Eds.), *Syntax and semantics* (Vol. 3, pp. 41–58). New York: Academic Press.

Grossman, L. K. (1995). *The electronic republic: Reshaping democracy in America.* New York: Viking.

Gunn, G. (2000). Introduction. In G. Gunn (Ed.), *Pragmatism and other writings* (pp. vii–xxxii). New York: Penguin Books.

Halavais, A. (2000). National borders on the world wide web. *New Media and Society, 2*(1), 7–28.

Hall, E. T. (1983). *The dance of life: The other dimension of time.* Garden City, NY: Anchor Doubleday.

Hansen, G. J., & Benoit, W. L. (2001). The role of significant policy issues in the 2000 Presidential primaries. *American Behavioral Scientist, 44,* 2082–2100.

Henderson, H. (2003). *Encyclopedia of computer science and technology.* New York: Facts on File.

Hill, T. (n.d.). *Alt.radio.talk.dr-laura FAQ, version 1.2.* Retrieved November 11, 2003, from http://www.angelfire.com/journal/artdljunkie/faq.html.

Ho, R. (2002, April 8). "Dr. Laura" tries to stay healthy in mixed ratings. *The Atlanta Journal-Constitution,* p. 1C.

Holquist, M. (1990). *Dialogism: Bakhtin and his world.* London: Routledge.

Holsti, O. R. (1969). *Content analysis for the social sciences and humanities.* Reading, MA: Addison-Wesley.

Holt, G. R. (1999, July). *"The world in a post": CMC as utterance and the case of Wen Ho Lee.* Paper presented at the Rochester Conference on Human Rights and Responsibilities, Rochester, NY.

Holt, G. R. (2001, November). *"My fellow 'Netizens": Year 2000 presidential campaigning on the Internet and its possible effects on civic discourse in the new millennium.* Paper presented at the annual convention of the National Communication Association, Atlanta, GA.

Holt, G. R., Chang, H.-C., & Sterigard, D. (1990). Taoism and the metaphoric analysis of international dispute mediation. In F. Korzenny & S. Ting-Toomey (Eds.), *Communicating for Peace* (pp. 118–130). Newbury Park: Sage.

Holt, R. (1989). Talk about acting and constraint in stories about organization. *Western Journal of Speech Communication, 53,* 347–397.

Holt, R. (2003a). Bakhtin's dimensions of language and the analysis of conversation. *Communication Quarterly, 51,* 225–245.

Holt, R. (2003b). Faces of the "new China": A comparison of touristic websites in the Chinese and English languages. *Information Technology and Tourism, 5,* 105–119.

Holt, R. (2003c). *The trials of Dr. Laura.* Unpublished manuscript, Northern Illinois University.

Horton, S. (2000). *Web teaching guide: A practical approach to creating course Web sites.* New Haven, CT: Yale University Press.

Husserl, E. (1970). *The crisis of European science and transcendental phenomenology, I* (D. Carr, Trans.). Evanston, IL: Northwestern University Press.

Husserl, E. (1975). *Experience and judgment.* Evanston, IL: Northwestern University Press.

Jacques, W. W., & Ratzan, S. C. (1997). The Internet's World Wide Web and political accountability. *American Behavioral Scientist, 40,* 1226–1237.

James, W. (1991). *Pragmatism.* Amherst, NY: Prometheus Press.

Jansen, E. (2002). *NetLingo: The Internet dictionary.* Ojai, CA: NetLingo.

Johnson, T. J., Braima, M. A. M., & Sothirajah, J. (1999). Doing the traditional media sidestep: Comparing the effects of the Internet and other non-traditional media with traditional media in the 1996 presidential campaign. *Journalism and Mass Communication Quarterly, 7,* 99–123.

Juliussen, E., & Petska-Juliussen, K. (1998). *Internet industry almanac.* San Jose, CA: Peer-to-Peer Communications.

Kamarck, E. C. (1999). Campaigning on the Internet in the elections of 1998. In E. C. Kamarck & J. S. Nye, Jr. (Eds.), *Democracy.com?: Governance in the networked world* (pp. 99–123). Hollis, NH: Hollis Publishing.

Kern, M. (2001). Disadvantage Al Gore in election 2000. *American Behavioral Scientist, 44*(12), 2125–2139.

King, D. C. (n.d.). Catching voters in the Web. Retrieved November 11, 2003 from http://ksghome.harvard.edu/~.DKing.Academic.Ksg/dck-files/voters-web.htm.

Klotz, R. (1998). Virtual criticism: Negative advertising on the Internet in the 1996 Senate races. *Political Communication, 15,* 347–365.

Kockelmans, J. J. (1999). Phenomenology. In R. Audi (Ed.), *The Cambridge dictionary of philosophy* (2nd ed., pp. 664–666). Cambridge, England: Cambridge University Press.

Kollock, P., & Smith, M. A. (1996). Managing the virtual commons: Cooperation and conflict in computer communities. In S. Herring (Ed.), *Computer-mediated communication: Linguistic, social, and cross-cultural perspectives* (pp. 109–128). Amsterdam: John Benjamins.

Kollock, P., & Smith, M. A. (1999). Communities in cyberspace. In P. Kollock & M. A. Smith (Eds.), *Communities in cyberspace* (pp. 3–25). New York: Routledge.

Kozulin, A. (2002). Vygotsky in context. In A. Kozulin (Ed.), *Thought and language* [L. Vygotsky] (pp. xi–lvi). Cambridge, MA: MIT Press.

Krug, R. (2000). *Don't make me think!: A common sense guide to Web usability.* Indianapolis, IN: Que.

Kuhn, T. (1996). *The structure of scientific revolutions* (3rd ed.). Chicago: University of Chicago Press.

Lave, J. (1988). *Cognition in practice: Mind, mathematics, and culture in everyday life*. Cambridge, MA: Cambridge University Press.

Lee, W. H. (2001). *My country versus me: The first-hand account of the Los Alamos scientist who was falsely accused of being a spy*. New York: Hyperion.

Lemay, L. (1996). *Teach yourself Web publishing with HTML 3.2 in 14 days*. Indianapolis, IN: Sams.net Publishing.

Lemay, L., Murphy, B. K., & Smith, E. T. (1996). *Creating commercial Web pages*. Indianapolis, IN: Sams.net Publishing.

Len-Rios, M. E. (2002). The Bush and Gore presidential campaign websites: Identifying with Hispanic voters during the 2000 Iowa caucus and the New Hampshire primary. *Journalism and Mass Communication Quarterly, 79*(4), 887–905.

Leont'ev, A. N. (1978). *Activity, consciousness, and personality*. Englewood Cliffs, NJ: Prentice-Hall.

Lessig, L. (1999). *Code and other laws of cyberspace*. New York: Basic Books.

Lessig, L. (2002). *The future of ideas: The fate of the commons in a networked world*. New York: Random House.

Linell, P. (1998). *Approaching dialogue: Talk, interaction, and contexts in dialogical perspectives*. Amsterdam: John Benjamins.

Luria, A. R. (1976). *Cognitive development: Its cultural and social foundations*. Cambridge, MA: Harvard University Press.

Luria, A. R. (1979). *The making of mind: A personal account of Soviet psychology* (M. Cole & S. Cole, Eds.). Cambridge, MA: Harvard University Press.

Lynch, P. J., & Horton, S. (2002). *Web style guide: Basic design principles for creating web sites*. New Haven, CT: Yale University Press.

MacIntyre, A. (1981). *After virtue: A study in moral theory*. Notre Dame, IN: Notre Dame University.

Margolis, M., & Resnick, D. (Eds.). (2000). *Politics as usual: The cyberspace "revolution."* Thousand Oaks, CA: Sage.

Margolis, M., Resnick, D., & Tu, C.-c. (1997). Campaigning on the Internet: Parties and candidates on the World Wide Web in the 1996 primary season. *The Harvard International Journal of Press/Politics, 2*, 59–78.

Margolis, P. E. (1999). *Random House Webster's computer and Internet dictionary* (3rd ed.). New York: Random House.

Markovà, I., & Foppa, K. (1990). *The dynamics of dialogue*. New York: Harvester Wheatsheaf.

Marks, P. (2000, September 15). Dropping all of his objections, Bush agrees to panel's debates. *The New York Times*, p. A1.

McLaughlin, M. L., Osborne, K. K., & Smith, C. B. (1995). Standards of conduct on Usenet. In S. G. Jones (Ed.), *CyberSociety: Computer-mediated communication and community* (pp. 90–111). Thousand Oaks, CA: Sage.

Mead, G. H. (1934). *Mind, self, and society from the standpoint of a social behaviourist* (C. W. Morris, Ed.). Chicago: University of Chicago Press.

Mead, G. H. (1938). *The philosophy of the act* (C. W. Morris, Ed.). Chicago: University of Chicago Press.

Mehta, M. D., & Plaza, D. E. (1997). Pornography in cyberspace: An exploration of what's in Usenet. In S. Kiesler (Ed.), *Culture of the Internet* (pp. 53–67). Mahwah, NJ: Erlbaum.

Menand, L. (1997). An introduction to pragmatism. *Pragmatism: A reader* (L. Menand, Ed.). New York: Random House.

Microsoft Corporation. (2002). *Microsoft computer dictionary* (5th ed.). Redmond, WA: Microsoft Press.

Millar, F., & Rogers, E. (1976). A relational approach to interpersonal communication. In G. R. Miller (Ed.), *Explorations in interpersonal communication* (pp. 87–104). Beverly Hills, CA: Sage.

Miller, D. L. (1973). *George Herbert Mead: Self, language, and the world.* Austin: University of Texas Press.

Mitnick, K. D., & Simon, W. L. (2002). *The art of deception: Controlling the human element of security.* New York: Wiley.

Mitra, A. (1997). Virtual commonality: Looking for India on the Internet. In S. G. Jones (Ed.), *Virtual culture: Identity and communication in cybersociety* (pp. 55–79). London: Sage.

Moll, L. C. (1990). *Vygotsky and education: Instructional implications and applications of sociohistorical psychology.* Cambridge, England: Cambridge University Press.

Moore, G. E. (1922). *Philosophical studies.* New York: Harcourt, Brace.

Morris, D. (1999). *Vote.com.* Los Angeles: Renaissance Books.

Morson, G. S., & Emerson, C. (1990). *Mikhail Bakhtin: Creation of a prosaics.* Stanford, CA: Stanford University Press.

Musciano, C., & Kennedy, B. (2002). *HTML and XHTML: The definitive guide* (5th ed.). Sebastopol, CA: O'Reilly.

Norris, P. (2001). Too close to call: Opinion polls in campaign 2000. *Harvard International Journal of Press/Politics, 6,* 3–10.

Novotny, P. (2002). Local television, the World Wide Web, and the 2000 presidential election. *Social Science Computer Review, 20,* 58–72.

Oder, N., & Rogers, M. (1999). ALA under attack from "Dr. Laura." *Library Journal, 124*(10), 20–21.

Patterson, T. E. (1983). *Out of order.* New York: Knopf.

Pfau, M., Cho, J., & Chong, K. (2001). Communication forms in U.S. presidential campaigns: Influences on candidate perceptions and the democratic process. *Harvard International Journal of Press/Politics, 6*(4), 88–105.

Popper, K. R. (1972). *Objective knowledge: An evolutionary approach.* Oxford, England: Clarendon Press.

Posner, R. A. (2003). *Law, pragmatism, and democracy*. Cambridge, MA: Harvard University Press.

Postman, N. (1985). *Amusing ourselves to death: Discourse in the age of show business*. New York: Penguin.

Powell, T. A. (2000). *HTML: The complete reference*. New York: McGraw-Hill.

Psathas, G. (1995). *Conversation analysis: The study of talk-in-interaction*. Thousand Oaks, CA: Sage.

Puopolo, S. (2001). The Web and U.S. senatorial campaigns 2000. *American Behavioral Scientist, 44*, 2030–2047.

Putnam, R. D. (2000). *Bowling alone: The collapse and revival of American community*. New York: Simon and Schuster.

Ramasastry, A. (2002, June 5). The law and politics of Internet activism: The Yes Men, Peta, Rtmark, and the phenomenon of parody websites. *FindLaw's legal commentary*. Retrieved November 11, 2003, from http://writ.news.findlaw.com/ramasastry/20020605.html.

Ray, E. T. (2001). *Learning XML*. Sebastopol, CA: O'Reilly.

Reddy, M. J. (1979). The conduit metaphor—a case of frame conflict in our language about language. In A. Ortony (Ed.), *Metaphor and thought* (pp. 284–297). Cambridge, England: Cambridge University Press.

Reese, W. (1996). *Dictionary of philosophy and religion*. Amherst, NY: Humanity Books.

Rescher, N. (1995). Pragmatism. In T. Honderich (Ed.), *The Oxford companion to philosophy* (pp. 710–713). Oxford, England: Oxford University Press.

Rorty, R. (1979). *Philosophy and the mirror of nature*. Princeton, NJ: Princeton University Press.

Rorty, R. (1982). *Consequences of pragmatism: Essays 1972–1980*. Minneapolis: University of Minnesota Press.

Russell, B. (1910). *Philosophical essays*. London: Longmans, Green.

Ryle, G. (1984). *The concept of mind*. Chicago: University of Chicago Press.

Sacks, H. (1992). *Lectures on conversation* (Vols. 1 & 2; G. Jefferson, Ed.). Oxford, UK: Blackwell.

Sacks, H., Schegloff, E., & Jefferson, G. (1974). A simplest systematics for the organization of turn-taking in conversation. *Language, 50*, 696–735.

Schegloff, E. A. (1968). Sequencing in conversational openings. *The American Anthropologist, 70*, 696–735.

Schegloff, E. A. (1991). Reflections on talk and social structure. In D. Boden & D. H. Zimmerman (Eds.), *Talk and social structure: Studies in ethnomethodology and conversation analysis* (pp. 44–69). Berkeley: University of California Press.

Schlessinger, Laura. (1997). *Current Biography, 58*, 40–43.

Schneider, S. M., & Foot, K. A. (2002). Online structure for political action: Exploring presidential campaign Web sites from the 2000 American election. *Javnost—The Public, 9*, 1–17.

Schneier, B. (2000). *Secrets and lies*. New York: Wiley.

Schooled in hate: Anti-semitism on campus. (n.d.). Anti-semitism and black student groups. Retrieved November 11, 2003, from http://www.adl.org/Sih/SIH-black_student_groups.asp.

Schrof, J. (1997). Stop whining! *U.S. News and World Report, 123*(3), 48.

Schrof, J. (1998). Honors and more controversy for Dr. Laura. *U.S. News and World Report, 125*(9), 4.

Schumpeter, J. (1947). *Capitalism, socialism, and democracy*. New York: Harper and Brothers.

Schutz, A. (1970). *Reflections on the problem of relevance* (R. M. Zaner, Ed.). New Haven, CT: Yale University Press.

Schutz, A. (1971). *Collected papers* (Vols. 1–2). The Hague, Netherlands: Nijhoff.

Schutz, A., & Luckmann, T. (1972). *The phenomenology of the social world*. London: Heinemann Educational Books.

Scribner, S. (1985). Knowledge at work. *Anthropology and Education Quarterly, 16*, 199–207.

Seabrook, J. (1997). *Deeper: My two-year odyssey in cyberspace*. New York: Simon and Schuster.

Segaller, S. (1999). *Nerds 2.0.1: A brief history of the Internet*. New York: TV Books.

Selected anti-semitic incidents around the world 2002. (n.d.). Anti-Defamation League of B'nai B'rith. Retrieved from the World Wide Web, July 7, 2003, http://www.adl.org/anti_semitism/anti-semitism_global_incidents.asp.

Seligmann, J., Reddick, C., & Pappas, L. (1998). Naked truth. *Newsweek, 132*(20), 94.

Servon, L. (2002). *Bridging the digital divide*. Oxford, England: Blackwell.

Shannon, C. E., & Weaver, W. (1949). *The mathematical theory of communication*. Urbana: University of Illinois Press.

Siegel, D. (1997). *Creating killer Web sites: The art of third-generation site design* (2nd ed.). Indianapolis, IN: Hayden Books.

Snyder, I. (1997). *Hypertext: The electronic labyrinth*. New York: New York University Press.

Sparks, C. (2001). The Internet and the global public sphere. In W. L. Bennett & R. M. Entman (Eds.), *Mediated politics: Communication in the future of democracy* (pp. 75–95). Cambridge, England: Cambridge University Press.

Spencer, H., & Lawrence, D. (1998). *Managing Usenet*. Sebastopol, CA: O'Reilly.

Sproull, L., & Faraj, S. (1997). Atheism, sex, and databases: The Net as a social technology. In S. Kiesler (Ed.), *Culture of the Internet* (pp. 35–51). Mahwah, NJ: Erlbaum.

Stallybrass, P., & White, A. (1986). *The politics and poetics of transgression*. Ithaca, NY: Cornell.

Sterne, J. (1997). *What makes people click: Advertising on the Web.* Indianapolis, IN: Que.

Stevens, W. R. (1994). *TCP/IP illustrated: Vol. 1, The protocols.* Reading, MA: Addison-Wesley.

Stivale, C. (1997). Spam, heteroglossia, and harassment in cyberspace. In D. Porter (Ed.), *Internet culture* (pp. 133–144). New York: Routledge.

Tannen, D. (1989). *Talking voices: Repetition, dialogue, and imagery in conversational discourse.* Cambridge, England: Cambridge University Press.

Tedesco, J. C., Miller, J. L., & Spiker, J. A. (1999). Presidential campaigning on the information superhighway: An exploration of content and form. In L. L. Kaid & D. G. Bystrom (Eds.), *The electronic election: Perspectives on the 1996 campaign communication* (pp. 51–63). Mahwah, NJ: Erlbaum.

Thimbleby, H. W. (2000). Java. In A. Ralston, E. D. Reilly, & D. Hemmendinger (Eds.), *Encyclopedia of computer science* (4th ed.). London: Nature Publishing Group.

Thing, Lowell. (2002). *The whatis?com's encyclopedia of technology terms.* Indianapolis, IN: Que.

Thomas, E., Brant, M., Gegax, T. T., Clift, E., Wingert, P., & Smalley, S. (2001, June 11). Busted again in Margaritaville. *Newsweek, 137*(24), 24–25.

Tittel, E., Gaither, M., Hassinger, S., & Erwin, M. (1996). *CGI bible.* Foster City, CA: IDG Books.

Turque, B. (1999, October 4). Reinventing Al Gore. *Newsweek, 134*(14), 44–46.

Van Natta, D. (2000, February 25). A daunting edge in campaign cash narrows for Bush. *The New York Times,* p. A1.

Vico, G. (1984). *The new science of Giambattista Vico: Unabridged translation of the third edition (1744) with the addition of "practice of the new science"* (T. G. Bergin & M. H. Fisch, Trans.). Ithaca, NY: Cornell University Press.

Vico, G. (1999). *New science: Principles of the science concerning the common nature of nations, third edition thoroughly corrected, revised, and expanded by the author* (D. Marsh, Trans.). London: Penguin.

Vygotsky, L. (1978). *Mind in society.* Cambridge, MA: Harvard University Press.

Vygotsky, L. (1981). The instrumental method in psychology. In J. V. Wertsch (Ed.), *The concept of activity in Soviet psychology* (pp. 134–143). White Plains, NY: Sharpe.

Vygotsky, L. (2002). *Thought and language* (A. Kozulin, Trans.). Cambridge, MA: MIT Press.

Warf, B., & Grimes, J. (1997). Counterhegemonic discourses and the Internet. *The Geographical Review, 87,* 259–274.

Watson, N. (1997). Why we argue about virtual community: A case of the Phish.Net fan community. In S. G. Jones (Ed.), *Virtual culture: Identity and communication in cybersociety* (pp. 102–132). London: Sage.

Watzlawick, P., Beavin, J. B., & Jackson, D. D. (1967). *Pragmatics of human communication: A study of interactional patterns, pathologies, and paradoxes.* New York: Norton.

Weigel, D. (2002, September). GOP pollster aims to expand Latino base. *Campaigns and Elections, 23*(9), 8.

Weinberger, D. (2002). *Small pieces loosely joined: A unified theory of the Web.* Cambridge, MA: Perseus.

Weiss, W. (1990). Challenge to authority: Bakhtin and ethnographic description. *Cultural Anthropology, 5,* 414–430.

Wertsch, J. V. (Ed.). (1981). *The concept of activity in Soviet psychology.* White Plains, NY: Sharpe.

Willard, W. B. (1997). I flamed Freud: A case study in teletextual incendiarism. In D. Porter (Ed.), *Internet culture* (pp. 145–159). New York: Routledge.

Wolff, K. H. (1978). Phenomenology and sociology. In T. B. Bottomore and R. Nisbet (Eds.), *A history of sociological analysis* (pp. 499–556). New York: Basic Books.

Index

About the Author

RICHARD HOLT is Associate Professor in the Department of Communication at Northern Illinois University.